JOSS WHEDON
C O N V E R S A T I O N S

TELEVISION CONVERSATIONS SERIES
DAVID LAVERY, GENERAL EDITOR

JOSS
WHEDON

CONVERSATIONS

Edited by David Lavery and Cynthia Burkhead

 UNIVERSITY PRESS OF MISSISSIPPI / JACKSON

www.upress.state.ms.us

The University Press of Mississippi is a member of the Association of American
University Presses.

First printing 2011
∞
Library of Congress Cataloging-in-Publication Data

Joss Whedon : conversations / edited by David Lavery and Cynthia Burkhead.
    p. cm. — (Television conversations series)
  Includes filmography and index.
  ISBN 978-1-60473-923-7 (cloth : alk. paper) — ISBN 978-1-60473-924-4 (pbk. :
alk. paper) — ISBN 978-1-60473-925-1 (ebook) 1. Whedon, Joss, 1964—Interviews.
2. Television producers and directors—United States—Interviews. I. Lavery, David,
1949– II. Burkhead, Cynthia.
  PN1992.4.W49A3 2011
  791.4302'33092—dc22
  [B]   2010043322

British Library Cataloging-in-Publication Data available

CONTENTS

INTRODUCTION

For its first half century, television, like its media rival the cinema, generated only minimal popular or scholarly interest in its makers. Until the publication in *Cahiers du Cinéma* of François Truffaut's "Une Certaine Tendance du Cinéma Français" ("A Certain Tendency in French Cinema," 1954), published in the very decade in which the small screen arrived in our living rooms, "auteurs" (authors) were not an essential factor in movie discourse, and only the last two decades have generated comparable awareness of those individuals making quality TV. Now the serious television watcher, whether scholar-fan or fan-scholar, is likely to be found talking, either around the water cooler or at the podium, about David Chase (*The Sopranos*), Tom Fontana (*St. Elsewhere*, *Oz*), Ron Moore (*Battlestar Galactica*), David Simon (*The Wire*), Amy Sherman-Palladino (*Gilmore Girls*), Matt Weiner (*Mad Men*), Alan Ball (*Six Feet Under*), or David Milch (*NYPD Blue*, *Deadwood*)—buzzing about their current shows, speculating about their new offerings. Now television viewing is characterized by what Jason Mittell deems a growing tendency to "push the operational aesthetic to the foreground, calling attention to the constructed nature of the narration and asking us to marvel at how *the writers pulled it off.*"[1] Because, in television, *writers* rule.

No recent television creator, no television author, has generated more critical and scholarly discussion or acquired as devoted a cult following as Joss Whedon. No less than thirty books concerned with his work have now been published (a forthcoming volume even offers a book-length bibliography) and ten international conferences have been held (in the United Kingdom, United States, Australia, Turkey).[2] So it is altogether fitting that this first volume in the University Press of Mississippi's Television Conversations Series would be devoted to the writer, director, showrunner who has given us *Buffy the Vampire Slayer* (WB, 1997–2001; UPN, 2001–2003); *Angel* (WB, 1999–2004); *Firefly* (2002); *Dr. Horrible's Sing-Along Blog* (webcast, 2008); and *Dollhouse* (Fox, 2009–2010).

Anyone whose work has inspired such academic attention, invited so many Whedon-worshiping websites (like Whedonesque), and inspired a t-shirt that proclaims, in an in-your-face George Lucas *Star Wars* font, that "Joss Whedon

Is My Master Now" may need no introduction, and several of the conversations included in this book—most notably James Longworth's—offer informative, preliminary partial overviews of Whedon's career. Suffice it to say that Whedon (born in 1964) is the son of a television writer (who was himself the son of a television writer) and an English teacher mother. After majoring in film studies at Wesleyan University in Connecticut under the tutelage of film historian Jeanine Basinger (*Silent Stars*, *A Woman's View*, *The Star Machine*) and scholar of American mythology Richard Slotkin (*Gunfighter Nation*, *Regeneration Through Violence*), Whedon would journey to California hoping to become a filmmaker and, breaking free from the family business, *not* a third generation television writer. He would nevertheless find himself writing for the sitcom *Roseanne* and the first incarnation of *Parenthood*.

In the mid-nineties, after his first movie script became the woefully disappointing *Buffy the Vampire Slayer* (Fran Rubel Kuzui, 1992), Whedon found himself an in-demand "script doctor," working, with varying degrees of success, on such films as *Speed*, *Toy Story*, *Twister*, *The X-Men*, and *Waterworld*. His original screenplay for *Alien Resurrection* (1997) resulted, like *Buffy*, in a film that was tremendously disappointing to its author.

That same year, however, Whedon would be given complete creative control over *Buffy*'s reincarnation on the WB, a new, youth-oriented network in search of signature shows. Though never a Nielsen success, *BtVS* did attract choice demographics, help to brand the network, and establish Whedon as not only an important writer and showrunner but one of the most creative directors in a medium in which directors are customarily for-hire craftsmen not known for their originality.

Though by his own admission he knew very little about directing and virtually nothing about creating a television show prior to helming *BtVS*, Whedon turned out some of the series'—and contemporary television's—most memorable, and most innovative, episodes, including "Innocence," in which Angel loses his soul and becomes the evil boyfriend from Hell Angelus after having sex with Buffy; "Becoming" (I and II), which was the first time the series shot on a soundstage and used historical settings and costumes; "Hush," a marvelous experiment, which broke him, he admits, out of a devolution into a "sort of a hack TV director" (Longworth in this volume), in which almost half the episode transpires in silence after fairy tale monsters The Gentlemen steal the voices of Sunnydale; "Restless," an all-dream episode, "basically a forty-minute poem" (as Whedon describes it [Longworth in this volume]), which has been described as a kind of television *8½* and compared to Eliot's "The Wasteland";[3] "The Body," an emotionally wrenching depiction of the aftermath of Buffy's mother's death; and "Once More with Feeling," an ingenious all-singing, all-dancing musical, the fulfillment of a long-time Whedon ambition—he dreams of being the next Stephen Sondheim.

Whedon's first series would lead to a successful spinoff, the darker, more adult set-in-L.A. *Angel*, which would run for five seasons on the WB. In the fall of 2002, an increasingly exhausted Whedon would have three series on air, with the science-fiction western *Firefly* debuting on Fox, but the short-lived show would perpetuate his ongoing clashes with network television. At the end of 2001, *BtVS* had been cut loose by the WB, despite its role as The Frog's flagship show, though it did succeed in finding a new home for its final two seasons on UPN. With *Firefly*, Fox would interfere from the outset, scheduling the series on the American television graveyard of Friday night, rejecting Whedon's pilot episode and requiring a more action-filled hour, showing subsequent entries out of their planned order (the original pilot would not air until December), and finally cancelling the series. Two years later, the WB would also cancel *Angel* peremptorily, giving Whedon and company only a severely limited time to wrap up its complex narrative.

Beginning in 2001, Whedon had begun funneling some of his energy and imagination into his long-time fanboy love for superhero comics, creating, for Darkhorse Comics, *Fray*—the story of a "Chosen One," inheritor of the Slayer tradition, trying to survive in a futuristic dystopia. With the end of *Angel* in the spring of 2004, writing for comic books would increasingly occupy Whedon's creative life. From 2004 to 2006, the long-time X-Men fan would take over Marvel's *Astonishing X-Men*. In 2006, Whedon would become prime author of Brian Vaughan's *Runaways*, a comic about children of supervillains seeking to becoming superheroes. And 2007 would see the launch of *Buffy the Vampire Slayer Season Eight*, a pen-and-ink version of his most successful series, with Whedon serving as one of many authors.

In 2005 came the potentially monumental news that Whedon had signed über-producer Joel Silver (*The Matrix*) to direct a big-budget summer block-buster version of *Wonder Woman*, but despite his insistence in a variety of interviews that he was making good progress on the script, the Marvel boy would finally admit (see the 2007 Onion A.V. Club interview included here) that, other than announcing, with typical Whedonian humor, that he had chosen Morgan Freeman to play the Amazon princess, he had gotten nowhere with the assignment to bring a DC superhero to the screen, and in 2007 he and Silver agreed to walk away from the project.

With his career having perhaps reached its nadir, Whedon found the necessary inspiration to begin again. He would contribute to other, much-admired television series, playing a small part in *Veronica Mars*, directing two episodes of *The Office* (one of which involved a vampire bat). Word that he was writing a film to be called *Goners* and that another movie, *Cabin in the Woods* (to be co-written and directed by *Buffy* and *Angel* alum Drew Goddard), had been greenlit had Whedon's fanbase again looking forward to the years ahead. (Though *Goners* is still in development, *Cabin* is now scheduled for a January 2011 release.)

During the Writer's Guild of America strike (November 5, 2007–February 12, 2008), Whedon, still bearing the scars from his conflicts with management, set out to circumvent Hollywood's normal chain-of-command by hatching a plan to put on a low-budget show that would stream for free on the web and only later charge admission (on ITunes, for a DVD release). The result was *Dr. Horrible's Sing-Along Blog*, which would air, one act at a time, July 15, 17, and 19, 2008. Though it has still not aired on TV, *Horrible* made many end-of-the-year's best television lists and even won an Emmy (for Outstanding Special Class—Short-Format Live-Action Entertainment Programs).

With *Dollhouse*, Whedon would return to actual TV. Created as a vehicle for former *Buffy* actress Eliza Dushku, *Dollhouse* would find Whedon, anxious to avoid the burnout he had experienced in his earlier television sojourn, delegating showrunner authority for the first time to others and writing and directing less frequently than on previous series. Fox, however, was again manipulative from the start, damning *Dollhouse* to Friday night (again), requiring a new pilot (again), reordering episodes (again), and shelving perhaps the first season's most brilliant episode: the made-on-a-shoestring-budget dystopian "Epitaph One" (which would be made available later on DVD). Despite disappointing ratings, Fox would nevertheless renew the series, though evicting it before the end of its fall 2009 run. The post-cancellation final episodes of the series did succeed in bringing the story to a truncated but powerful end.

As we write, Whedon has signed to write and direct Marvel Enterprises' *The Avengers*. The watershed assignment to helm a big-budget summer blockbuster will surely determine Whedon's creative future. If the movie about a team of superheroes is a success, then Whedon is likely to remain a filmmaker for the rest of his career, perhaps never again working in television. If *Avengers* fails, Whedon could well return to working for both the big and small screens.

If Whedon has shown himself to be a virtuoso screenwriter/script doctor, director, comic book author, and librettist, the very embodiment in a single creative individual of psychologist Howard Gardner's "multiple intelligences," he is as well a masterful conversationalist. As a DVD commentator, for example, a mostly improvisational form understandably not represented here, the consistently hilarious, reliably insightful, frequently moving Whedon has no real rival known to us. In his many, many interviews—we had no shortage of conversations from which to choose—he likewise shines. Whether answering a hundred rapid-fire, mostly silly questions from fans on the internet ("Joss Whedon Answers 100 Questions"), fielding serious inquiries about his craft and career from television pros like James Longworth or David Bianculli, or assessing his disappointments with Tasha Robinson (Onion A.V. Club Interview [2007]), Whedon seldom fails to provoke laughter and reflection.

A forthcoming intellectual biography of Whedon identifies a score of stylistic and thematic signatures in his creative work contributing to what might be deemed the Whedonian.[4] Not surprisingly, these pages are redolent with the Whedonian as well. Again and again, these interviews bring "the funny," exhibit the same kind of self-deprecating, often naughty wit that characterizes all his scripts. Whedon in conversation (WIC) embraces and exhibits a love for and a deep understanding of the nature and function of the cultic. Throughout Whedon embraces collaboration with genuine humility. WIC shows him to be as genre defying/genre bending as a thinker about media as he is as a maker of popular culture forms. We glimpse repeatedly the breadth and depth of his knowledge of film history. Without pretension, WIC demonstrates his impressive cultural literacy, both low and high brow, and we understand better the seeds of his own signature intertextuality. We find him in conversation, as in all his scripts, always playful with language, quick with metaphor, ready and able to create a neologism at the drop of a hat. WIC is no more afraid of declaring his atheism than he is in his work. In his interviews we find him as ready to embrace the same "loser aesthetic" identified by Richard Burt and elucidated by Matt Hills that *Buffy*, *Angel*, *Firefly*, and *Dr. Horrible* all exhibit.[5] At the third *Slayage* Conference on the Whedonverses, his mentor Jeanine Basinger referred to her prized student as an "A+ All the Way" film major in his student days. These interviews show that same superb student, still learning, still inquiring, always imaginative.

In the final episode of *Buffy the Vampire Slayer*, Whedon has his greatest creation seek to metaphorically explain her growth:

OK, I'm cookie dough. I'm not done baking. I'm not finished becoming whoever the hell it is I'm gonna turn out to be. I make it through this, and the next thing, and the next thing, and maybe one day I turn around and realize I'm ready. I'm cookies. And then, you know, if I want someone to eat . . . or enjoy warm, delicious cookie me, then . . . that's fine. That'll be then. When I'm done.

Like Buffy, Whedon is far from done. We could see another twenty years of his films, his movies, his television, his interviews. Which is not to say that the conversations included here are half-baked ("It's not," as Dr. Horrible might say, "a perfect metaphor").

In selecting the content of this book we had, as we have already indicated, a lot to choose from. Whedon conversations can be found all over the Internet, in books, on National Public Radio. We narrowed our choices based on several factors. We wanted to represent the full continuum of Joss Whedon's career, both chronologically—our first interview is from 2000, our last from 2009—and in regard to subject matter—in these interviews Whedon discusses virtually all of his work for television, from *Roseanne* to *Dollhouse*, his film experiences, his script doctoring, his comic book authorship. We wanted to represent Whedon in a variety of contexts, engaging informally with fans, speaking at length and in depth with experienced journalists, chatting amiably with the editor of an online journal devoted to crocheting about Captain Hammer's sweater vests (*Dr. Horrible*) and Jayne's hilarious hat (*Firefly*).

Due to length limitations and our occasional inability to acquire permission for reprinting here, we were not able to include every piece we would like to have offered in these pages. We feel certain, however, that both avid fans and newcomers to the Whedonverses alike will find this book of value, offering as it does the opportunity to meet with and talk to Joss Whedon in the pages of a book. The experience of Whedon on the screen (small or silver), in the panels of a comic book, on a webcast, will, we trust, be richer thanks to conversing with him here.

DL
CB

NOTES

1. Jason Mittell, "Narrative Complexity in Contemporary American Television." *The Velvet Light Trap* 58 (Fall 2006): 29–40.

2. See these two excellent bibliographic resources: Alyssa Hornick's "Whedonology: An Academic Whedonstudies Bibliography," http://www.alysa316.com/Whedonology/; and Don Macnaughtan's *Bibliographic Guide to "Buffy the Vampire Slayer" and "Angel"* (Jefferson, NC: McFarland Publishing, 2011).

3. David Lavery, "The Genius of Joss Whedon." Afterword to *Fighting the Forces: What's at Stake in "Buffy the Vampire Slayer"* (Boulder, CO: Rowman and Littlefield, 2002): 251–56; Wilcox, *Why "Buffy" Matters: The Art of "Buffy the Vampire Slayer"* (London: I. B. Tauris, 2005) 162–73.

4. David Lavery, *Joss: A Creative Portrait of the Maker of the Whedonverses* (forthcoming from I. B. Tauris).

5. Richard Burt, *Unspeakable ShaXXXspeares: Queer Theory and American Kiddie Culture* (New York: St. Martin's, 1998); Matt Hills, *Fan Cultures* (London: Routledge, 2002).

CHRONOLOGY

1964—Joss Whedon born

1973—Tom Whedon and Lee Stearns, Joss's parents, divorce

1976—Begins reading comic books

1979—Accompanies his mother to England, where he becomes a student at Winchester College (1979–1981)

1983—Enrolls at Wesleyan University in Connecticut (1983–1987)

1988—Moves to California

1989—Writes for *Roseanne* (1989–1990)

1992—Lee Stearns dies; *Buffy the Vampire Slayer* (the movie, written by Whedon) released

1994—*Speed* (rewritten by Whedon) released; Columbia reportedly pays $1.5 million for his script for *Afterlife*; spends six months (from Christmas 2004 into 2005) rewriting *Toy Story*

1995—Weds Kai Cole

1997—*Alien Resurrection* (written by Whedon) released

1997–2003—*Buffy the Vampire Slayer* on television (WB, 1997–2001; UPN, 2001–2003)

1999–2004—*Angel* on the WB

2000—*Titan A.E.* (co-written by Whedon) released

2001—First issue of *Fray* (2001–2004) published

2002—Arden Whedon born; *Firefly* on Fox (cancelled in December)

2004—Cancellation of *Angel* announced; production of *Serenity* begins in June; Squire Whedon born; takes over *Astonishing X-Men* (2004–2006)

2005—Signs to direct Wonder Woman film; *Serenity* premieres; plays an employee of the month for a car rental agency in *Veronica Mars*

2006—Makes "Equality Now" speech; *Buffy Season Eight* (comic book) begins its run (2006–2010)

2007—Withdraws from Wonder Woman film; directs two episodes of *The Office*; begins authorship of *Runaways* comic book (2006–2007)

2008—*Cabin in the Woods* (a film) greenlit; *Dr. Horrible's Sing-Along Blog* broadcast on the Internet and released on DVD

2009–2010—*Dollhouse* on Fox (cancelled, fall 2010); directs one episode of *Glee* (2010)

2011—*Cabin in the Woods* (co-written by Whedon) to be released

FILMOGRAPHY

Roseanne (CBS, 1989–90)
Created by Matt Williams and Roseanne Barr
Three Season One episode written by Joss Whedon
Cast:
Roseanne Barr—Roseanne Conner
John Goodman—Dan Conner
Laurie Metcalf—Jackie Harris
Michael Fishman—D. J. Conner
Sara Gilbert—Darlene Conner
Alicia Goranson—Becky Conner
Johnny Galecki—David Healy

Buffy the Vampire Slayer (1992)
Director: Fran Rubel Kuzui
Writer: Joss Whedon
Cast:
Kristy Swanson—Buffy Summers
Donald Sutherland—Merrick
Paul Reubens—Amilyn
Rutger Hauer—Lothos
Luke Perry—Pike
Michele Abrams—Jennifer
Hilary Swank—Kimberly
Paris Vaughan—Nicole "Nicki"
David Arquette—Benny

Speed (1994)
Director: Jan DeBont
Screenplay: Graham Yost
Script Doctored by Joss Whedon
Cast:
Keanu Reeves—Officer Jack Traven

Dennis Hopper—Howard Payne
Sandra Bullock—Annie Porter
Joe Morton—Capt. McMahon
Jeff Daniels—Det. Harold "Harry" Temple
Alan Ruck—Stephens
Glenn Plummer—Jaguar Owner
Richard Lineback—Norwood
Beth Grant—Helen
Hawthorne James—Sam
Carlos Carrasco—Ortiz
David Kriegel—Terry
Natsuko Ohama—Mrs. Kamino

Toy Story (1995)
Director: John Lasseter
Screenplay: Joss Whedon, Andrew Stanton, Joel Cohen, Alec Sokolow
Voice Cast:
Tom Hanks—Woody
Tim Allen—Buzz Lightyear
Don Rickles—Mr. Potato Head
Jim Varney—Slinky Dog
Wallace Shawn—Rex
John Ratzenberger—Hamm
Annie Potts—Bo Peep
John Morris—Andy
Erik von Detten—Sid
Laurie Metcalf—Andy's Mom
R. Lee Ermey—Sergeant

Twister (1996)
Director: Jan DeBont
Screenplay: Michael Crichton and Anne-Marie Martin
Script Doctored by Joss Whedon
Cast:
Helen Hunt—Dr. Jo Harding
Bill Paxton—Bill Harding
Cary Elwes—Dr. Jonas Miller
Jami Gertz—Dr. Melissa Reeves
Philip Seymour Hoffman—Dustin Davis
Lois Smith—Meg Greene
Alan Ruck—Robert "Rabbit" Nurick
Jeremy Davies—Laurence

Alien Resurrection (1997)
Director: Jean-Pierre Jeunet
Screenplay: Joss Whedon
Cast:
Sigourney Weaver—Ellen Ripley
Winona Ryder—Annalee Call
Dominique Pinon—Vriess
Ron Perlman—Johner
Gary Dourdan—Christie
Michael Wincott—Frank Elgyn
Kim Flowers—Sabra Hillard
Dan Hedaya—Gen. Martin Perez
J. E. Freeman—Dr. Mason Wren
Brad Dourif—Dr. Jonathan Gediman
Raymond Cruz—Vincent Distephano
Leland Orser—Larry Purvis

Buffy the Vampire Slayer (WB, 1997–2001; UPN, 2001–2003)
Created by Joss Whedon
Cast:
Sarah Michelle Gellar—Buffy Summers
David Boreanaz—Angel
Nicholas Brendon—Xander Harris
Alyson Hanigan—Willow Rosenberg
Charisma Carpenter—Cordelia Chase
Seth Green—Oz
Anthony Stewart Head—Rupert Giles
James Marsters—Spike
Emma Caulfield—Anya
Amber Benson—Tara
Marc Blucas—Riley Finn
Mark Metcalf—The Master

Angel (WB, 1999–2004)
Created by Joss Whedon and David Greenwalt
Cast:
David Boreanaz—Angel
Charisma Carpenter—Cordelia Chase
Glenn Quinn—Doyle
Alexis Denisoff—Wesley Wyndham-Pryce
Amy Acker—Winifred Burkle
J. August Richards—Charles Gunn

Vincent Kartheiser—Connor
Andy Hallet—Lorne
Stephanie Romanov—Lilah Morgan
James Marsters—Spike
Christian Kane—Lindsey McDonald
Julie Benz—Darla
Mercedes McNab—Harmony Kendall
Elisabeth Röhm—Detective Kate Lockley

Titan A.E. (2000)
Directors: Don Bluth, Gary Goldman, Art Vitello
Screenplay: Ben Edlund, John August, Joss Whedon
Voice Cast:
Bill Pullman—Capt. Joseph Korso
John Leguizamo—Gune
Nathan Lane—Preed
Janeane Garofalo—Stith
Drew Barrymore—Akima
Ron Perlman—Professor Sam Tucker
Alex D. Linz—Young Cale
Tone Loc—Tek (as Tone-Lōc)
Jim Breuer—The Cook
Christopher Scarabosio—Queen Drej
Jim Cummings—Chowquin
Charles Rocket—Firrikash / Slave Trader Guard
Ken Hudson Campbell—Po

Firefly (Fox, 2002)
Created by Joss Whedon
Cast:
Nathan Fillion—Captain Malcolm "Mal" Reynolds
Gina Torres—Zoe Washburne
Alan Tudyk—Hoban "Wash" Washburne
Morena Baccarin—Inara Serra
Adam Baldwin—Jayne Cobb
Jewel Staite—Kaylee Frye
Sean Maher—Dr. Simon Tam
Summer Glau—River Tam
Ron Glass—Shepherd Book
Christina Hendricks—Saffron
Mark Sheppard—Badger

Serenity (2005)
Director: Joss Whedon
Screenplay: Joss Whedon
Cast:
Nathan Fillion—Mal
Gina Torres—Zoe
Alan Tudyk—Wash
Morena Baccarin—Inara
Adam Baldwin—Jayne
Jewel Staite—Kaylee
Sean Maher—Simon
Summer Glau—River
Ron Glass—Shepherd Book
Chiwetel Ejiofor—The Operative
David Krumholtz—Mr. Universe
Michael Hitchcock—Dr. Mathias
Sarah Paulson—Dr. Caron
Yan Feldman—Mingo
Rafael Feldman—Fanty

The Office (2007)
"Business School" (episode 3.16) and "Branch Wars" (episode 4.6)
Director: Joss Whedon

Dr. Horrible's Sing-Along Blog (2008)
Created by Joss Whedon
Cast:
Neil Patrick Harris—Billy
Nathan Fillion—Captain Hammer
Felicia Day—Penny
Simon Helberg—Moist

Dollhouse (Fox, 2009–2010)
Created by Joss Whedon
Cast:
Eliza Dushku—Echo
Harry Lennix—Boyd Langton
Fran Kranz—Topher Brink
Tahmoh Penikett—Paul Ballard
Enver Gjokaj—Victor
Dichen Lachman—Sierra

Olivia Williams—Adelle DeWitt
Miracle Laurie—Mellie
Amy Acker—Dr. Claire Saunders
Reed Diamond—Laurence Dominic
Alexis Denisof—Senator Daniel Perrin
Summer Glau—Bennett Halverson
Alan Tudyk—Alpha
Keith Carradine—Matthew Harding
Felicia Day—Mag

Glee (2010)
"Dream On" (episode 1.19)
Director: Joss Whedon

The Cabin in the Woods (2011)
Director: Drew Goddard
Screenplay: Joss Whedon and Drew Goddard
Cast:
Richard Jenkins—Steve Hadle
Bradley Whitford—Richard Sitterson
Jesse Williams—Holden McCrea
Chris Hemsworth—Curt Vaughan
Fran Kranz—Marty Mikalski
Kristen Connolly—Dana Polk
Anna Hutchison—Jules Louden
Amy Acker—Wendy Lin

JOSS WHEDON

CONVERSATIONS

Fresh Air Interview with Joss Whedon

DAVID BIANCULLI/2000

From *Fresh Air*, NPR, May 9, 2000. Reprinted by permission.

Bianculli: That's Sarah Michelle Geller and Anthony Stewart Head from the very first episode of *Buffy the Vampire Slayer*, a 20th Century Fox production that airs on the WB. The show and the character were created by my guest, Joss Whedon. Viewers put off by the silly *Buffy the Vampire Slayer* title, or by monster dramas in general, are missing something really special here.

Despite its paranormal situations and characters, and sometimes because of them, *Buffy* is turning out some of the best stuff on TV right now. Genuinely funny jokes and seriously dramatic situations are doled out in equal measure. The show is full of metaphors about how loved ones can turn into monsters, how high school and college life is a particular type of hell and how everyone, to some extent, is haunted by his or her own demons. Characters grow, change, and sometimes even die. And Buffy, through the course of the series so far, has survived high school, left home and her first serious relationship behind, and moved on to college while still fighting demons on the side. She's gotten older and wiser, but life hasn't gotten any easier.

This season, *Buffy* generated its first spinoff series, *Angel*, starring David Boreanaz as a heroic vampire, and the two series currently run back to back on WB's Tuesday schedule.

Bianculli: Joss Whedon, welcome to *Fresh Air*.
Whedon: Thanks for having me.

Bianculli: I'm wondering if you can think back to that first episode [of *Buffy*] so long ago and how you feel about where her character has grown and whether you anticipated any of that back in season one.
Whedon: The character of Buffy has grown a lot. I had always imagined I would take her on a pretty long journey. I didn't realize exactly how far we'd go. I didn't realize how far the actress could go when we first started. I knew

that I wanted somebody who had to deal with the responsibility of this great weight, this burden of being a slayer, and that that would help her to grow up as a person. But I didn't know until I worked with Sarah for a while, you know, how far she could take it, how deep she could go in terms of the grief she could experience and the growth and the intelligence she would bring to it.

Bianculli: Did you know what you wanted to do in terms of this TV series, having come from places like *Roseanne* and doing movies and stuff, what you wanted out of the TV experience?

Whedon: Well, what I wanted was to create a fantasy that was, emotionally, completely realistic. That's what really interests me about anything. I love genre, I love horror, I love action, I love musicals, I love any kind of genre, and *Buffy* sort of embraces them all. But, ultimately, the thing that interests me the most is people and what they're going through, and that's why I loved *Roseanne*, that's why I wanted to work on it, because it was the only sitcom I felt was genuinely funny and also very real and very kind of dark. And that's what I wanted to bring to this.

Bianculli: There's one thing I'm really curious about in terms of your work, and that's if you see it, what you're doing every week in *Buffy*, as writing different chapters of a novel. That by being in control—because you spend so much time reflecting on past history of the characters and past things that they've done, if you're careful about the sequence and if I'm correct in presuming that you allow ramifications to spread on down the line with what these characters do from week to week.

Whedon: Well, I'm very, very much aware of it as being like a novel. You know, the only equivalent to what you can do with a soap opera to me is what Dickens was doing, and he happens to be my favorite novelist, the idea that you can get invested in a character for so long and see it go through so many permutations. It's fascinating to me, the shows that I've always loved the best, *Hill Street Blues*, *Wiseguy*, *Twin Peaks*, have always been shows that did have accumulative knowledge. One of the reasons why *The X-Files* started to leave me cold was that after five years, I just started yelling at Scully, "You're an idiot. It's a monster," and I couldn't take it anymore. I need people to grow, I need them to change, I need them to learn and explore, you know, and die and do all of the things that people do in real life.

And so we're very, very strict about making sure that things track, that they're presented in the right way. Because, ultimately—and this is one of the things that I did find out after we had aired, the soap opera, the characters, the interaction between them is really what people respond to more than anything else. And although we came out of it as a sort of monster-of-the-week format, it was clear that the interaction was the thing that people were latching onto.

So we were happy to sort of go with that and really play it up and really see where these characters were going to go. So now it is very much a continuing show, and we're always aware of that.

Bianculli: Now what part of—what seasons of *Roseanne* did you work on, and what basically were the story arcs at the time?
Whedon: I came in in the second season; I was there for one year. It was—I guess Jackie was becoming a cop and—well, they're all very young. It was very early on. Roseanne had just quit her job and was unemployed for a while. It was the beginning of her hunt for work. And I quit after a year, just because it was kind of chaos there.

Bianculli: Would you like to comment on the type of chaos?
Whedon: The type of chaos was merely that they had a bunch of writers who really didn't know how to write the show, or a show. They were sort of not the right people to be there, and then they had—you know, Roseanne was difficult. I don't think I'm breaking a big news story by explaining that.

Bianculli: Right.
Whedon: And for a while, the chaos worked for me because I got to write a lot of scripts and I really got to work; I got in there. And then I sort of got shut out of the process by the producers. As it got more insane there, they got more insular and they just sort of locked themselves in a room and I found myself with nothing to do, so I'd come in, work on *Buffy*, the movie script, and go home. And I realized that was not what I wanted to do, so I quit.

Bianculli: You were also pretty much a puppy then, weren't you? How old were you?
Whedon: I was twenty-four when I started.

Bianculli: Yeah.
Whedon: That qualifies me for puppy status.

Bianculli: I guess. Well—but, you know, one interesting thing about your doing television, even though you're working on film and stuff at the time, is that you're one of the few people that I've interviewed in terms of writer/producers where you don't imagine a scene where you have to go home and tell your parents, "Oh, I'm going to write for television." Because, you know, it's in your line with both your father and your grandfather writing for TV.
Whedon: Yes, it's true. Well, I do think there was a bit of 'Oh, maybe he'll do something better than we did.' But, no, my father was extraordinarily supportive.

Bianculli: Now in terms of your grandfather's credits, the only one that I know of is *Donna Reed*.

Whedon: *Donna Reed*. There was *Mayberry, R.F.D., Dick Van Dyke*. I know there was a *Room 222* I saw in college that he wrote. But those were the "Make it stupid or make it lighter. Make it fluffier. Take away the edge." And, in fact, they very much encouraged the dark side of it.

Bianculli: . . . Now is it unfair to ask someone who creates all of these characters if there is one that you either relate to more or have more fun writing when you drop into the various skins?

Whedon: You know, I have fun writing all—I love to write all of them, and part of that comes from the actors, because their voices are so unique that the more I know them, the more—like I started to write Willow the way Alyson spoke throughout the first season, because she has such a particular cadence and she and Nicky are both so witty. It's—of the characters that—you know, Spike is always going to be fun to write, because he's always going to have the meanest opinion about anything, and therefore, you know, he's always got a good attitude. He's never just going to be there and be sincere and give exposition. He's always going to put a spin on something.

As far as who I relate to, Xander was obviously based on me, the sort of guy that all the girls want to be best friends with in high school, and who's, you know, kind of a loser, but is more or less articulate and someone you can trust. That part wasn't like me, but the rest was. And I also sometimes identify with Giles, particularly when I'm working and I just—I feel like I'm supposed to be the grown-up in an insane group of children who are not paying attention to me when we have this mission which, in my case, is to create this show. But I also went to English boarding school, and so knew a lot of Gilesy people, so he has a particular resonance for me.

Bianculli: When you build this show, even though it was set in high school, when it came time for them to graduate, you allowed them to graduate and then moved on to a different venue in terms of college. Number one, is that a reaction against, you know, the AARP card-carrying members of *Beverly Hills 90210* and that sort of thing? And is it just the idea of the ongoing Dickensian story that you want to tell?

Whedon: Yeah. You know, I wanted to do the next thing, and sometimes I thought, "Oh, I wish I could've kept them in high school a little bit longer," but it would have started to look silly. I did make one compromise. I had Oz repeat a grade because I wanted him to be there for Willow, and he had ostensibly already graduated. So that was my one cheesy maneuver. But I really felt like, yes, I want to keep him in high school, and that's probably the way they feel. Yes, I'm worried that college is going to be different and not as cool and we won't be as popular as a show, and that's what they'd feel.

The important thing is always to match whatever your characters are going through to whatever you're going through as a creator to what the audience is going through. When people worried about, "How are you ever going to give Buffy a boyfriend after Angel? How are they ever going to get over each other?," well, that's exactly what Buffy was worried about, that's exactly what Angel was worried about. You know, it's taking the challenges, it's taking the fears that you have and letting everybody go through them, because, ultimately, everybody always does.

Bianculli: And then you also get the metaphors as well when she goes to college and has a roommate from hell that pretty much is a roommate from hell.

Whedon: Oh, yeah. Yeah. Well, there wasn't anybody I know who didn't say, "Oh, yeah, that was me." You know, everybody thought that was based on them.

Bianculli: Whenever a program is not set in regular, present-day, normal stuff—I mean, everything from *Star Trek* to *Bonanza*, those shows are able, if they want to, to talk about certain issues at the time, or to get away with some things that they can't otherwise. And I'm wondering if, well, the title of *Buffy the Vampire Slayer* and the idea of monsters, in some respects, may make it a little harder for you to get respect from the Emmy community or something else. Does it also make it easier for you to tell certain stories or explore certain ideas?

Whedon: Absolutely it makes it easier. You know, *Star Trek* dealt with a lot of issues that other people weren't dealing with. As I said before, *Buffy*'s not really an issues show; it's more emotional. But it allows us to get into some very hairy emotional places week to week in a way that you just couldn't with a normal show. You'd think your characters were schizophrenic. When you have the fantasy element of "Oh, here's my evil twin," you can really examine another side of a character and you can go to a very dark place if you want to. You can kill people off, you can bring them back, you can do all these things. You can put everybody through intense emotional paces, and that emotional realism is the core to the show. It's the only thing I'm really interested in. But when you have just a normal show, you can't really take them to that many different places without it just seeming very fake. It's like—you know, soap operas, it's like, "Who's going to get kidnapped today?" You can only do that so many times. But when your show is structured around a genre show—horror or fantasy or science fiction—then you have great license.

What we don't have, which is what some science fiction shows have, is we can't just do a thing because it seems cool. Everything that we pitch, everything that we put out there, whether or not it works, is based on the idea of: The audience has been through this. A normal girl goes through this. A normal guy deals with this. You know, it's issues of sexuality, popularity, jobs. Whatever it is, it's got to be based in realism. We can't just say, "The warship's come and, you know, they transmogrify, the—blah, blah, blah." We can't do that. We can go to some pretty strange places, but at the start, we always have to be about, "How does the audience relate to having done this themselves?"

That's why when we aired "Innocence," when Buffy slept with Angel and his curse went into effect and he became evil again, I went on the Internet and a girl typed in, "This is unbelievable. This exact thing happened to me," and that's when I knew that we were doing the show right . . .

Bianculli: [to the audience] Whedon has also written a number of the episodes, including a recent two-part episode, [in which] the character, Faith, a slayer who started using her power for evil instead of good, found a way to switch bodies with Buffy. So Sarah Michelle Gellar had to play Faith pretending to be Buffy. She's a bad Buffy, but her friends and enemies don't know that . . . [B]ad Buffy is at a club and runs into Spike, played by James Marsters. Spike is a vampire adversary who no longer is able to bite people.*
Bianculli: You wrote that, didn't you?
Whedon: Yes, I did, actually.

Bianculli: OK. So what's that like to write? What's it like to hand out to the different actors and what's it like to have it done on the floor?
Whedon: Well, it's—the most fun is writing it—is figuring out what these characters need to say to each other and pushing the envelope sometimes in terms of the kind of content we get. Obviously, that could be taken to be a little bit dirty, that speech. But, you know, Faith is very much somebody who uses her sexuality to wield power over people. It's—once I give it to the actors at this point, they're pretty much—they just go with it, you know, I can't surprise them anymore. They're used to having to do everything. The stranger things get, the more they have to play somebody who's not them, the more they take it in stride.

And shooting it is, you know—it just depends on the day. It's always fun to shoot the scenes with James. Sarah loves working with him because he has a great rapport with everyone and people don't get that many scenes with him— Spike—so they always relish them because he always brings a very different perspective. And for him to be completely controlled by somebody else in the scene, Faith, who is basically just badder than he is, you know, is a different experience for him. So that's always fun. But then you have to shoot like nineteen angles of it, and then it becomes less fun. And then it gets genuinely boring.

Bianculli: Right. I know it eventually ends up as work. Plays well on the screen. When you talk about the flexibility and the versatility, that's also definitely true of the co-stars and just about everybody who appears in the show. And I'm wondering, you came to *Angel* as the spin-off and to David Boreanaz as his character, but you could have gone—it would seem—with a half dozen of them and spun off. How did you decide upon *Angel*?

Whedon: Well, I have always been of the opinion that any one of these guys could sustain their own show. I think they're that good. I think they're that interesting. And I think they're pretty. But Angel became the logical choice for a few reasons, and that was clear early on. One, he is like Buffy, bigger than life, you know. He, for the first couple of seasons anyway, was the only superhero on the show, in a sense, that Buffy was. You know, he had something more. Now, Oz became a werewolf, Willow became a witch. Everybody sort of had something to make them more than they'd been. But at the time, everyone else was normal, mortal, whereas, Angel was kind of a bigger-than-life character. And if people responded to him like that, then he was gonna have a kind of heat that would certainly make the network interested in making a show about him.

I also knew that the romance between Buffy and Angel could go so far before it became incredibly tired. And we found interesting ways to shake that up, obviously. The moment she slept with him, he turned evil, which, as I was saying before, in that episode, "Innocence" was a huge benchmark for the show. But ultimately there were so many variations we could play. And so, even though people are constantly yelling at me and screaming on the Internet that I have to get them back together, we knew that there was gonna come a time where there wouldn't be as much of a place for Angel on the show, so it made sense to give him his own.

Bianculli: The idea of getting to the point where you have him trying to redeem the bad character of Faith because he had been a bad character himself, and then having Buffy come in and almost be the villain in this triangle—not the villain, per se, but just that it changed the dynamics so much. These seem to be pretty high stakes chess moves with these characters.

Whedon: Well, you can't—I mean, you can't bring Buffy to Angel without a good reason, without it making an impact. You can't just drop by and borrow a cup of sugar. For one thing, it's too difficult production-wise. For another thing, it sort of lessens their impact as mythic characters. We brought her back once before and they'd had the grand love that they'd always been denied, in an episode called "I Will Remember You." And then, of course, he was forced to take it all back and she remembered none of it. So we had played great tragic romance in that respect and it was a lot of fun and very much felt like a culmination of where they'd been going, but what do you do the next time?

And when we realized the kind of conflict they were gonna have over Faith and how they would have two totally different perspectives about it, we realized that that was what we needed to play in terms of creating the mythic story with the big characters. Here are three characters, you know, coming at an issue from three totally different angles, so they really have conflict on a higher level, but at the same time emotionally, it's that thing of, "You can't stay away from your old boyfriend or girlfriend, but you can't get along even remotely."

Bianculli: . . . One of the things that you do from time to time in *Buffy* and in *Angel* is to establish a very important character and then ruthlessly and unexpectedly kill them off. And you have said that you like surprises. But with Jenny, for example, in *Buffy* and with Doyle who was a co-star in *Angel*, you just set up these people and then take them from us. *St. Elsewhere* did that. *Twins Peaks* did that. Not a lot of TV shows do that. Why do you do that, and what reaction do you get from fans when you do it?

Whedon: Well, I do it because I want to keep [everyone] afraid. I want to keep people in suspense. I want people to understand that everything is not perfectly safe. The problem with doing a horror show on television is that you know your main characters are coming back week to week, and you're not— you don't really care about, you know, somebody who just showed up for one episode. So, you know, every now and then you have to make the statement, "You know, nothing is safe." And that's a very effective way of doing that. If somebody objects, if somebody says, "How could you kill that character? You have to bring that character back. You have to bring that character back." I know I've done the right thing. If they go, "Oh, they're dead," then I killed the wrong person because nobody cares. One of the things that people always shy away from is killing a sympathetic character.

When I worked on *Speed*, there was a character who died—a lawyer that Alan Ruck played, and I took out the lawyer; he was a bad man, he was terrible, he was causing trouble and he ended up dying. And I turned him into a likeable, sort of a doofy tourist guy, and they're like, "Well, now we can't kill him." And I—my opinion was, "Well, now you should because now people will actually care when he dies." But nobody wants to kill a good guy; it makes them twitchy, particularly on a series. And we were very careful about it because if there's somebody we know we're gonna want for future episodes—but then again, Jenny Calendar worked more episodes probably after she died than she did before because on our show everybody's a ghost, everybody's a whatnot. But it does inflame emotion sometimes, but that is, in fact, what I'm trying to do.

Bianculli: When you talk about the resonance of characters and keeping the history going, back in the episode "Doppelganger," I guess a couple of seasons ago now, there was a reference made to Willow, Alyson Hannigan's character,

as, at least in this other existence, having a bisexual sexuality, and that supposedly based on the Doppelganger rules, that that might mean something
on this real *Buffy* world. And in the most recent episode of *Buffy the Vampire
Slayer*, which I think was, by the way, a very dramatic and very well-done hour
of television . . .
Whedon: Thank you.

Bianculli: . . . it culminated with a readjustment of Willow's sexuality, and yet,
if you'd been watching the show for a couple of years, it wasn't like an *Ellen*
move or anything else—it seemed very organic and natural to the story, and I
was wondering how the decision was reached to go that way and with as much
restraint as the episode presented it?
Whedon: Well, the arc between Willow and Tara has kind of a long and sort
of tortured history. We had thought about the idea of someone exploring their
sexuality, expanding it a little bit in college, because that's felt like one of the
things that might happen in college. Since we tend to work inside metaphor
for most of the show, you know, we talked about Willow and her being a witch
because it's a very strong female community, and it gives her a very physical
relationship with someone that isn't necessarily sexual at first. And then when
we decided to go that way, part of it was because Seth Green wanted to step
out and do movies, and we knew that he was going to be out of the picture
and, you know, we had to do something with Willow, and it seemed like a
good time for her to be exploring this.

Then the question just became how much do we play in metaphor and how
much do we play as her actually expanding her sexuality? And you're walking
a very fine line there. The network obviously has issues. They don't want any
kissing. That's one thing that they've stipulated. And they're a little nervous
about it. Ultimately, they haven't interfered at all with what we've tried to do,
but, you know, they've raised a caution about it. And, you know, at the same
time, you have people—the moment Tara appeared on the scene—saying,
"Well, they're obviously gay. Why aren't they gay enough? They're not gay
enough. You need to make them more gay." You know, people want you to
make a statement. They want you to turn it into an issue right away. So you
sort of have forces buffeting you and you're trying to come up with what is
both emotionally sort of correct as a progression and also sort of mythically
significant in terms of your greater arc. You're trying to wield all these things
and, week to week, sort of make this thing progress.

Bianculli: Now when you do these major moves for your characters, the story
meetings that you have with the other writer-producers, how far ahead are you
working? What's your bible like or whatever it's called?
Whedon: Generally speaking, I come into a season with the arc for the season,

the main fill-in, you know, the main sort of journeys for each of the characters, where are they going to go and some benchmarks—certain episodes. Somewhere around episode 10, this has to happen. Somewhere around episode 15, this has to happen. We have to keep it flexible, because you come up with better ideas or an actor falls out or something happens, you know. The process of creating TV is entirely fluid. You always have to be ready to be thrown a curve, and in our case, every time we have, I think it's helped us out a great deal. I really think what we're doing with Willow and Tara is interesting. And Amber Benson's a wonderful actress. That might not have happened if we hadn't lost Seth.

You always have to be ready for those things, and they tend to work out really well if you are. But at the same time, you must have a bigger plan, both emotionally and structurally. Because I make each year on *Buffy* work as a separate arc. I did that with the first season because I didn't know if we were ever going to air again, and I absolutely hate a show that ends in the middle before everything's over. It drives me insane if the story isn't finished. So with "Prophecy Girl," on the last episode of the first season, I finished the story, and if we had never aired another show, it would have still been a self-contained union of twelve episodes that told a story. So that's how we designed every year. And right now, we're in the process of discussing year five of *Buffy* and year two of *Angel*, figuring out the benchmarks for those seasons.

Bianculli: And I guess my last question then is: Is there anything in general you can tell us about any of those story arcs in general, or if not, what you can tell us about what you're doing next?

Whedon: Well, I can't tell you much about what's going to happen next year because I don't like to spoil things. I'm a great believer in the surprise. And although it's incredibly difficult actually to have a surprise, especially with the Internet, I do like to try every now and then to shock people. It's going to be a very different year on *Buffy* than it was certainly—this last year was about college. It was about the sudden freedom and how you try on new personas and how your gang kind of falls apart, and at the end of your first year of college, you're in a very different place. Next year is really about family, is about getting the group back together and really working within the group. It's about sort of refocusing, and so I think people who feel like the Scooby gang, Buffy's friends and whatnot have become a little peripheral, they're going to be pleased. We're going to see much more intense interaction between all our main characters, who all sort of got scattered in this last year. And what I'm going to be doing next is figuring out what all that literally means, because right now, we're starting to break stories for both shows and I don't really have time for a whole lot else.

Bianculli: Well, you made me feel guilty about taking up this much of your time, but thank you very much for being here.
Whedon: Damn you. No.

Bianculli: It's a pleasure to have you here.
Whedon: I really appreciate it. Thank you. It's good to talk to you.

*Here is the speech Bianculli and Whedon speak of:
Buffy: 'Cause I could do anything I want, and instead, I choose to pout and whine and feel the burden of slayerness? I mean, I could be rich, I could be famous, I could have anything. Anyone. [Buffy moves closer and puts her hands on Spike's chest.] Even you, Spike. I could ride you at a gallop until your legs buckled and your eyes rolled up. I've got muscles you've never even dreamed of. I could squeeze you until you popped like warm champagne, and you'd beg me to hurt you just a little bit more. And you know why I don't? [She moves closer and looks up at him pursing her lips.] Because it's wrong. Humh humh.

Joss Whedon Gets Big, Bad, and Grown-Up with *Angel*

PATRICK LEE/2000

From *Science Fiction Weekly*, 2000. Reprinted by permission.

Joss Whedon, creator of the WB network's hit show *Buffy the Vampire Slayer*, takes on added duties this year with the *Buffy* spinoff *Angel*. Whedon's creations have won him a broad fan following, particularly on the Internet, where fans gather to share their enthusiasm for all things Sunnydale. Whedon, one of Hollywood's best-known script doctors, has also been working on a rewrite of the upcoming feature film version of *The X-Men*. Whedon took a few minutes last week to talk to *Science Fiction Weekly* about his two shows, his fans, his film career, the decision by the WB to postpone two controversial *Buffy* episodes last season in the wake of real-life high school shootings, and more.

Lee: You've got a full plate this television season; the fourth for *Buffy* and the first for *Angel*. How are you going to juggle the two shows?
Whedon: I really have no idea. I am burned out already. [*Angel* executive producer] David Greenwalt and I just stare at each other balefully and say, "What were we thinking?" I think my life is over, and that's just something I have to deal with. [Seriously], I don't know how it's done. Basically, it just means I work harder. We were working sixteen hours a day on *Buffy*, and now we work sixteen hours a day, but more concentrated. It's more mentally exhausting. But it's not like you can let it slide. I still don't work on Sundays when I can avoid it. Now I'm actually firm about not working Sundays, since I'm so burned out after the week, more so than before.

Lee: What changes do you have in store for Buffy and the gang this season? Will college be a kinder environment for Buffy? If high school was hell, what will college be like?
Whedon: College is similar hell. Everyone's emotions are still a roller coaster, and there are themes aplenty. Basically it's a new experience for Buffy—a lot of new freedoms, new restrictions, new fears—but at the same time a lot more fun. Last year was harsh for her; this year she explores a lot of new personalities

and relationships and emotions with all the freedom and fun of college, but also the fear that it brings. There's the lack of security and all the fear. [Her mother] Joyce will be in it less, since Buffy's not living at home.

Lee: Will you turn Amy, the witch, from a rat into a human?
Whedon: Someday we'll probably figure a way to do that.

Lee: Will there be new villains?
Whedon: Yes. Much more I cannot say. We have a season arc planned, and there's definitely stuff going on around her that's new, and very strange, but we're keeping it a mystery.

Lee: What can you tell us about how *Angel* will differ from *Buffy*? You've said it will be more adult. It's been said it will be darker; people have described it as a vampire *Batman*. How will you sustain a distinct voice for the show?
Whedon: It brings with it certain elements that necessarily make it different from *Buffy*, the first and foremost among them being [star] David [Boreanaz]. He's a different performer playing a different character. He's intense, dark, a solid moral person you trust. Buffy was a constant underdog and open to everyone. Angel is someone you see from afar; he's more closed. The kind of attraction they emit is different, almost the opposite, which is why they made such a good couple. We're also not dealing with high school or college; we're dealing with the big, bad grown-up world and the people first entering it. We're looking at a lot of the things people go through: getting their apartments, trying to date outside the controlled environment of a campus, getting married. These rituals happen to people in their twenties. But of course, they'll all be scary and horrible. [The dark look of the show] is very much intentional, necessitated because Angel's not wearing pink. And it's L.A. and, also, he's a vampire, so not a lot of daytime. Of course, we don't want it to be unrelentingly dark, blue-colored. There will definitely be lightness and humor.

Lee: How much of a commitment has the WB given you for *Angel*?
Whedon: Thirteen episodes. So far, [the reaction from the WB has] been very positive. They seem very pleased, and we're still finding our footing in some ways. The show is discovering itself, as they do in the first few episodes. We're turning out good stories as we find our way, and the WB seems quite pleased.

Lee: How do you feel about the WB's decision last year to postpone both "Earshot"—about a potential high school massacre—and "Graduation Day, Part 2," the season finale in which students take up arms against a giant serpent?

Whedon: I agreed with the postponement of "Earshot," but not "Graduation Day," but I respected their motivations for doing it. I didn't think they needed to, but I didn't hate them for it either.

Lee: What did you think of the fans' efforts to distribute the episodes in bootleg form? And what did you think of the full-page ad the fans took out in *Daily Variety* over the summer protesting the decision?
Whedon: I got in big trouble for saying I thought it was cool [that fans were bootlegging the episodes], but ultimately it was nice to know that people cared about the show. [The WB] thought they would get terrible ratings, but they did fine when they finally aired. [The bootlegs] did not hurt us that much in terms of the network's needs. We were all just tremendously touched [by the *Variety* ad]; it was very cool. I have a framed copy of it in my office.

Lee: You've developed quite an Internet-based following for *Buffy*. What do you think of that? Do you read fan comments, and do they influence your thinking about the show? Or do you ignore most of it?
Whedon: I think it's really neat. I haven't had as much time as I used to to check in and see what people are talking about. [But] sure, I'll read the posting board. I'm always interested to see what people are responding to, and what they're not. To an extent it does [affect me]. For example, when I saw that people were rejecting the Oz character when he was first introduced, I realized how carefully I had to place him. I wrote scenes where Willow falls in love with him in a way where fans would fall in love with him too. You learn that people don't take things at face value; you have to earn them. It was clear that David was a popular figure fairly early on.

Lee: Do you share William Shatner's opinion of the most ardent fans that they need to get a life?
Whedon: I have never had any particular life of my own, so I don't see any particular reason why anyone should run out to get one. Of course, if they're dressing up like Willow and staying in their basement for nine months at a time, that's not good. But the show's designed to foster slavish devotion; it has it from me, and I entirely respect it in others.

Lee: How do you feel about the cultural impact of *Buffy*? The comics, merchandise, fan fiction, etc.?
Whedon: Again, the show was designed to be the kind of show that people would build myths on, read comics about, that would keep growing. So naturally, I'm wicked pleased that it's entering people's consciousness. I obviously can't read [fan fiction], but the fact is there seems to be a great deal of it, and that's terrific. I wished I'd had that outlet as a youngster, or had the time to do it now.

Lee: Let's talk about your feature film plans. You've said that the studio won't be using your rewrite of *The X-Men*. Are there pet projects you'd like to see produced?

Whedon: I'm not too hopeful my version [of *The X-Men*] will show up; there may be some stuff left when the dust settles, but no, it looks like they went a different way. The difference between my movie career and my TV career is, my TV career has been successful. I'm very unhappy with my movie career. There's stuff I'm proud of, but some really big disappointments, *Alien Resurrection* being first and foremost among them. [I have lots of ideas], but there are none I can actually describe. I've had such bad luck seeing things turn up before I have a chance to develop them. A *Buffy* movie would be a thrill; it would be totally good for the cast and they deserve it. They'd be terrific on the big screen. But it's nothing resembling a reality at this point, and it certainly isn't something we'd do while the show is still on the air. But it's something that would be wicked cool to me.

Lee: What's Oz's last name?
Whedon: Osborne.

Lee: What's Angel's? Do we ever find out?
Whedon: I'm not sure. We will find out one day.

Lee: Do you believe in vampires?
Whedon: I do not. I think that they are something we made up that's cool.

Westfield Comics Joss Whedon Interview

ROGER ASH/2001

From *Westfield Comics*, July 2001. Reprinted by permission.

Joss Whedon is best known as the creator of *Buffy the Vampire Slayer* and *Angel*. He's also written or co-written scripts for films including *Alien Resurrection*, *Titan A.E.*, and the original *Toy Story*. This month he sets his sights on comics with *Fray* from Dark Horse. Worlds of Westfield Content Editor Roger Ash recently spoke with Whedon about *Fray*.

Westfield: What can you tell us about *Fray*?
Whedon: It's a slayer story, but one that's not connected at all to the *Buffy* mythos, except that it's about a slayer. I wanted to do a futuristic, slightly sci-fi adventure, but I didn't want to create a whole new universe. I wanted to stay sort of in the world that I had already created, so I had some of the groundwork already laid. At one point, I had thought about doing a story about Faith, but then we brought Faith back to be on *Angel*, so I can't really interfere with that myth. I thought if I go a few hundred years into the future, I probably won't step on any toes. Then I can do whatever I want in the series and I can have fun with the comic.

Westfield: Who are some of the major characters in *Fray*?
Whedon: The major character would be Melaka Fray, she's the heroine. She's the slayer, although she has no idea of this at first. She is a professional thief who works for a guy named Gunther who is, among other things, a big fish. In the future, there's a lot of mutations out there. She's confronted by UrKonn, who's an extremely powerful demon, early on. But her nemesis, the vampire that she first met up with when she was younger, is called Icarus. He's a particular bad-ass. He's in the mix a lot. There's her sister, Erin Fray, who's a cop. They have a very contentious relationship because Melaka's a crook. They have very different reactions to the crappy lives they've had. Those are the major players, except that Icarus is working for a higher being that we don't meet for a while.

The other thing is that, not only has there not been a slayer called for a couple hundred years in this, there hasn't been any vampires or demons or magic of any kind in the world. Vampires are reoccurring, and nobody even knows what they're called. When Fray's first told that she has to fight vampires, she doesn't know what the word means. They don't even have them in legends, so it's all a whole new world for her. It takes place in Manhattan, which they call Haddyn, because everything's sort of shortened. Manhattan is exactly as it is now, only more so. They just kept building straight up.

Westfield: Why did you decide to do *Fray* as a comic?

Whedon: Because there's no way on God's green earth I could afford to do it any other way. There's a bunch of flying cars in it. I wanted to do a comic. I love comics. I've read them my whole life. I've always wanted to write one. I thought about this story and thought, "Instead of creating a whole new world, I can just do this and maybe it'll be self contained and it can be a little journey into comics." I had hoped just to do a couple issues of something, then it ballooned into an eight-part story because I can never shut up.

Westfield: How much work did you do on creating this new version of the world before you actually started working on the comics and what were some of the influences you drew on?

Whedon: In terms of creating the world, we kept it pretty simple. Artist Karl Moline looked a lot at the movies *Blade Runner* and *Fifth Element* because those are both urbanization gone mad. Stylistically, those were obviously influences just in terms of creating the world. I didn't spend a lot of time coming up with a brilliant vision of the future. I wanted to keep it simple. My excuse is always, and it's the same thing I did in *Alien Resurrection*, for the rich people, for the normal people, for the people who actually live inside the law; yes, computers have changed everything and everyone is young and beautiful, and it's a whole new world and there's all sorts of ramifications. But if you're poor, nothing has really changed. Especially if you're crooked. That gets me out of having to actually imagine a lot of things because I'm not the sci-fi visionary that some people are, although it would be fun to get into a world like that. I wanted to tell a pretty basic story. I just wanted to have that scope, that feel. I love stuff in the future.

Westfield: How is writing *Fray* similar or different to what you do when you write for TV or films?

Whedon: It's surprisingly both, actually. It's similar in that you're looking for the big moments, you're looking for the big emotions, and you're constantly saying these guys are overacting. It's different in the sense that you have to choose a still picture that will convey what usually you would have movement to convey. When you're taking off in the air or landing, which one is the one you need to show? How much do need to convey visually? How much can you do in one panel? That's different and pretty exciting just because it's new.

Westfield: How did you feel when you first saw Karl Moline's art for *Fray*?
Whedon: I love it. I'm pretty blown away by it. We've definitely gone back and forth on a couple of things, conceptual things. There're certain things that I stress that he doesn't. We're feeling each other out in that sense. But I think his pencils are really lovely. His character stuff is really beautifully detailed. I love Melaka. I love the look of the world. It's very dynamic. I'm pretty thrilled. I just got the colored pages for the first issue and I've been just giggling like a school girl.

Westfield: Do you have any plans for *Fray* past this mini-series?
Whedon: We're doing a book, *Tales of the Slayers*, a one-shot that me and a bunch of the writers from the show are doing that will encompass a lot of different slayers in stories, and there will be a short Fray story in that. Beyond that, I have no immediate plans. But if people really respond and they're like "hey, we want a *Fray* book," certainly it would be open. The story will be self-contained, but I'm not going to blow up the world at the end of it.

Westfield: You're also working on an *Angel* comic that's coming out soon. Can you tell us anything about that?
Whedon: Brett Matthews, who is on my staff and who has spent hours and hours talking comic books and films with me, we both went to the same college, studied film at the same place; we're both comic book freaks. We've spent a lot of time talking about the *Angel* book and what we thought we should do. He said, "Why don't we just do that?" And we called editor Scott Allie and said, "Can we write a couple?" And Scott's like, "OK." That's one of the things I love about Dark Horse, they're really nice about everything. What we've been trying to do is get the *Angel* book to be more of a comic book. The template was so locked to the show that it was starting to feel a little stale because a TV show is not a comic book. Let's have the character with the big, long tail. Let's have the two-story Jack Kirby monster. Let's have this guy swoop from the shadows in an alley in the dark of night and save somebody, not unlike that guy with the cape. Let's accentuate that. Let's make it a real bigger-than-life comic book. Give it some of that sexy feel. So we came up with a four-part story arc. Brett's doing most of the heavy lifting. We've been bringing the story together, and I've been working dialog on him, but in terms of laying it out, it's mostly his. I think it's going well. It's fun. Some very cool pencils from Mel Rubi.

Westfield: Can you say anything more about the *Tales of the Slayers* book?
Whedon: We don't have a date for it, but we talked about this when we were shooting the seventies flashback of Spike killing a slayer on a subway. I said to Doug Petrie, who's one of my writers and who's written some of the *Buffy* comics and is, like me, a comic book nut, "God. We should do a compendium of stories of slayers throughout history." And he was like "I get to do the seventies slayer on the subway." He's actually doing it with Gene Colan. There was so much of the original *Blade* and *Tomb of Dracula* in that whole sequence. We were so into that. We pitched that to Scott and he was all over it and it turned out that practically my entire staff wanted to do it. They all picked an era and we talked about length and I'm doing three little pieces in it myself. It's a different artist for every piece and we're getting some really exciting people to draw it. Luckily, a little more contained than this eight-issue monster.

Westfield: Can you mention any of the other artists who are working on it?
Whedon: Karl's going to do, obviously, the Fray story for me. I think Tim Sale is going to do one of my pieces, which I'm just freaking out about. Craig Russell is doing something, and, like I said, Gene. I'm not sure who else at this point. We're still fairly early in the process. But cool guys. [Note: Editor Scott Allie says we can add Ted Naifeh and Steve Lieber to the list of artists working on the book.]

Westfield: Is there anything you'd care to share about what we can look forward to on the *Buffy* and *Angel* TV series?
Whedon: Lots o' fun. [laughter] Hey, I'm not wrong. Both shows are gearing up for season finales of just insane adventure. The last four episodes of both shows just kick into enormous high gear. It's gonna be really fun, really hard to shoot, really expensive, and I'll be really tired afterwards. [laughter] Hopefully, things will wrap up emotionally as well as adventuresomely.

Westfield: Do you plot out the story arc for the entire year before you start doing anything?
Whedon: Actually, we plotted out the story arc for this year before last year. It was in the third year that we figured out what we wanted to do for the next two years. So, yes. We plot it out leaving room for disasters or fortuitous occasions. Anything could change. Basically, we plot it ahead always, because if you don't know where you're going, you're not going anywhere.

Westfield: With that in mind, do you have an eventual end in mind for *Buffy*?
Whedon: No, I really don't. I end every year as though it's the last year, just in case, so that you don't feel that sense of "but there was all that left unresolved."

Instead of doing cliffhangers, I like to leave every year with a sense of closure. But no, I don't see any end in sight. I've already got plenty of extraordinary ideas for next year.

The Onion A.V. Club Interview with Joss Whedon (1)

TASHA ROBINSON/2001

From *The A.V. Club*, September 5, 2001. © Onion Inc. Reprinted by permission.

Joss Whedon is a third-generation television scriptwriter, possibly the first one. As he tells the story, he never intended to follow in his father's footsteps: He started his career as a snobby film student who never watched television and intended to write movies, until he found out how much TV writing paid. Ultimately, he did both, working as a scriptwriter on *Roseanne* and the TV series *Parenthood* before selling his script to the 1992 *Buffy the Vampire Slayer* movie. For several years, he was a film writer and a script doctor, doing uncredited touch-ups on *Twister*, *Speed*, and *Waterworld*, and writing drafts of projects such as *X-Men*, *Toy Story*, *Titan A.E.*, Disney's *Atlantis*, and *Alien: Resurrection*. But Whedon came into his own with the television incarnation of *Buffy*, which has, over the past few years, grown from a cult classic into a cottage industry. As the original creator of the Buffy character, Whedon—now a writer, director, and executive producer of the *Buffy the Vampire Slayer* TV show—has a hand in virtually all of its spinoffs, including the WB series *Angel*, a line of comic-book tie-ins distributed by Dark Horse, and an upcoming animated series and BBC TV show. Whedon recently spoke to The Onion A.V. Club about the *Buffy* phenomenon, his bitterness over his movie career, and the fans who share in his worship of his creations.

The Onion: So, how are you bringing Buffy back? [The character died at the end of this past season.—ed.]
Whedon: Aw, I'm not supposed to tell.

The Onion: I'm teasing. I know you get that a lot.
Whedon: Yeah, it's the first thing everybody asks, including my developers. And the answer is, I can't say, because that's why you watch the show. The one thing I can say is, I think we earn it. There's no Patrick Duffy in the shower, there's no alternate-universe Buffy. It's not going to be neat. Bringing her back is difficult, and the consequences are fairly intense. It's not like we don't take these death-things seriously. But exactly how she comes back, I can't reveal.

The Onion: When your actors get questions like that in interviews, they always seem to answer with horrific threats: "I can't tell, Joss will rip out my tongue and feed it to wolves," and so forth. Do they actually get these threats from you?

Whedon: I'm a very gentle man, not unlike Gandhi. I don't ever threaten them. There is, sort of hanging over their head, the thing that I could kill them at any moment. But that's really just if they annoy me. They know that I'm very secretive about plot twists and whatnot, because I think it's better for the show. But anybody with a computer can find out what's going to happen, apparently even before I know. So my wish for secrecy is sort of pathetic. But they're all on board. They don't want to give it away, and a lot of times, they just don't know.

The Onion: How closely were you involved with the making of the *Buffy* movie?

Whedon: I had major involvement. I was there almost all the way through shooting. I pretty much eventually threw up my hands because I could not be around Donald Sutherland any longer. It didn't turn out to be the movie that I had written. They never do, but that was my first lesson in that. Not that the movie is without merit, but I just watched a lot of stupid wannabe-star behavior and a director with a different vision than mine—which was her right, it was her movie—but it was still frustrating. Eventually, I was like, "I need to be away from here."

The Onion: Was it a personality conflict between you and Sutherland, or was he just not what you'd envisioned in that role?

Whedon: No, no, he was just a prick. The thing is, people always make fun of Rutger Hauer [for his *Buffy* role]. Even though he was big and silly and looked kind of goofy in the movie, I have to give him credit, because he was there. He was into it. Whereas Donald was just . . . He would rewrite all his dialogue, and the director would let him. He can't write—he's not a writer—so the dialogue would not make sense. And he had a very bad attitude. He was incredibly rude to the director, he was rude to everyone around him, he was just a real pain. And to see him destroying my stuff . . . Some people didn't notice. Some people liked him in the movie. Because he's Donald Sutherland. He's a great actor. He can read the phone book, and I'm interested. But the thing is, he acts well enough that you didn't notice, with his little rewrites, and his little ideas about what his character should do, that he was actually destroying the movie more than Rutger was. So I got out of there. I had to run away.

The Onion: What was Paul Reubens like? He seems to be the actor people remember most from the movie.

Whedon: [Adopts weepy, awed voice.] He is a god that walks among us. He is one of the sweetest, most professional and delightful people I've ever worked with. [Normal voice.] He was my beacon of hope in that whole experience, that he was such a good guy, and so got it. I mean, most of the people were sweet. Most of them were actively out there trying . . . They were good people. Paul was a delight to be around, trying to make it better. He actually said to me, "I'm a little worried about this line, and I want to change it. I realize that it'll change this other thing, so if that's a problem . . ." I'm like, "Did I just hear an actor say that?"

The Onion: How early on did it occur to you to re-do *Buffy* the way you'd originally intended?

Whedon: You know, it wasn't really my idea. After the premier of the movie, my wife said, "You know, honey, maybe a few years from now, you'll get to make it again, the way you want to make it!" [Broad, condescending voice.] "Ha ha ha, you little naïve fool. It doesn't work that way. That'll never happen." And then it was three years later, and Gail Berman actually had the idea. Sandollar [Television] had the property, and Gail thought it would make a good TV series. They called me up out of contractual obligation: "Call the writer, have him pass." And I was like, "Well, that sounds cool." So, to my agent's surprise and chagrin, I said, "Yeah, I could do that. I think I get it. It could be a high-school horror movie. It'd be a metaphor for how lousy my high-school years were." So I hadn't had the original idea, I just developed it.

The Onion: You joke a lot in interviews about how you wanted to write horror because you experienced so much of it in high school. Did you have an unusually bad high-school experience, or was it just the usual teen traumas?

Whedon: I think it's not inaccurate to say that I had a perfectly happy childhood during which I was very unhappy. It was nothing worse than anybody else. I could not get a date to save my life, but my last three years of high school were at a boys' school, so I wasn't actually looking that hard. I was not popular in school, and I was definitely not a ladies' man. And I had a very painful adolescence, because it was all very strange to me. It wasn't like I got beat up, but the humiliation and isolation, and the existential "God, I exist, and nobody cares" of being a teenager were extremely pronounced for me. I don't have horror stories. I mean, I have a few horror stories about attempting to court a girl, which would make people laugh, but it's not like I think I had it worse than other people. But that's sort of the point of *Buffy*, that I'm talking about the stuff everybody goes through. Nobody gets out of here without some trauma.

The Onion: How much of your writing made it into the final versions of *Twister* and *Speed*?

Whedon: Most of the dialogue in *Speed* is mine, and a bunch of the characters. That was actually pretty much a good experience. I have quibbles. I also have the only poster left with my name still on it. Getting arbitrated off the credits was un-fun. But *Speed* has a bunch. And *Twister*, less. In *Twister*, there are things that worked and things that weren't the way I'd intended them. Whereas *Speed* came out closer to what I'd been trying to do. I think of *Speed* as one of the few movies I've made that I actually like.

The Onion: What about *Waterworld*?
Whedon: [Laughs.] *Waterworld*. I refer to myself as the world's highest-paid stenographer. This is a situation I've been in a bunch of times. By the way, I'm very bitter, is that okay? I mean, people ask me, "What's the worst job you ever had?" "I once was a writer in Hollywood . . ." Talk about taking the glow off of movies. I've had almost nothing but bad experiences. *Waterworld* was a good idea, and the script was the classic, "They have a good idea, then they write a generic script and don't really care about the idea." When I was brought in, there was no water in the last forty pages of the script. It all took place on land, or on a ship, or whatever. I'm like, "Isn't the cool thing about this guy that he has gills?" And no one was listening. I was there basically taking notes from Costner, who was very nice, fine to work with, but he was not a writer. And he had written a bunch of stuff that they wouldn't let their staff touch. So I was supposed to be there for a week, and I was there for seven weeks, and I accomplished nothing. I wrote a few puns, and a few scenes that I can't even sit through because they came out so bad. It was the same situation with *X-Men*. They said, "Come in and punch up the big climax, the third act, and if you can, make it cheaper." That was the mandate on both movies, and my response to both movies was, "The problem with the third act is the first two acts." But, again, no one was paying attention. *X-Men* was very interesting in that, by that time, I actually had a reputation in television. I was actually somebody. People stopped thinking I was John Sweden on the phone. And then, in *X-Men*, not only did they throw out my script and never tell me about it; they actually invited me to the read-through, having thrown out my entire draft without telling me. I was like, "Oh, that's right! This is the movies! The writer is shit in the movies!" I'll never understand that. I have one line left in that movie. Actually, there are a couple of lines left in that are out of context and make no sense, or are delivered so badly, so terribly . . . There's one line that's left the way I wrote it.

The Onion: Which is?
Whedon: "It's me." "Prove it." "You're a dick." Hey, it got a laugh.

The Onion: It's funny that the only lines I really remember from that movie are that one and Storm's toad comment.

Whedon: Okay, which was also mine, and that's the interesting thing. Everybody remembers that as the worst line ever written, but the thing about that is, it was supposed to be delivered as completely offhand. [Adopts casual, bored tone.] "You know what happens when a toad gets hit by lightning?" Then, after he gets electrocuted, "Ahhh, pretty much the same thing that happens to anything else." But Halle Berry said it like she was Desdemona. [Strident, ringing voice.] "The same thing that happens to everything eeelse!" That's the thing that makes you go crazy. At least "You're a dick" got delivered right. The worst thing about these things is that, when the actors say it wrong, it makes the writer look stupid. People assume that the line . . . I listened to half the dialogue in *Alien 4*, and I'm like, "That's idiotic," because of the way it was said. And nobody knows that. Nobody ever gets that. They say, "That was a stupid script," which is the worst pain in the world. I have a great long boring story about that, but I can tell you the very short version. In *Alien 4*, the director changed something so that it didn't make any sense. He wanted someone to go and get a gun and get killed by the alien, so I wrote that in and tried to make it work, but he directed it in a way that it made no sense whatsoever. And I was sitting there in the editing room, trying to come up with looplines to explain what's going on, to make the scene make sense, and I asked the director, "Can you just explain to me why he's doing this? Why is he going for this gun?" And the editor, who was French, turned to me and said, with a little leer on his face, [adopts gravelly, smarmy, French-accented voice] "Because eet's een the screept." And I actually went and dented the bathroom stall with my puddly little fist. I have never been angrier. But it's the classic, "When something goes wrong, you assume the writer's a dork." And that's painful.

The Onion: Have you done any other uncredited script work?
Whedon: Actually, my first gig ever was writing looplines for a movie that had already been made. You know, writing lines over somebody's back to explain something, to help make a connection, to add a joke, or to just add babble because the people are in frame and should be saying something. We're constantly saving something that doesn't work, or trying to, with lines behind people's backs. It's almost like adding narration, but cheaper. I did looplines for *The Getaway*, the Alec Baldwin/Kim Basinger version. If you look carefully at *The Getaway*, you'll see that when people's backs are turned, or their heads are slightly out of frame, the whole movie has a certain edge to it. I also did a couple of days of looplines and punch-ups for *The Quick and the Dead*, just to meet Sam Raimi.

The Onion: I attended your Q&A session at a comics convention last year, and many of the people who got up to ask questions were nearly in tears over the chance to get to talk to you. Some of them could barely speak, and others couldn't stop gushing about you, and about *Buffy*. How do you deal with that kind of emotional intensity?

Whedon: It's about the show, and I feel the same way about it. I get the same way. It's not like being a rock star. It doesn't feel like they're reacting to me. It's really sweet when people react like that, and I love the praise, but to me, what they're getting emotional about is the show. And that's the best feeling in the world. There's nothing creepy about it. I feel like there's a religion in narrative, and I feel the same way they do. I feel like we're both paying homage to something else; they're not paying homage to me.

The Onion: Does knowing that you have fans who are that dedicated put extra pressure on you, or does seeing the show as something outside yourself make it easier to deal with?

Whedon: You don't want to let them down. The people who feel the most strongly about something will turn on you the most vociferously if they feel you've let them down. Sometimes you roll your eyes and you want to say, "Back off," but you don't get the big praise without getting the big criticism. Because people care. So. Much. And you always know that's lurking there. It does make a difference. If nobody was paying attention, I might very well say, "You know what, guys? Let's churn 'em out, churn 'em out, make some money." I like to think I wouldn't, but I don't know. I don't know me, I might be a dick. Once the critics, after the first season, really got the show, we all sort of looked at each other and said, "Ohhh-kay . . ." We thought we were going to fly under the radar, and nobody was going to notice the show. And then we had this responsibility, and we got kind of nervous. You don't want to let them down. But ultimately, the narrative feeds you so much. It's so exciting to find out what's going to happen next, to find the next important thing in the narrative, to step down and say, "That's so cool."

The Onion: Are you ever surprised by your fans' passion for the show?

Whedon: No. I designed the show to create that strong reaction. I designed *Buffy* to be an icon, to be an emotional experience, to be loved in a way that other shows can't be loved. Because it's about adolescence, which is the most important thing people go through in their development, becoming an adult. And it mythologizes it in such a way, such a romantic way—it basically says, "Everybody who made it through adolescence is a hero." And I think that's very personal, that people get something from that that's very real. And I don't think I could be more pompous. But I mean every word of it. I wanted her to be a cultural phenomenon. I wanted there to be dolls, Barbie with kung-fu grip. I wanted people to embrace it in a way that exists beyond, "Oh, that was a wonderful show about lawyers, let's have dinner." I wanted people to internalize it, and make up fantasies where they were in the story, to take it home with them, for it to exist beyond the TV show. And we've done exactly that. Now I'm writing comics, and I'm getting all excited about the mythology. We're doing a book of stories about other slayers, and I'm all excited about that, and it's all growing in my mind, as well. I think she has become an icon, and that's what I wanted. What more could anybody ask?

The Onion: Do you ever feel a responsibility to society, to use your massive power for good?

Whedon: Yes and no. I mean, I've always been, and long before anybody was paying any attention, very careful about my responsibility in narrative. How much do I put what I want to put, and how much do I put what I feel is correct? People say, "After Columbine, do you feel a responsibility about the way you portray violence?" And I'm like, "No, I felt a responsibility about the way I portrayed violence the first time I picked up a pen." I mean, everybody felt . . . It's a ridiculous thing to ask a writer. But you feel it, and at the same time—and I've said this before—a writer has a responsibility to tell stories that are dark and sexy and violent, where characters that you love do stupid, wrong things and get away with it, that we explore these parts of people's lives, because that's what makes stories into fairy tales instead of polemics. That's what makes stories resonate, that thing, that dark place that we all want to go to on some level or another. It's very important. People are like, [whining] "Well, your characters have sex, and those costumes, and blah blah . . ." And I'm like, "You're in adolescence, and you're thinking about what besides sex?" I feel that we're showing something that is true, that people can relate to and say, "Oh, I made that bad choice," or "Oh, there's a better way to do that." But as long as it's real, then however politically correct, or incorrect, or whatever, bizarre, or dark, or funny, or stupid—anything you can get, as long as it's real, I don't mind.

The Onion: Speaking of sex and reality, the Tara-and-Willow relationship has been controversial from several angles, with one side of the spectrum accusing you of promoting a homosexual agenda while the other side accuses you of exploiting lesbian chic.

Whedon: You just have to ignore that. I actually went online and said, "I realize that this has shocked a lot of people, and I've made a mistake by trying to shove this lifestyle—which is embraced by, maybe, at most, 10 percent of Americans—down people's throats. So I'm going to take it back, and from now on, Willow will no longer be a Jew." And somebody was actually like, [adopts agitated whine] "What do you mean she's not going to be a Jew any-more?" I was like, "Can we get a 'sarcasm' font?" But, you know, the first criti-cism we got was, "She's not gay enough. They're not gay enough." We were playing it as a metaphor, and it was like, "Why don't they come out? They're not gay enough!" And eventually we did start to say, "Well, maybe we're being a little coy. They've got good chemistry, this is working out, why don't we just go ahead and make them go for it?" And, of course, once you bring it out in the open, it's no longer a metaphor. Then it's just an Issue. But we never played it that way. Ultimately, some people say "lesbian chic," I say, "Okay, whatever." Those criticisms don't really bug me. You look at shows like *Ally McBeal* and *Party of Five*, which both did lesbian kisses that were promoted and hyped for months and months, and afterwards the characters were like, "Well, I seem to be very heterosexual! Thank you for that steamy lesbian kiss!" Our whole mission statement was that we would bury their first kiss inside an episode that had nothing to do with it, and never promote it, which I guess caught people off-guard at the WB. The reason we had them kiss was because if they didn't, it would start to get coy and, quite frankly, a little offensive, for two people that much in love to not have any physicality. But the whole mission statement was, "We'll put it where nobody expects it, and we'll never talk about it." I mean, there are people who are genuinely concerned—are we falling into a pattern that other shows are falling into? It's very possible. The WB was like, "We have gay characters on all our shows. Why didn't you tell us you were making characters gay?" "Well, I don't watch your other shows. I didn't know." I'm sort of not really aware of what's going on out there. So the accusations of, "You shouldn't have a gay character on your show," those people are just—they should just be tied to a rock. "Whatever, you dumb people." Not that I feel strongly. But the other ones, "Oh, you just do that because it's sexy" . . . Well, the writers, and the men and women on the set, are like, "Yeah, it is pretty sexy!" I mean, so were Buffy and Angel. If it's not sexy, then it's not worth it. Like those two guys in *thirtysomething* sitting in bed together, looking like they were individually wrapped in plastic. They did a scene with two guys in bed, and it was a big deal, on *thirtysomething*, and it was the most antiseptic thing I've ever seen in my life. They were sitting ramrod-straight, far away from each other, and not even looking at each other. I was like, "Ahhh, sexy!"

The Onion: One aspect of your fans' dedication is that they become very threatened by perceived changes in the show, like Giles becoming a lesser character as Anthony Stewart Head moves to Britain, or the show itself moving to UPN.

Whedon: Change is a mandate on the show. And people always complain. [Agitated voice.] "Who is this new guy, Oz?" "Where'd that guy Oz go?" They have trouble with change, but it's about change. It's about growing up. If we didn't change, you would be bored. The change as far as Tony Head is concerned, the man has two daughters growing up in England, and he'd like to live there. The kids [on *Buffy*] are old enough now that they don't really need a mentor figure, and this is a period in your life when you don't really have one. So it made sense for him to go back, and he chose to be on the show as a recurring character. But change is part of the show, and people always have a problem with it. But I think it's why they keep coming back.

The Onion: How do you think the move to UPN will affect the series?
Whedon: I don't think it'll affect it one iota. Any change that happens in the show will happen naturally because the show evolves. UPN has never said, "Skew it this way, do this thing," and they never will, because I'm not going to do it. I've had an unprecedented amount of control over the show, even for television, considering the show is a cult show. From the very start, the WB left me alone. You know, they collaborated, they didn't disappear, but they really let me do what I wanted. They trusted me. And UPN is on board for letting me do the show the way that works. I don't think anything will change. I mean, there'll be wrestling. But tasteful wrestling. Wrestling with a message behind it.

The Onion: I've got a quote here from a recent interview with James Marsters [who plays Spike on *Buffy*]: "Joss likes to stir it up. He likes a little chaos. He likes to piss people off. He likes to deny them what they want. He loves making people feel afraid." Do you agree with that?
Whedon: First of all, if you don't feel afraid, horror show not good. We learned early on, the scariest thing on that show was people behaving badly, or in peril, morally speaking, or just people getting weird on you—which, by the way, is the scariest thing in life. In terms of not giving people what they want, I think it's a mandate: Don't give people what they want, give them what they need. What they want is for Sam and Diane to get together. [Whispers.] Don't give it to them. Trust me. [Normal voice.] You know? People want the easy path, a happy resolution, but in the end, they're more interested in . . . No one's going to go see the story of Othello going to get a peaceful divorce. People want the tragedy. They need things to go wrong, they need the tension. In my characters, there's a core of trust and love that I'm very committed to. These guys would die for each other, and it's very beautiful. But at the same time, you can't keep that safety. Things have to go wrong, bad things have to happen.

The Onion: What's your method for balancing humor and drama when you're writing the show?
Whedon: We get bored of one, and then switch to the other. I thought we got very dramatic last year, and I was like, "We need more jokes this year!" Every year the balance falls one way or another. You've just got to keep your eye on it. All of my writers are extremely funny, so it's easy to make [*Buffy*] funnier. The hard part is getting the stuff that matters more. Our hardest work is to figure out the story. Getting the jokes in isn't a problem. We wanted to make that

sort of short-attention-span, *The Simpsons*, cull-from-every-genre-all-the-time thing. "You know, if we take this moment from *Nosferatu*, and this moment from *Pretty in Pink*, that'll make this possible. A little *Jane Eyre* in there, and then a little *Lethal Weapon 4*. Not *3*, but *4*. And I think this'll work."

The Onion: Does the writing itself come naturally to you, or do you have to set hours and force yourself to sit down and get it done?
Whedon: It's like breathing. I'm not un-lazy, and I do procrastinate, but . . . Some of my writers sweat. The agony, they hate doing it, it's like pulling teeth. But for me, it comes easy. I love it. I don't rewrite, almost ever. I basically just sit down and write. Now my wife is making gestures about what a pompous ass I am. [Laughs.] And she's not wrong. But that's how it is. I love it. And I know these characters well enough that it comes maybe a little more naturally to me.

The Onion: Have you gotten good at delegating, or do you really want to be doing all the writing yourself?
Whedon: No, I have, and that was really hard for me. It was hard because I had such a specific vision, and nobody was seeing it. And so you have to do everything—props, costumes. Gradually, you surround yourself with people who do see it your way. I've worked for producers, and I know producers, who are true megalomaniacs, and need to write everything, and be responsible for everything, and get all the credit. And, although I am something of a control freak, if somebody does something right, I will not change a word. If the script works, if a costume is right, if an actor gets it, I'm not going to get in there just so I can have gotten in there. I've spent five years culling the most extraordinary staff, which I trust to share my vision and my experience. So if somebody gets it right, I leave it alone.

The Onion: Do you think you'd ever be able to completely let go of a *Buffy* spin-off, leave it totally in someone else's hands?
Whedon: It's possible. It's possible that I could. A while ago, I would have said, "No." But now I'm working on what will be four *Buffy* shows and three *Buffy* comics, and eventually you sort of go, "Uh, maybe somebody else could do that other thing." Would I be able to not have any hand in it at all? I think I just said "yes" and meant "no." I don't want it to have my name on it if it doesn't reflect what I want to say. Because once you get to the position of actually getting to say something, which is a level most writers never even get to, and is a great blessing, you then have to worry about what it is you're actually saying. I don't want some crappy reactionary show under the *Buffy* name. If my name's going to be on it, it should be mine. Now, the books I have nothing to do with, and I've never read them. They could be, "Buffy realized that

abortion was wrong!" and I would have no idea. So, after my big, heartfelt, teary speech, I realize that I was once again lying. But I sort of drew the line. I was like, "I can't possibly read these books!" But my name just goes on them as the person who created *Buffy*.

The Onion: Now that you've actually appeared in an episode of *Angel*, do you have the acting bug? Are you going to write yourself into more scripts?
Whedon: I do and I don't. I've always had it, and I think it's part of being a writer and a director. It's knowing how you want things to be played. But I don't have the face—that's the problem—and I don't want the giant ego. I don't want to become Kevin Costner, singing on the soundtrack to *The Postman*.

The Onion: If you had *Buffy* to do over from the start, this time knowing how popular it would get, would you do anything differently?
Whedon: Not in terms of popularity. I mean, there were certain things on the show that I learned the hard way, but not really. I love the show, and I love the people. I love the stories we told. I mean, I'm angry about every single edit, and line, and costume change, and rewrite, but that's part of the business. So ultimately, I wouldn't change anything.

Joss Whedon Answers 100 questions

SFX MAGAZINE/2002

From *SFX*, Future Publishing, 2002.

1. How are you?
JW: So very sleepy.

2. Where are you right now?
JW: I'm behind you.

3. What are you doing for the rest of today?
JW: Working and playing piano.

4. What's your favorite British show?
JW: *Python*. Still.

5. What's your favorite British swear word?
JW: C**t. It's horrible when Americans say it, but oddly endearing with a British accent.

6. Are you running out of ambitions?
JW: Haven't written a ballet yet, or directed a film, or known a woman sexually. So no.

7. Which is your favorite Western?
JW: *Once Upon a Time in the West.*

8. Which is your favorite science fiction movie?
JW: *The Matrix.*

9. Which is your favorite musical?
JW: My head just exploded, but *The Bandwagon* kicks ass.

10. Who is your favorite James Bond?
JW: Connery.

11. Who is your favorite Doctor Who?
JW: Oddly, Timothy Dalton.

12. Who's your favorite other person called Joss?
JW: Ackland! *A Little Night Music*, dude!

13. When were you drunk last?
JW: Now-ish.

14. Superman or Spider-man?
JW: Spidey.

15. Beatles or Stones?
JW: Beatles.

16. Is this the final season of *Buffy*?
JW: God, I hope so.

17. Is this the final season of *Angel*?
JW: No.

18. Is this the final season of *Firefly*?
JW: God, I hope not.

19. Who did you take to the prom?
JW: Didn't have one (self pity . . .).

20. Are you spreading yourself too thinly, and is this a good thing?
JW: Yes, no, maybe.

21. What's your favorite biological function?
JW: Who doesn't love poo?

22. Who is your hero?
JW: I'm giving it up for Van Gogh. He produced epic shit with zero approbation. All about the work.

23. What would you do if all your shows ended tomorrow?
JW: A film. Also, a drunken party.

24. Which show do you enjoy writing the most?
JW: The one I'm writing now.

25. Which show do you enjoy directing the most?
JW: See above.

26. Which actor gives you the most backtalk?
JW: The one I fired.

27. Which writer never agrees with you?
JW: The one I killed and ate.

28. Which movie would you loved to have written?
JW: *Revenge of the Jedi.*

29. Which movie do you regret having any involvement in?
JW: *Alien Resurrection.*

30. How many hours of sleep do you get at night?
JW: 6–8.

31. What's the most irritating question a journalist has ever asked you?
JW: "Angel is a vampire?"

32. Which book would you recommend everybody should read?
JW: *Abe*, by Richard Slotkin, though it's very much an American thing.

33. Who is the most overlooked person on television?
JW: Alexis Denisof.

34. Who should be the most overlooked person on television?
JW: Regis.

35. Kirk or Picard?
JW: Well, Stewart, but yes, Kirk.

36. If you could live anywhere in the world, where would you be?
JW: London, actually.

37. Has anyone ever come up to you and said "I loved you in *The Shawshank Redemption?*"
JW: Not nearly enough.

38. What's the worst part of making a television show?
JW: It never ends.

39. And what's the best?
JW: It's living theatre meets film—it's immediate.

40. What's the worst line of dialogue you've ever written?
JW: No clue.

41. And what's the best?
JW: "It's not the demon in me that needs killing—it's the man" is up there.

42. Is the character of Wash in *Firefly* based on you?
JW: A bit.

43. Would you do *Faith the Vampire Slayer* if Eliza Dushku would commit to it?
JW: Sure.

44. Does it worry you that Spike is such a popular character—he's evil!
JW: So am I.

45. If you could do a crossover episode of *Buffy*, *Angel*, or *Firefly* with any other show, what would it be?
JW: *The Simpsons*.

46. What do you think of fan fiction: flattering or embarrassing?
JW: Lots o' both.

47. For budgetary reasons, you have to do a "clip" episode of *Angel*. How would you make it different from the norm?
JW: It would only be the clips of Wesley falling over.

48. What was your nickname in school?
JW: "Who are you again?"

49. If they did *Buffy Big Brother*, who would win?
JW: Never seen it.

50. Is Hamlet mad?
JW: If the person playing him gets there, yes.

51. Do you see the influence of *Buffy* on other shows (i.e., *Smallville*)?
JW: Sadly, yes.

52. Can I show you my script?
JW: Uh, show it to my people. I have people.

53. Who are the best people to hang out with—actors, writers, producers, or directors?
JW: Actors and writers are the most neurotic, therefore the most fun.

54. How good are you in a fight?
JW: Let's not find out.

55. How many times have you been asked if you believe in vampires?
JW: Too many.

56. What's the best dessert in the world?
JW: Chocolate mousse.

57. Can you tell us a joke?
JW: My deal at Fox won't allow it.

58. Do you feel Saddam Hussein might become a better person if he watched *Buffy*?
JW: Couldn't hurt. Bush could use it, too.

59. What's the record that changed your life?
JW: *Decade*, the Neil Young compilation.

60. When was the last time you felt wide awake?
JW: Writing.

61. What's the best time of day?
JW: Just before dawn.

62. Will you write and direct the very last episode of *Buffy*?
JW: Yup.

63. Given a choice, would you be a vampire and live forever?
JW: Probably, because I'm weak.

64. When *Buffy* ends, will any of the characters end up on *Angel*?
JW: Mebbe.

65. Do you think that the series would stand more chance at the Emmys with a different name?
JW: *Buffy the Vampire Slayer, MD.*

66. What scares you?
JW: People. And large insects.

67. How did you vote in the last election?
JW: Against that ass-wipe, thank you.

68. Are you afraid of Virginia Woolf?
JW: Well, who isn't?

69. Which was your favorite Golden Girl?
JW: Bea, dude! Bea!

70. What was the last film you saw at the cinema?
JW: *Punch Drunk Love.*

71. What story will you never tell on *Buffy*, *Angel*, or *Firefly*?
JW: "Wow, smoking pot is wrong, I see that now!"

72. What are your pets called?
JW: Tok, Vinnie.

73. How long will we have to wait for *Ripper*?
JW: A while.

74. Do you believe in God?
JW: Not a jot.

75. Would John Wayne have been out of place in *Firefly*?
JW: He'd damn well have made a place for himself.

76. Have you played the *Buffy* computer game?
JW: No.

77. How big is your television?
JW: Big enough.

78. Have you ever broken the law?
JW: Mostly just kidnapping . . .

79. Which car do you drive?
JW: Mine.

80. Were you at Sarah Michelle Gellar's wedding?
JW: No, but I was at her Bat Mitzvah. What are the odds?

81. Would you eat at Doublemeat Palace?
JW: Jesus, no! Okay.

82. Has anyone ever mentioned that the Serenity looks a bit like a plucked parrot?
JW: That was its original name. What are the odds?

83. Which is your favorite member of The Magnificent Seven?
JW: Yul!

84. Which show does your wife prefer, *Buffy*, *Angel*, or *Firefly*? Or won't she tell you?
JW: "They all fulfill a different need," she says.

85. Which show on U.S. TV at the moment do you love . . . other than your own?
JW: There are other shows?

86. Who let the dogs out?
JW: Timothy Dalton. What are the odds?

87. How many series do you think you could run at once without exploding?
JW: Actually, only 2.

88. Can you speak Chinese?
JW: Nope. My wife can.

89. Can you ride a horse?
JW: If it's under me.

90. If you could write a song for any artist, who would you choose?
JW: After Sinatra, Jill Sobule.

91. Would YOU have survived Sunnydale High?
JW: Big no.

92. What's the thing you're proudest of in this world?
JW: Art and feminism; my little show that changed things.

93. What makes you happy?
JW: Work, Kai, my friends, more work.

94. What makes you sad?
JW: My chemical imbalance.

95. Do you find Benny Hill funny?
JW: I did in school—haven't seen him since.

96. Who put the bob in the bob sh-bop? Who put the ram in the ram-a-lam-a-ding-dong?
JW: That was me, sorry.

97. Can you justify Twinkies to everyone in the UK?
JW: Dude, they never see an oven. They're science that's soft!

98. *SFX* is 100 issues old. Where do you want to be when you're 100?
JW: Standing.

99. Does the internet ever scare you?
JW: Often.

100. Are you pleased this questionnaire is over?
JW: Sweet muscular Jesus, I never thought I'd get through it. I mean, no.

Joss Whedon, Feminist

JAMES LONGWORTH/2002

From *TV Creators: Conversations with America's Top Producers of Television Drama, Volume 2* (Syracuse: Syracuse University Press, 2002). Reprinted by permission.

"Even a man who is pure at heart and says his prayers by night, may become a wolf when the wolfbane blooms, and the autumn moon is bright." Those lyrical strains from Curt Siodmak's 1941 classic screenplay *The Wolf Man* describe the tormented lycanthrope Larry Talbot. But they might also apply to *Buffy the Vampire Slayer*'s one-time heart throb, Angel, who, because of his conflicted nature, is more akin to a werewolf than to a Dracula-like figure.

Still, while vampires and wolf men can sometimes be sympathetic characters, Buffy's pal Willow observed that "Men can be jerks, dead *or* alive." Translation? It is a man's world out there, and that is why the world needs Buffy, an empowered woman who fights not just her own battles but also those of others—all the while protecting the meek against any adversary, regardless of its manifestation.

So, what radical feminist invented this superchick? None other than Joss Whedon, a yuppie-era scribe with a love of Gothic horror films and a passion for arming the disenfranchised against the modern horrors and villains that confront us every day. Thus, Whedon's TV tandem of *Buffy the Vampire Slayer* and *Angel* works on a number of levels. Both breakthrough dramas appeal to horror fans of all ages. They appeal to girls looking for a strong role model. They appeal to young men with an eye for beautiful slayers and young women with an eye on hunky vampires. Finally, they appeal to anyone who knows what it is like to be a victim and how good it feels (albeit vicariously) to exact a pound of flesh from a bossy bully or a bullying boss.

Joss Whedon is a mild-mannered, highly imaginative man whose talents are as varied as the demographics of his programs and as diverse as his mix of genres. Whedon is a writer, producer, and director, whose work is a veritable smorgasbord of drama, comedy, action, science fiction, and romance. Says former WB executive Susanne Daniels, "Joss has a genius mind like television has never seen. I think *Buffy* is that rare combination of humor and suspense. It makes you laugh and makes you scared at the same time, which is very difficult to achieve, in a way that these scary movies like *Scream* haven't achieved, because they rely very much on gimmicks, and parody, and extreme violence."

Marti Noxon, Whedon's co-executive producer on *Buffy*, told *TV Guide*, "[Joss] is a student of creating mythologies to get to the heart of real emotional matters" (February 10, 2001). Perhaps through writing and presenting primetime parables on social equality, Whedon has created a mythology that has transcended the 3:4 aspect ratio and given society a lesson in tolerance and respect. The best part is that Whedon's mythologies are also fun. And, as Mary Poppins (herself an empowered female) said, "A spoonful of sugar helps the medicine go down." Thanks to Whedon, we twenty-first-century males are learning to take our medicine with less and less resistance.

Joss Whedon was born into a family of letters in 1964. His grandfather and his father wrote episodic television, with the former contributing to such shows as *Leave It to Beaver* and *The Donna Reed Show*, and the latter composing dialogue for *Alice* and *Benson*. His mother, a teacher, also wrote. Growing up in Manhattan, Joss had two older brothers. His family later expanded following his parents' divorce when he was just nine years old. With both his mom and dad remarrying, Joss would gain two half brothers and a stepsister. Prior to the amicable breakup of his parents, Joss was influenced greatly by his father's creative spirit. "I think my father's best work was probably done at our dinner table," Joss says laughing. "It was great to live around a writer, and my mother also wrote in her spare time, so the sound of typewriters was probably the most comforting sound in the world to me. I loved that. And while I really enjoyed all of the funny things my dad was working on, it was really just being *around* someone who was that funny. And all of his friends were comedy writers. So the house was constantly filled with these very sweet, erudite, intelligent guys just trying to crack jokes—my father's friends, my mother's friends, teachers, drama people. It just had a great air to it, and what you wanted to do is to go into that room and make those guys laugh."

After the divorce, Joss lived with his mother and came to respect her strength and independence. For ten years, Whedon attended Riverdale, the same school where his mother taught. But a change in venue was in store for Joss. "She was going on sabbatical to England, and since I couldn't stay in New York, and since she didn't think there were actual schools in California [laughs], she suggested that I go to boarding school in England," Joss recalls. "By incredible happenstance, and I stress that because I in no way earned it, I ended up at the best school in the country (Winchester), and when my family returned to America, I stayed on there for two more years."

While attending Riverdale, Whedon had been both bullied and ignored, but at Winchester he enjoyed his role as an outsider. "I wouldn't trade it for the world, and I wouldn't wish it on a dog," he says laughing. "This was a six-hundred-year-old, all-male school where you have to wear a suit and a straw hat to class every day. Not long on fun, also 'chickless' in the extreme, and I don't mean Michael, I mean, *lack* of women. [Laughs.] When I left there I found out how much they hated us [Americans]. Every Fourth of July I walked around saying, "We won, we won!" [Laughs.]

Joss the Yank also went on to win a diploma from Winchester, *and* with a special guest in attendance. "There was no prom, and the only reason we had a celebration was that the Queen came for the school's six hundredth anniversary."

Whedon left England, but he would eventually return to the world of old Gothic architecture, and the Brits would love him for it. While attending Wesleyan University, Whedon became more focused on his future. "I said, 'Film is what interests me. Film is what I'm going to study. I'm going to give up my drawing, I'm going to give up acting. I'm going to give up all the other stuff that I've done and just focus on one thing, making movies.'" Upon receiving a degree in film studies and literature from Wesleyan, Joss moved to Los Angeles in hopes of catching a break. "I got out here with nary a dime, and thought I could perhaps write a spec TV script, and maybe sell it and get enough money to get myself started," Joss says. "That was the first time I had ever sat down and said, 'I'm going to write something, and try to be a writer.' And it was like, 'Where have you been all my life?' And then I realized that I just never loved anything as much, and *will* never love anything as much as writing. The first time I sat down just to write, just to create a script, was extraordinary."

In the meantime, Whedon took a job in a video store to support himself, but the experience would later pay huge dividends in helping him devise a tide for what would become his signature project. After penning several spec scripts. Joss landed his first steady job in show biz, working for the ABC hit comedy, *Roseanne*. "I thought it was the best show on TV, and it was the last spec I wrote," he recalls. "I sort of knew the format of a script, I knew generally how they looked because I had read a lot of them that my father did. So I knew the structure, and my father, when he read my stuff, was extraordinarily supportive, which was a big, nervous moment for me. He showed it to his agency, where I still am, or they might have shown it to him. I'm not sure who read it first, but obviously they wouldn't have read it, or it would have been harder to have them read it, if it had not been for my father."

Staff positions on *Roseanne* and *Parenthood* followed. But the idea for *Buffy* had been brewing for some time. While still working on *Roseanne*, Whedon began scripting and pitching the slayer concept but found no takers. Joss was back to writing specs and hoping for his first film deal. "I wrote a spec called *Suspension*," Joss says. "It was a rip-off of *Die Hard*, where terrorists take over a bridge. Loads of fun. [Laughs.] Having then written *Suspension* and *Buffy*, I got a lot of comedy pitches, and I was like, 'I want to write hard action. I want to write big summer movies because so many of them suck.' [Laughs.] Seeing my two scripts, Jorge Saralegui at Fox asked again if I was interested in trying to revive the *Alien* franchise, because he had seen me write action, and he had seen a woman hero in those two different scripts, so he just thought I had the right qualifications."

In addition to writing *Alien Resurrection* (1997), Joss had also penned *Speed* (1994) and *Toy Story* (1995). But it was his earlier screenplay for *Buffy the Vampire Slayer*, which was made into a movie in 1992, that would lead him to a rendezvous with the medium in which the Whedons had worked for generations. Says Joss, "Without Fran Kuzui there would have been no movie. She produced it and put it together. She directed it. She made it her own. As a creator, every writer will think of themselves as that. It's frustrating, because I have a very specific vision when I write, directorially speaking, about everything, about camera angles. Somebody said that mine was the first script they had ever read by a wannabe costume designer because I was very specific about the way things should look, and feel, and because, inevitably, my vision was not going to be the same as Fran's. She was interested in making more a sort of head-on comedy, and I wanted to make an action horror movie that was funny. And we had different sensibilities."

Five years later, Whedon, who had already followed in his father's footsteps as a television writer, would now also create and produce his own series, the vehicle for which would be the saga of his old, familiar teenage vampire vigilante. Susanne Daniels, former president of the WB network, recalls the beginning of *Buffy*'s TV incarnation. "When the network first started out, we were in a position where writers weren't really coming to us," Daniels recalls. "For the most part, we were going to them. At the time we were pitching two things, teenage female superheroes, and a contemporary version of *The Nightstalker*. And so, when Joss walked in and told us he was going to do *Buffy* the movie as a TV series, he immediately responded to the two things we were looking for. I didn't have a lot of drama experience then, and that really worked to our advantage [laughs], so we didn't know enough to say, 'You don't buy a drama series based on a failed movie.' [Laughs.] We just did it. And we loved Joss's work. I was very familiar with the movie version of *Buffy* and familiar with what I felt were the flaws. Joss really had worked out so many improvements and acknowledged those flaws, and how he was going to make the show stronger and better, and it was just very appealing to us for all of those reasons."

Disappointed with the campy tone of the movie, Whedon was determined to make TV's *Buffy* more three dimensional. Joss wrote and directed a twenty-four-minute presentation pilot. *Buffy the Vampire Slayer* premiered in March of 1997 and soon became one of the fledgling WB's biggest and most reliable hits. Like Brenda Hampton's *7th Heaven* and Kevin Williamson's *Dawson's*

Creek, Buffy would help the WB to balance its mostly young, mostly African American programming with a mix of dramas that could attract more broad-based demographics. *Buffy* was also an instant hit with critics. *TV Guide's* Matt Roush proclaimed *Buffy* to be "smart, with unfailingly glib dialogue" (January 2, 1999), while Frederick Szebin wrote in *Cinefantastique* magazine that "*Buffy* may have finally kicked asunder that tired cliché of the screaming maiden in distress" (October 1999). *Time* noted that the show was a "post-feminist parable on the challenge of balancing one's personal and work life." And David Graeber, assistant professor of anthropology at Yale University, wrote, "Joss is responsible for subverting the message of the horror genre . . . and making it a form of empowerment for women" (*Entertainment Weekly*, April 2000).

Of course, there have been some bumps in the road. *Buffy* is, after all, a drama that contains more violence than some action hours, and that's something that Congressional crusaders have been critical of as they suggested a link between television drama and real-life crime. In a February 2000 interview with *Dreamworks* magazine, *Buffy* star Sarah Michelle Gellar weighed in: "I just got back from Europe where they have the same TV shows and movies, yet this problem really only exists in *our* country. So how can we blame entertainment?" Still, there are unfortunate extremes with any issue. In the spring of 1999, on the heels of the Columbine High School shootings, Joss (who once described his relationship with the WB for *Cinescape's* Edward Gross by saying [November 1997] "they let me get away with murder" [from *Terror Television* by John Kenneth Muir]) was directed by the WB to reschedule and make changes to remaining episodes containing particularly violent themes or scenes. Susanne Daniels defends her decision. "I didn't want to overreact, but it seemed important for us and for our affiliates to feel like we were responding, not just to the Columbine families, but to all of the families in America who were affected by it and have been affected by local shootings," she says. "And even though Joss's show, that episode, works so clearly on a level of fantasy and is not at all realistic, even despite that, I now believe that we did absolutely the right thing, without a doubt . . . I was proud of that decision."

But despite mounting pressures from politicians, Whedon and the WB launched a *Buffy* spin-off, starring a two-hundred-and-forty-four-year-old vampire given to violence in the name of protecting the innocent. *Angel* premiered in the fall of 1999 and, like its mother-ship series, met with rave reviews. Ken Tucker of *Entertainment Weekly* called it "fully satisfying across a whole range of emotions." And *TV Guide* wrote, "We are intrigued by the deft blend of classic film noir and hip, horror allegory" (September, 1999). The magazine's Matt Roush later proclaimed *Angel* to be "The best of this season's spin-offs" (November 13, 1999). John Kenneth Muir in his book *Terror Television* deemed *Angel* to be a "darker, more adult version of *Buffy*, one that labors on the idea of redemption."

Ironically, it was the maturing of Whedon's cast and audience that became a sticking point during the embattled licensing negotiations of 2001. *Buffy* had helped the WB broaden its viewer base. In fact, the show has consistently increased its numbers across every demographic category. From 1999 to 2000, for example, the series saw a 100 percent jump in men, eighteen to thirty-four years old, with significant gains among both males and females in the eighteen to forty-nine-year-old demographic. However, Jamie Kellner (a former WB executive who later became CEO of Turner Broadcasting, a division of AOL, as a result of the AOL/Time Warner mega-merger) suggested that *Buffy*, which is produced by 20th Century Fox, had an aging audience base. But faced with rising production costs, Whedon entertained offers to move his franchise from the WB. Whedon told *Entertainment Weekly*, "The idea that *Buffy* viewers are getting too old now is a spurious argument for not paying for a show that has as much to do with the WB being the WB as anything else" (March 23, 2001). Eventually the battle was won by UPN, which outbid the WB. Much like baseball's Curt Hood, who tested the waters of free agency, Whedon became one of the first TV creators forced to deal with the impact of vertical integration. (Newscorp, the parent of 20th Century Fox, was negotiating a dual ownership of UPN *with* Viacom, the parent of CBS.) But regardless of its home base, *Buffy* will continue to be a marketing phenomenon. The series has generated comic books, magazines, novels, dolls, trading cards, videos, and a huge following on the Internet. Hollywood insiders may finally even be succumbing to the random frenzy. Perennially locked out of Emmy contention, Whedon snagged his first nomination, for writing the December 1999 episode "Hush," in which a supernatural "force" robs the main characters of the ability to speak. It was a brilliantly crafted script, replete with imaginative nonverbal communication, and should have earned its author a gold statue.

Rich, successful, and happily married, Joss the aging feminist is growing a bit more comfortable with his lifestyle—but not so much as to lose his edge. His mind is still teeming with innovative stories that continue to slay us each week.

To my relief and surprise, he agreed to be interviewed in broad daylight.

Longworth: First of all, how can I be sure that I'm really talking to Joss Whedon and not some otherworldly imposter?
Whedon: There is nothing even remotely supernatural about me, it's all just a bunch of fakery. Why do you think I'd be so desperate to make shows about it, if I thought it was real? [Both laugh.] We'd never come near it.

Longworth: As a writer, does it offend you that my all-time favorite *Buffy* episode, "Hush," contained the least amount of dialogue?
Whedon: Not at all. That was actually one of the best experiences I've ever had

as a writer because it forced me to think through things differently. Writing is not about the number of words. Very often there should be fewer than there are, although I love words. I love the sounds of words. I love syllables. I love the whole deal. Sometimes you gotta shut up. [Both laugh.] Particularly me.

Longworth: You seem to enjoy nonverbal humor as well. I'm thinking, for example, when Lindsay points to a sign near a broken elevator that reads, "In case of emergency use stairs." There's another one where Seth is on his way to a party, and someone asks him who he is going as, and he points to his name tag that says "God." This kind of nonverbal humor threads its way through your work. It's seamless, and yet there are no spoken words.

Whedon: The thing has to work visually. It all has to be in concert. This show, because it's a fantasy show obviously we knew it was going to rely on visuals to a great extent, but creating visual humor is much more difficult to do because so much of TV is just radio with faces.

Longworth: And so much of what kids are exposed to is manic and frantic, whether on TV, the Internet, or in video games, whereas you offer up a more intelligent product with moments of nonverbal communication.

Whedon: Ultimately, if it's not working on that level, you're not going to make it scary by talking about it. And while you can make a lot of jokes, what differentiates it from a sitcom is by really embodying it "filmically" so that its visually funny and so that the frame is working, and it's not just standing there.

Longworth: Since you brought up jokes, let me ask you about your father and grandfather, who both wrote comedy. What is the difference in writing comedy for a sitcom like *Roseanne*, which is supposed to be funny, and writing comedy for a *Buffy* or *Angel* series, which is a drama?

Whedon: Well, in a way *Roseanne* would be easier to write because you don't have to write blocking. But the thing about *Buffy* is you don't have to make a joke, you don't have to make dense, wall-to-wall jokes. But if there aren't a couple of jokes on a page, I still get nervous. I'll never get over that.

Longworth: Why?

Whedon: Because when a joke works, I know it. I can hear the audience laugh, and I still watch the show with a bunch of people. I still watch it with people who haven't worked on it, so I can see when they laugh, and when they get scared, and when they think it's ridiculous, and when they cry, and all that good stuff. And that's the fun. So it's very hard for me *not* to make a joke, because I know that a laugh is a surefire reaction, whereas if you're playing something more dramatic, I don't know if they liked it till it's over [laughs] because they'll just sit there, and that's very nerve racking.

Longworth: OK, so I know that you have written some funny lines for *Buffy* and that you did *Toy Story*, but your writing career veered off a hundred and eighty degrees from the sort of things that your grandfather and dad wrote. I don't recall either of them writing horror, Gothic, sci-fi screenplays, for example.

Whedon: My grandfather did write *Island at the Top of the World*, possibly David Hartman's finest movie. [Both laugh.] But yeah, I'm very much attracted to the dramatic, and though I enjoy half-hour [shows] I don't see myself working in there much because the shows that really move me are always dramatic. In fact, my father wrote a script for *United States*, a very short-lived show. The script never aired, and it was one of my favorite things I ever read because it was one of those early attempts at a dramedy that everybody said wouldn't work, around the time of *Slap Maxwell*. And to read something that was very serious and very moving and very personal, and not schtick, schtick, schtick, not only was it very gratifying, but when the jokes hit, they hit ten times as hard because you were in the middle of something dramatic. That to me is the essence of what I'm interested in. It's something you see in the Hong Kong films that [Quentin] Tarantino has followed. You don't *know* what kind of scene you're in. Something can be very funny and then suddenly very terrifying—very exciting, and suddenly very ridiculous. I think that's what life is like, that's what interests me. But ultimately, while humor is definitely the voice that I'm the most comfortable with, drama is the structure that will always attract me.

Longworth: You mentioned your affection for half hours, and that your father dabbled in dramedy. Why is it that producers won't do half-hour dramas anymore?

Whedon: You know I think certain things get locked down, format wise, Even though sometimes I think, "God, if my show were only a half hour long!" [Laughs.] But if somebody's going to give me a half an hour more to talk, I'm going to do it. Also, there is a very big difference in terms of visual information and telling a story. Every "hour guy" is going to say, "We're making a little movie every week." In our case, God help us, they're not that little.

Longworth: But suppose the network said you had to do *Buffy* as a half hour?

Whedon: It was originally supposed to be a half hour, *Power Rangers*–type afternoon adventure with some comedy. That was what they first approached me with, and I developed it as a half-hour drama. Now I knew that it would be funny, but I thought that you could also really get into the characters, and, actually, it was my agent, Chris Harbert, he said, "This is an hour. You have too much. With all the action and suspense you want to create in a half hour, you're never going to get a chance to get into the character, and that's what's interesting and that's what you're interested in." And an hour gives us time to do all of that. Yes, you could do all of that in a half an hour, there is no reason why you *couldn't* have a half-hour drama except structurally people would be like, "Oh, what will we pair it with? What will we do?" But if you're going to give me an hour, I'm going to take an hour.

Longworth: You could have a *Buffy*/*Angel* hour though.
Whedon: But I have a *Buffy*/*Angel* two hours. [Both laugh.] It's like I produce a movie every week, and the fact [is] that I may die at any moment.

Longworth: Well, we don't want anything to happen to you. What's your diet like when you're working, by the way?
Whedon: Sometimes it's good, and sometimes it's bad. I'm actually getting better at living during these shows. The first year I was sick constantly. And this year I didn't get sick once. Two shows, no sickness. I'm a god. Except having to go into the hospital, but that's different; it was my appendix, not exhaustion. But you learn to live the life of nothing but your shows.

Longworth: Well, let's see if anything about those shows is autobiographical. Did things happen to you at Riverdale or Winchester, for example, that in any way made writing *Buffy* somewhat cathartic for you?
Whedon: Oh yeah. When I devised the show, it was very different from the movie. The movie had "the girl you think is going to get killed turns out to be a superhero," that type of thing. That's enough for a movie but it's not enough for a show. And the show was, "High school is a horror movie." And there are not a lot of people I know who don't relate to that. I sold the show with *Invisible Girl* as part of my pitch, and that was the girl who was just so unremarkable that she had gradually disappeared. That was based on, when I was fifteen I actually drew a picture of myself becoming transparent.

Longworth: That's kind of sad.
Whedon: It was, because I felt myself feeling extraordinarily alienated.

Longworth: Did you save that picture?
Whedon: You know, I think it's somewhere in my closet. I mean it was really a cartoon. But it was very specific, and when you're able to be that, it is very gratifying, because even though the show had a lot of problems, [was] very difficult to write, the filming didn't go that well, and every now and then we get a kid watching it who, you can tell on their face that "this has happened to me."

Longworth: But I think most of us have experienced some of that unless you were the star football player.

Whedon: But part of the point of the show is that even if you were the star football player, there comes a point in every human's life where they realize that they are alone in their mind, and they can't help but feel alienated. That's why anybody can relate to the show.

Longworth: What was the first time you remember writing stories, and when did you realize this was something you wanted to do in earnest?
Whedon: Sort of always, and never. I always wrote things. Stories, poems, songs, plays, comic books. Whatever came to mind. And I always sort of vaguely associated writing with my life, in that I thought I could make movies. I always assumed making them meant writing them, but I never really thought about that. I thought about directing, and when we studied film we really didn't study writing at all. I was doing various things, but I wasn't doing any heavy writing and I never studied at all. I never thought of myself as definitely becoming a writer. I tried to write several novels as a kid, and I'd usually get to page twelve. [Both laugh.]

Longworth: So even sitting around the dinner table with your father, you still didn't make that connection early on?
Whedon: Not specifically. I mean, I knew I wanted to do something that wasn't a real job, because I just can't do it. I'm pathetic that way. I knew I wanted to be an artist. I loved drawing, I loved singing, I loved acting, I love every kind of art that there is. So I had never really narrowed it down, and it wasn't like I was slaving away. I did write a couple of screenplays when I was a kid, but I always thought that was just part of the process. I didn't think of myself as a writer. And then I got out of college, and I swore that I wasn't going to write for TV because I had actually not been raised on American TV much. I was more into the sort of highbrow British stuff that my mother watched. I was a PBS kid.

Longworth: That's weird. Your father is writing all of these shows on commercial television, and your mother wants you to watch PBS.
Whedon: Well, you know, my father and my mother are divorced, and I was living with my mother, but, no, actually they got along splendidly. But yeah, we weren't a huge TV family. And my father, one of the things about working in television is that you never have time to watch any. So my father wasn't an avid TV watcher either. He would enjoy himself, there were things we watched, but it wasn't like we all sat down.

Longworth: What did you like to watch on television when you were growing up?
Whedon: The things that made an impression were all like *Masterpiece Theatre*, *Monty Python*, and the BBC Shakespeares.

Longworth: I think that college students and young people breaking into the business could benefit from hearing how you actually picked up work. You did *Roseanne*, then the films *Speed*, *Alien Resurrection*, and *Toy Story*. How do you get those kinds of jobs? Do you wait by the telephone until someone calls your agent and says, "Hey, I loved *Speed*; can he write *Toy Story*?"

Whedon: Basically I'm never satisfied with where I am. I always want to be doing more: I always want to be doing the next thing. So when I was on *Roseanne*, I started to write *Buffy* (the film) because I wanted to make movies also. And then, when it was clear that there was no more for me to do on *Roseanne*, I sort of got shut out by the producers, I quit. *Buffy* went around, I got a job on *Parenthood* that lasted half a season, that show disappeared, and I sort of backed off from TV at that point. But *Buffy* had gone around, and I then also wrote a spec *Die Hard* rip-off called *Suspension*, about terrorists taking a bridge. Loads of fun. [Laughs.] The person who told me to write *Suspension*, Jorge Saralegui, I had pitched it to him as a joke while we were having lunch. He was pitching me a movie about a dog, and I think it later became a movie about a pig. [Both laugh.] And I told him how little I wanted to be pitched another dog movie, and I told him my funny *Die Hard* rip-off, and he said, "Write it, don't pitch it. Just go and write it. You will never be pitched another dog movie again."

Longworth: Very prophetic.

Whedon: He was smart. But anyway, while we were working on a treatment *of Alien* together, he was also in charge of *Speed*, and production was coming up, and he needed someone. So he set me up with Walter Parks and Laurie McDonald.

Longworth: So it really *is* all about connections?

Whedon: Well, it's in doing good work. If I get the job done for somebody, they're going to think of me for somebody else. I hear the word "connections," and I think it doesn't matter how you write. I believe I had a very easy start. I didn't work as a production assistant. I didn't work in the industry at all until I worked as a writer. And I had the advantage of my father, who told me, "When somebody tells you to get a job as a production assistant, don't do it. Hold out, and you're going to be employed as a writer."

Longworth: Really?

Whedon: Yeah, it was beautiful because he was the guy that I wanted to be like.

Longworth: So how did you get the idea for creating the character of Buffy?

Whedon: It basically came through my love of horror movies and having seen all of the ones that had been made [laughs] and seeing the trend of the blonde girl who always got killed, like P. J. Soles in *Halloween*, who was cute, had sex, was bouncy and frivolous, always got her ass killed. I just felt really bad for her. I thought, I want to see the movie where she walks into a dark alley, a monster attacks her, and she just wails on him. And a lot of that came from me, as well, because I have been mugged a lot of times.

Longworth: Seriously?

Whedon: Yeah. Four times. I've been picked on; I was the little brother, not somebody anybody ever took seriously, so, in a weird way, I identified with this extremely pretty, blonde, frivolous person who was the polar opposite of myself. Nobody ever expected she could take care of herself, or turn around and become a superhero. And not just a superhero, but a hero in the classical sense. To me that's extraordinarily gratifying and I think it is to other people, too, because everybody thinks of themselves as something more significant than the world believed.

Longworth: You spoke earlier about how the TV series was originally slated to be sort of an afternoon kids' show, but prior to that, while writing the screenplay for *Buffy*, did you think it could ever be a great TV series one day?

Whedon: No, I really didn't. I thought this could be an icon. I thought, in a very small way, this movie was designed, even with the title, to be one of those movies picked off the video shelf because it had a funny title. This was around the time they were making *Revenge of the Killer Bimbos*, or whatever, and that bothered me.

Longworth: I missed that one.

Whedon: Well, maybe it was *Attack of the Killer Bimbos*, I can't remember. [Both laugh.] But titles like that leap out at me because I *want* them to have their revenge because everybody's been calling them bimbos. But these movies weren't really about that; they were "T&A" fests. So I wanted to make a movie that would grab you in that same way. That juxtaposition of something very frivolous versus something very serious. *Buffy the Vampire Slayer* was actually a good, responsible, feminist, exciting, enjoyable movie, and not just a titty bash.

Longworth: Every episode of *Buffy* jumps between genres. One minute there's high drama, the next there's comedy, then science fiction. How would you, then, categorize the show?

Whedon: As an action, comedy, romance, horror, musical. [Both laugh.] It is a hodgepodge. Structurally it is a drama. We break it like a drama. Everything is about the momentum of the storytelling, whether the story is somewhat farcical, or straight-ahead action, or horror. So, if I had to choose one, I'd choose drama. If I had chosen comedy, who knows, maybe we'd have an Emmy. [Both laugh.]

Longworth: Ouch!

Whedon: No, I very much doubt that would happen in any category. [Both laugh.] But that question did come up after *Ally McBeal* did that, and they were the first ones [in drama] to call themselves a comedy. But I can't anymore. It gets so schizophrenic at this point that drama sort of covers everything. But comedy/horror/drama/action, those are the big four.

Longworth: OK, since you brought it up, what about the Emmys? Sarah Michelle Gellar was quoted as saying that Emmy voters don't consider the WB to be a real network. Do you agree with her assessment, and, if so, is that prejudice likely to abate any time soon?

Whedon: I don't know. Sarah knows a great deal more about these things than I do. And when I don't understand what's happening, I'll go to her and ask, "What does this mean?" She's the insider. She knows all the awards. She knows all the machinations of the studios, and things like that. But I don't have a clue.

Longworth: She is empowered.

Whedon: [Laughs.] Dangerously so. She's absolutely the expert. And she's very much in charge of her career, which I admire. There's a lot of confluence between her and the young Buffster. She may well be right. I've heard people say nice things about how we should get an award, and I work so very hard on this show that, of course, in my heart, I believe it, but I never expected that we would. I do think it's a little strange, a bit of a hybrid, and it is tough. You know, I think the Academy has proved itself kind of stodgy in the last couple of years. Not to say that we should be getting it. I watched the first *Sopranos* and was like, "Give it to *these* guys. Oh my God!" I watch *The West Wing* and say, "Give it to these guys!" There's great shows out there. I'm not like, "Oh those stodgy voters, they don't get how great we are, blah, blah, blah," because the fact that I'm *ever* having a conversation about the Emmys in regards to a show called *Buffy the Vampire Slayer* means that something's gone horribly right [both laugh], so the critical understanding of this show has been so gratifying. The fact that the critics got it and appreciated it from day one, and the rabid, almost insane fan base is great. Anything else is just gravy. The thing, though, about the show that I think holds it back is the wacky title. You know, people don't like the wacky title. It's not serious drama if you have a wacky title. But it's the fact that it is so schizophrenic and has so many elements. One of the things that TV is about is comfort, is knowing exactly where you are. I know they're going to invite Jessica Fletcher over, one of them is going to get killed, she very politely is going to solve it. I know what's going to happen when I tune in to a particular show. With *Buffy* we'll do French farce one week and *Medea* the next week. We try very hard structurally not to fall into a pattern either, so there's not a shoot-out in a warehouse every episode; because there *are* elements of comfort, obviously, Buffy will appear in the film at some point, but, at the same time, I'm very much committed to keeping the audience off their feet. It's sort of antithetical to what TV is devised to do. Not that there aren't surprising and delightful shows out there, but not to have that particular comfort level would throw people to a certain extent. It's like when we decide what show to send to the Academy voters, it's always a big question. Do we send the drama, the comedy, the horror show?

Longworth: I'm a big fan of the old Universal horror films principally because of the Gothic mood they struck. Not a lot of gore or violence. And I think that's what draws me to your two shows. I feel that this Gothic tone is going to thread its way through the episodes regardless of the story line. Do you work hard to make sure you are maintaining that tone?

Whedon: Ultimately this was designed as a horror that is funny and exciting, so visually we want to keep those rich blacks, we want to keep that suspense. It's never been a gorefest because the one thing that leaves me really cold in a horror movie is excessive gore. I think I'm just a wuss, really, but that's the fact. We've pushed it sometimes, because when something horrible is happening it's sometimes better if it looks really painful, rather than sort of blithe. But, yeah, I'm much more interested in the suspense and the implied, in the unseen.

Longworth: But while you do the violence thing tastefully, you have pushed the envelope with some of the sexual scenes and innuendo. Like the episode where Buffy's imposter says to Buffy, "Oh, so Willow's not driving stick anymore?"—referring to Willow's lesbian tendencies.
Whedon: I loved that. [Laughs.]

Longworth: And then, to go back to the "Hush" episode, where Buffy, who can't speak, is trying to gesture to her friends how they might drive a wooden stake through the villain's heart. The hand motion that she used to gesture resembled the international symbol for male masturbation. Has the WB Standards and Practices office ever rapped your knuckles?
Whedon: We go back and forth. We have our episodes, but we have a pretty good relationship with them. I mean, it's always handled politely. I'm not one of these guys who says, "Fuck the network, fuck these executives." Obviously they have a different agenda than we do, and I respect that, and they let us get away with murder, so it works out nicely. But things like that [Buffy's

gesture], they're pretty harmless, you know? It's not going to disturb a four year old that somebody made a gesture with his hand, because that four year old categorically can't understand. "Willow's not driving stick anymore" is going to go over the heads of everybody it needs to go over the heads of. Ultimately, because it's a show about teenagers and young adults, and because it's a horror show, there's going to be a heightened emotion and, particularly, a heightened sexuality that's inevitable. Because that's part of that time of your life, and because it's dealing with fantasy and horror. Your best dreams and your worst nightmares are going to come out of that.

Longworth: Did you support or oppose the network's decision to reschedule the famous prom episode in the wake of the Columbine shootings?
Whedon: It wasn't actually the prom episode. They rescheduled two episodes. One was about a kid bringing a gun to school [episode number eighteen] that was supposed to air three days after Columbine, and I absolutely supported that because, let's say we came down against it. Any comment on the situation *after* that horror would have been offensively trite. So that was not a problem. They then started making us make cuts in the last show. We had to cut down explosions when it turned out that the kids had been trying to bomb the place but the people hadn't known right away. And Xander trying to blow up the school had to go. And then they said they were going to reschedule episode number twenty-two, the season finale, as well. At that point, I got a little, well I was not crazy about that situation, but I understood it. They were worried because there was violence at the graduation. Now admittedly it was crossbows against a sixty-foot snake, but, still, had there been any violent incident at a graduation [after that], there would have been a very bad taste in everyone's mouth.

Longworth: OK, let's suppose the network hadn't changed a thing, and a violent incident had occurred in real life following the broadcast of your show. What's your responsibility as a producer, or do you feel a certain obligation toward young people and how your product may influence them?
Whedon: I have always felt an enormous obligation, I mean, since I was a kid. Since I was writing stories alone in my room that nobody else was going to read, I worried about how much I needed to mix what my political beliefs were with the story I wanted to tell. How much I needed to protect good role models, how much I needed to make a statement, and how much I needed just to dig to some dark place and write whatever the hell I wanted. That's a huge part of it. I've thought about this a lot, particularly when I've been confronted by it, by events like this. To an extent, I think we have a grave responsibility. I think it would be belittling our audience to say that if we poke a stick in somebody's eye on the show they're all going to go do it, because they're a little

more intelligent than that. But you absolutely have to think about what it will mean. At the same time, I feel strongly, and I've only come to realize this in the last few months, that we have a responsibility to be irresponsible. As storytellers, I've always been very offended by the whole, "let's rewrite all the fairytales" where the three little pigs settle their differences with the wolf by talking about their feelings.

Longworth: So that makes you very conflicted on this broad issue of responsibility versus creative latitude, doesn't it?

Whedon: Well, it does, and it doesn't because, ultimately, stories come from violence, they come from sex. They come from death. They come from the dark places that everybody has to go to, kind of wants to, or doesn't, but needs to deal with. If you raise a kid to think everything is sunshine and flowers, they're going to get into the real world and die. And ultimately, to access these base emotions, to go to these strange places, to deal with sexuality, to deal with horror and death, is what people need and it's the reason that we tell these stories. That's the reason fairy tales are so creepy [laughs], because we need to encapsulate these things, to inoculate ourselves against them, so that when we're confronted by the genuine horror that is day-to-day life we don't go insane.

Longworth: Do you ever attempt to moralize on an issue? For example, Buffy's first sexual encounter with Angel, which went badly in the aftermath. Was that your way of sending a message to young people to say, "You better abstain?"

Whedon: Absolutely not. When I say we have a responsibility to be irresponsible, I'm not just talking about, "Oh, I'm trying to help kids deal with the world." I'm talking about the process of telling a story. These stories come from this place, and I think that stories are sacred. I think that creating narrative is a basic human function. It's why we remember some things and not everything. It's why everybody's version of the same event is different. Everybody creates narrative all the time. I think it's a really important function. And it has to come from this base place to be pure, to be art, to be anything other than a polemic. So I'm not just talking about "Well, I've got to help kids deal with their problems by showing them scary stuff." I mean, I've got to fulfill that human need for scary stuff, and sexy stuff, and racy stuff, and wrong stuff, and disturbing stuff. Because I think that's what storytelling is. Now, am I saying that sex is bad? Unfortunately, because it's a horror show everything that happens is bad. [Both laugh.] Everything that can go bad, will. Buffy's gonna drink beer, and it's going to turn her into a caveman. Now, I've been to college, and that's what happens. [Both laugh.] But we sort of undercut that specifically at the end of the show when Xander said, "And what have we learned about beer?" And Buffy says, "Foamy." I don't want to make a reactionary statement. I don't want to say, "Never have sex." I don't want to say, "Quick, go have it now." I want to say, "Some people have it. Everybody thinks about it. Here's how we deal with it." The thing with Angel wasn't, "Don't sleep with your boyfriend." Giles very clearly comes out and says, "I think you were rash, but I know you loved him and he loved you, and I'm not going to upbraid you for that." That wasn't about that. It was about what happens when you sleep with a guy and he stops calling you. What happens if you give him what he wants, and he starts treating you like shit. It was about the emotion of it. And that's a very real, emotional thing that everybody goes through. You consummate a relationship, and it disappears out from under you, and it happens to both sexes.

Longworth: I know you talked about being mugged and identifying with women, but why *are* you so good at writing for women and at understanding and empowering your female characters?
Whedon: I've struggled with my ability to write women. My whole life I've wanted to make sure that I didn't idealize them, that I just didn't sort of scratch the surface. And sometimes I don't get it right. When I don't understand, I go to Marti Noxon, one of our female writers, and ask, "What did you go through?" But I have always been interested in feminism, partially because I was raised by a very strong woman, and partially because being small and fragile, and not taken seriously by anybody, I could identify with the way I perceived women were being treated once I got out of my house, where they were treated like equals. Gender and feminism has just always been a big area of study for me. It's what I concentrated on in film. And I think the other side of that is I'm a fella. One of the reasons why I was always able to do well in my feminine studies is that I never came from a knee-jerk, lesbian separatist sort of perspective. I understand the motivation of the man with the murderous gaze, of the animal, of the terrible objectifying male, 'cause [laugh] I'm him. So it was very easy for me to sort of get into the mind set of, shall we say, the enemy.

Longworth: What kind of feedback or letters does the show get from young people? And I don't mean fan letters like, "I love your hair."
Whedon: I know, but I have *really* great hair. [Both laugh.] I have great hair, just less and less of it. You know, we *do* get letters where people say the show has really helped them.

Longworth: So do you feel as though you've actually helped kids in dealing with life's situations?
Whedon: I really do. I've had so many people say, and that includes people on my writing staff, "This [character] wasn't around when I was little. I needed this person to look up to and identify with." Creating Buffy is about creating not just a character who can take care of herself, but a world that accepts that.

She's surrounded by men who not only don't mind that she takes charge in a situation but find it kind of sexy. So in a way, it's kind of Utopian, this group of people. But it's how I was until I went to a place where they didn't grow any. Most of my best friends were girls, and I'm very comfortable with them.

Longworth: Everyone assumes that the demos for your shows are thirteen to twenty, but what's the truth?
Whedon: They charted it in our second year, and the median viewer age is twenty-six. There are young kids watching it, but I consider it as a college kind of show. The thing about it is, a lot of teen shows are all about, "Look at the crazy, bumbling grown-up." And we have some of those, some authority figures that we hate because I'll never get over that [both laugh], but the show is not designed to be exclusive to anyone. I was raised by teachers, so I had a very different idea of school than most of the kids around me. I tended to see the school as the way it functioned. I saw how tired my teacher was, 'cause I'd come home with my mom and she'd be more exhausted than I was. And the character of Giles is there to give that perspective.

Longworth: OK, so we know you can write for women, and young people, and vampires, and teachers, but let's suppose the studio came to you tomorrow and asked you to write a movie about senior citizens. Are you so ensconced in your genre that you either couldn't or wouldn't take the assignment?
Whedon: Sometimes I'm like, "Oh my God, I just want to work with Abe Vigoda. Get me away from these fucking teenagers." [Both laugh.] Especially because at the WB there's a rotation of actors, you just go, "Oh my God, I'm so sick of this world." But then, I *tend* toward stories about adolescents. I tend toward young-adult fiction, toward that moment in life. I'm interested in that. Yeah, I definitely want to tell other stories. I want to tell stories about grown-ups, and, to an extent that's what *Angel* is. Here's a guy who's living with decisions he's made, and so he's like a recovering alcoholic. What he's going through is not an adolescent experience. It's much more of a middle-age experience. But absolutely, sometimes I just want to run as far from here as I possibly can. It may be that as far as I can get is half a block [both laugh], but this to me isn't a teen show in the sense of, say, four years of giggling by the locker and "Will he ask me out," even though that's part of the human experience of it. The show exists on a much bigger level, and it deals with so much of life. She's changing so much, going to college. And what I have in store for her next year is so different from what happened last year that I don't feel stuck.

Longworth: You mentioned *Angel*, and as you know, some critics have said that the spin-off is better than the original. Do you agree with that assessment, or is it like being the parent of two kids, and—
Whedon: It's basically like saying, "Girls, girls, you're *both* pretty."

Longworth: But when you raise a second child, you're automatically benefitting from your experiences in raising the first.

Whedon: Oh yeah. But you know, you learn every day the exact same lesson. Every story we break, halfway through the story we're like, "Well, what if this was actually about Buffy? What if we cared about what Buffy was going through? That might make it better. Let's try that!" I mean, it's incredible how stupid you can be and how everything is a lesson. The same thing with *Angel*. *Buffy* to me is my first child. It's a phenomenon that says more about what I want to say about the world than anything I've ever worked on. *Angel* has the potential to be that, too, and is starting to. But you look at the first scene in *Angel*, there's the blonde woman in the alley, and here comes Angel to save her. And I thought, "Oh my God, have I just betrayed everything I believe in by doing this scene?" But *Angel* works at a different level. *Angel* is about something else. But in terms of just creating an icon that I know exists in the endless sort of fantasy lives of young people, in a way that there hadn't been one that did before, or that's what *Buffy* is, I don't think I'm ever going to match that.

Longworth: I've talked at length with producers who have had multiple shows on the air at once, so I'll ask you the same question I asked of them. Do you feel that either of your dramas suffers because you're stretching yourself too thin?

Whedon: Yes, a little bit. A little bit. I work really hard, not just on both shows, but to surround myself with really smart people who can get a great deal done without me. But yeah, there have been things in *Buffy* where I was like, "I could have spent a little more time tweaking that scene. I could have edited that for a little more excitement." You know, the extra yard that I could have gone. I see it inevitably. I'm still working as hard on *Buffy* as I possibly can, and doing as much on *Angel* as well, and I'm very pleased with the quality of the show. I think the problems we've had on *Buffy* have not been a question of my involvement so much as we're throwing a lot of new stuff up against the wall, and you never know what's going to stick.

Longworth: Is it hard to let go and entrust other writers with your creations?

Whedon: No. When we came into it, I hired a staff. It took me four years to get a really, really solid staff. If I don't like something, if it's not right, I'll rewrite it. And I've rewritten a dozen scripts from the words "fade in" on this show. I've written half or three-quarters of the scripts. Now I have a staff where that's happening much, much less, because they are really solid. If somebody else is getting it right and is embodying what the show should be, I don't need to do it. I've worked for producers who need to do every goddamn thing, no matter what. If you turn in a perfectly good script, they're going to rewrite it anyway, just so they could be the one to have written it. I do not like to create work for myself, and if somebody is getting it right, I like them to know it. So I'll never rewrite anything that I don't have to.

Longworth: In doing two shows at once you must have to be a disciplined person. Describe that discipline.

Whedon: You know, I am incredibly undisciplined. I'm very lazy. I'm a big procrastinator. I happen to love doing this, which makes it easier. And, sometimes I can stay up all night if I have to, because I have no choice. Any discipline that I have comes from my desire to make the shows as good as I possibly can before I let them go. I reach a level of exhaustion, and this year I only reached it sooner, because I had two shows going. But ultimately, how disciplined I am doesn't matter because I have this huge amount of work to do, and I get scripts in late, and it's not great in that sense. But I don't really have the opportunity to be as lazy as I really am because the show just doesn't allow it. I've often said that everyone who does movies should be forced to work in television for two reasons. One, the story actually matters, and two, you have to get it done. I think movies get sort of mired in this place of, "Well, we can do anything we want. We don't know what the fuck we're doing." [Both laugh.] In TV you have to tell the story, and you have to bring them back next week. And it has great discipline in terms of structure, in terms of meaning, in terms of what matters, and it's got to be done by tomorrow.

Longworth: Has writing become a chore for you, or is it still fun?

Whedon: It is the most fun I'm ever going to have. I love to write. I love it. I mean, there's nothing in the world I like better, and that includes sex, probably because I'm so very bad at it. [Both laugh.] It's the greatest peace when I'm *in* a scene, and it's just me and the character; that's it, that's where I want to live my life. I've heard about guys who find it strenuous and painful and horrible, and I scratch my noggin. I don't get it. I definitely get tired of rewriting, something that I'm not creating from whole cloth is tough. So every now and then I have to drum up the enthusiasm to write this exposition scene. It's a real drag. But, ultimately, the moment I break into a scene, the moment I figure out what it is, I'm there, I'm loving it.

Longworth: What, if anything, do you watch on TV when you have free time? I know you said you like *The West Wing*.

Whedon: That's pretty much it. *The Simpsons is* starting to lose me. It's starting to happen, but, Jesus, it was only the best goddamn show on TV for ten years. But *The West Wing* I don't miss, and, quite frankly, I watch *Buffy*.

Longworth: How will you keep *Buffy* and *Angel* from getting stale after they've been on for a decade?

Whedon: By dying of exhaustion.

Longworth: Are you going to know when to get out?

Whedon: Maybe. Is the network? Is the studio? Are the actors? Who knows. It's clear to me that, even if I were to walk away, the show would continue to exist beyond me, which is the beauty and the horror of it. I do think this show will stop either before or soon after it starts getting stale. I don't think anybody wants that. I don't think the audience would put up with it. I don't think the actors would, either. It's hard for them to stay at the challenge, to come at it with the same joy that I do when I'm writing it. After seven years, some of it can be even harder.

Longworth: You mention the network, but your shows have a tremendous fan base on the Internet now. Stephen King tried his hand at a direct-to Internet book. In that same vein, do you ever see a point where you or any producer would be able to bypass networks and make a good living taking your creations directly to the Internet?

Whedon: Very possibly. Who the hell knows what's going to be possible in five years? Clearly, things are getting more spread out. Clearly, the TV and the computer are edging closer together, and I expect them to meld sometime within the next ten years for sure. And there's fifty-seven channels and all that good stuff. It's definitely possible. I'm not a great pioneer of technology and new thinking. I'm not great independent maverick, either. I've always thought of myself as kind of a company man. I hope that I'm doing something original. I hope I'm pushing the envelope a little bit. I've always wanted to work with the studios doing great big hit shows and big summer movies. I love those things, and I always want to maintain a good relationship with the people I work with. I have a network that lets me put on a rather strange show.

Longworth: Speaking of strange shows filled with vampires and demons. You once said that everyone has demons. What are your demons?

Whedon: Whop, doggie! [Laughs.] Some of them I can't even describe. Generally, I'm a very depressive kind of person, and I think the world is a horrible, scary place where you die. And human interaction is kind of meaningless, and that's why I so desperately enjoy narrative, which provides me with that experience. So if I'm not writing, I'm pretty much just not fun to be around. There's a sense of failure and mortality, and depression over, "Is my nose really going to look like this for the rest of my life?" [Both laugh.] I can be a real bummer.

Longworth: Your characters sometimes hang around graveyards, so I'll ask the obvious question. What's going to be inscribed on your tombstone?

Whedon: If I'm lucky? [Pauses.] "He was getting better." Whatever I do, I just want to get better at it. I just want to keep trying, because I think of narrative and everything I do, whatever form it takes, as this sort of great, vast library that can be explored, that you'll never, ever see all of, but that you can just try and see as much of it as you can. I've learned more *this* year writing *Buffy* than I probably have in three years before, doing shows like "Hush," where everybody shut up for three acts. Writing "Restless," which is the season finale, which took place entirely in dreams and is basically a forty-minute poem. The fact that I'm working in year four of a show that is giving me completely new challenges without becoming completely silly, self-referential, and pointless is a great thing.

Longworth: Well, not to belabor the point, but, again, "Hush" I believe will stand as one of the single greatest episodes in series drama. So you *are* getting better. Oh, say, before I let you get away, I need your advice on something. Can a vampire be repelled or killed over the telephone?
Whedon: [Laughs.]

Longworth: The reason I ask is that I'm so damn tired of these telemarketers calling me.
Whedon: A lot of them *have* risen from the grave, but I don't think so. Not unless you say, "Hey, look, sun's coming out!" [Both laugh.]

Longworth: Well, thanks for spending time with me.
Whedon: There's just one more thing that I want to say about "Hush," because you've got me started on it, and something I've never gotten to talk about is this. The great thing about that episode was, I knew I wanted to do it silent, because I was starting to devolve into sort of a hack TV director, and I wanted to push myself visually. But what it became about was the way language interferes with communication. The amazing thing about it was, when you're writing about that, every word is on theme. Every single thing that happens in that show inevitably is about communication. And that was the most pure experience of language I ever had, just writing the first act. People were using words wrong, somebody who needs to communicate because they're too busy talking, all that stuff. People just talking around the point. It all became so centrally thematic. That's never happened before. That was really *cool!*

Longworth: Of course, it's ironic that you and I have spent so much time verbalizing about a basically nonverbal episode. Shouldn't we be gesturing about it instead?
Whedon: No, not on the phone. It's like killing vampires; it's harder on the phone. [Both laugh.]

Must-See Metaphysics

EMILY NUSSBAUM/2002

From *New York Times*, September 9, 2002. Reprinted by permission of the author.

"Every once in a while, I'll just look up and say, 'My spaceship!'" says Joss Whedon, bouncing on the tips of his sneakers. The thirty-eight-year-old creator of *Buffy the Vampire Slayer* grins and gazes up at the *Serenity*, a pirate vessel of the future. The ship dominates the Hollywood set of Whedon's newest genre-bender, *Firefly*—a show that is part cowboy shoot-'em-up, part space opera, with a sneaky existential streak. At once majestic and junky, the *Serenity* resembles a blown-up kid's toy, and its interior has been filled with oddball details. A tiny plastic bobble-headed dog sits on the dashboard, and the ship's low-tech engine is reminiscent of an overgrown eggbeater.

As he delivers notes to Nathan Fillion, the strapping actor who plays the *Serenity*'s captain, Mal Reynolds, Whedon looks notably less than strapping—and more like a frazzled grad student who missed laundry day. ("Write 'doughy,'" he suggests, hovering over my reporter's notebook. "Write 'jowly.'") But his schlubbiness is a bit of an act, concealing a charismatic, prickly intensity. After one successful take, he jumps up with a cry of "Sweeeet!" then murmurs: "Don't give him coffee! You don't know what he will become." Between scenes, he edits scripts for *Buffy* and its spinoff, *Angel*. Like more than one ex-nerd of my acquaintance, Whedon compulsively peppers his speech with self-deprecating asides: "Oh, my God, I am a hack," he moans as we watch Fillion, his thumbs hooked in the belt loops of his skintight slacks, swagger back onto the ship's bridge. But like his show's hero, Whedon exudes confidence.

And why shouldn't he? After all, Whedon has created one of the most intelligent, and most underestimated, shows on television. Like the *Serenity*, *Buffy* might look at first sight like a disposable toy, something cobbled from materials that most adults dismiss out of hand: teen banter, karate chops, and bloodsucking monsters. Before the show went on the air in 1997, executives at the fledgling WB network begged him to change the whimsical title, arguing that the show would never reach intelligent viewers. But it did. *Buffy* is about a teenage girl staking monsters in the heart, but her true demons are personal, and the show's innovative mix of fantasy elements and psychological acuity transcends easy categorization. Despite being perpetually snubbed at the Emmy Awards, *Buffy* has become a critics' darling and inspired a fervent fan base among teenage girls and academics alike. The show's influence can be felt everywhere on television these days, from tawdry knockoffs like *Charmed* to more impressive copycats like *Alias.*

Firefly, which began its run this Friday on Fox, is an opportunity for Whedon to build a fresh new mythology, what he calls a "drama with landscape." Audaciously combining two more neglected juvenile genres, westerns and science fiction, the series began as Whedon's most experimental yet—until Fox rejected the pilot and forced him to whip up a more accessible premiere episode. But although the new season opener has a kickier and more commercial structure than the meditative pilot he originally devised, Whedon was able to maintain his central vision. Yes, it's a space show, but it's also an intellectual drama about nine underdogs struggling in the moral chaos of a postglobalist universe. Adventure and ethical debate are melded in one sexy package. "It's about the search for meaning," he explains. "And did I mention there's a whore?"

As technicians nudge a glowing white spaceship into the sky, Whedon talks about his frustration with those who mistake his creations for guilty pleasures. "I hate it when people talk about *Buffy* as being campy," he says, scarfing takeout chicken with a plastic fork. "I hate camp. I don't enjoy dumb TV. I believe Aaron Spelling has single-handedly lowered SAT scores." But despite these inevitable misreadings, Whedon's heart will always be with genre fiction. Like Buffy herself, genre fiction is easily undervalued, seen as powerless fluff. But Whedon finds it uniquely forceful: using its vivid strokes, you can be speculative, philosophical—and create stories that are not merely true to life but are metaphors for a deeper level of human experience. "It's better to be a spy in the house of love, you know?" he jokes. "If I made 'Buffy the Lesbian Separatist,' a series of lectures on PBS on why there should be feminism, no one would be coming to the party, and it would be boring. The idea of changing culture is important to me, and it can only be done in a popular medium."

Joss Whedon's family has worked in television for generations: his father wrote scripts for *Alice* and *The Golden Girls*, while his grandfather worked on *The Donna Reed Show* and *The Dick Van Dyke Show*. But in many ways, Whedon says, his deepest influence is his mother, Lee Stearns, a high-school teacher who wrote novels during her summers, novels that were never published. "She was very smart, uncompromising, cool as hell," he recalls. "You had to prove yourself—not that she wouldn't come through if you didn't, but she expected you to hold your own."

His parents divorced when he was nine (a "good divorce," he says). He lived with his dad, but he spent summers with his mom and stepdad at an artists' commune in upstate New York. As a teenager, Whedon attended a private boys' school in England; he became "the world's biggest Sondheim freak" as well as an avid comics fan. But at Wesleyan University, his sights narrowed to film. "I'd go out and see three classic films, stagger home at 2 A.M. and then watch whatever was on HBO," he recalls. "It was glorious." Majoring in film and immersing himself in women's studies, Whedon became convinced that the pop genres he loved—sci-fi and horror movies among them—could be more than just entertainment. They could carry subversive ideas into the mainstream.

After college, Whedon drifted out to Los Angeles. An eccentric wannabe auteur with bright red hair down to his waist, he fiddled with weird projects like a musical parody of the Oliver North hearings; despite his father's industry connections, he had disastrous pitch meetings. Then he got his big break: a staff writer's job on *Roseanne*. By the time he left, he had a solid writer's rep. For several years, Whedon worked as a bored but well-compensated script doctor, contributing to good films (*Toy Story*, for which he received an Oscar nomination) and many bad ones (*Waterworld*). But he had an escape plan in the works, a screenplay with a mission statement. Whedon wanted to create an iconic female hero, but also "a world in which adolescent boys would see a girl who takes charge as the sexiest goddamn thing they ever saw." His mother died in 1992, but they had talked about his *Buffy* screenplay, and, he says, she knew he was on his way.

Then, in a classic Hollywood tale of disillusionment, he lost control of his screenplay—only to see his vision of "populist feminism" turned into a schlocky comedy. He recalls sitting in the theater, crying. "I really thought I'd never work again," he recalls of the experience. "It was that devastating." But in a second chance few get, Whedon was able to resurrect *Buffy* on television, restoring the show's powerful central metaphor: adolescence is hell, and any girl who makes it through is a superhero.

With each of *Buffy*'s six television seasons, Whedon's reputation grew. The show took startling structural risks. There was the silent episode, "Hush"—a virtuoso spook show with wordless scenes as witty as any dialogue. In "The Body," Whedon broke television taboo by treating the death of Buffy's mother with raw, mournful realism. In the fifth-season finale, the heroine herself died, a scenario that managed to resonate as both a beautiful Christ-like sacrifice and an act of suicidal despair. Last season featured her painful resurrection— she literally dug herself out of a grave—as well as an exhilarating all-musical episode, "Once More with Feeling." (The soundtrack comes out on Tuesday.) Over time, the show's mythology has become as rich and multilayered as any work of literature—eternally complicating its own notions of morality, allow- ing characters to grow up in a way rare for television and generating enough internal allusions to fuel its own media-studies department. Indeed, several academic anthologies focus on the show; other high-flown analyses appear on *Slayage: The Online International Journal of Buffy Studies*. The show's daring and complexity have earned it many smarty-pants fans, from those who contribute to the show's insanely challenging Internet discussion groups (some of which feature posts from Whedon himself) to Ira Glass, the host of the radio program *This American Life*.

Television creators like David E. Kelley and Aaron Sorkin may be better known, but to many critics, Whedon is the more original artist, one who has been unfairly denied prizes and high ratings. To J. J. Abrams, creator of *Alias*—a show about a tough female spy—Whedon is a pioneer, stubbornly resisting the pressure to take the easy route to cultural respect. "He's not the normal adult in any way that I can see," Abrams says. "He's the mischievous kid and the wise-adult kid in one package. You know, if he wanted to be taken seriously in the conventional way, he could write a medical show or a legal show. But he cares more about telling stories he wants to tell, and he's being taken seriously on his terms. It's like the title *Buffy the Vampire Slayer*: if you don't smile, you're not going to get the show anyway."

The messy anteroom to Whedon's office at Mutant Enemy, his Los Angeles production company, is filled with *Buffy* memorabilia and piles of videotapes. On the walls hang glossy framed posters: *The Matrix*, *Written on the Wind*, a pen-and-ink drawing of Mickey Mouse hanging by a noose. Whedon hands me a snapshot of a fellow redhead with a wicked grin; it's his wife, Kai Cole. "The funniest woman I've ever met," he says. On their honeymoon, Whedon scribbled the names of *Buffy* characters in a notepad. And it was on a long-overdue London vacation with Kai that Whedon found the inspiration for *Firefly*. When the jet-lagged couple read through the night, Whedon dived into *The Killer Angels*, Michael Shaara's fictional re-creation of the Battle of Gettysburg. "I thought, That's the show I want to make!" he recalls. "It was about the minutiae of the soldiers' lives. And I wanted to play with that classic notion of the frontier: not the people who made history, but the people history stepped on—the people for whom every act is the creation of civilization. Then again, there's also gunfights and action."

From this blueprint, Whedon has built a show that, like *Buffy*, twists comic-book structures into novel shapes. It's science fiction, but there are gunfights instead of laser battles, and no alien foreheads to be seen. "This is my first non-latex show," he tells me, grinning. "The show is set five hundred years in the future, but humans are still acting worse than any monster." It's a character-rich drama, but one full of violence and slapstick comedy. And while *Firefly* contains plenty of Whedon's favorite TV-friendly tropes—whip-smart caper plots and ricocheting sexual subtext—the show has a grubby, realistic look to it, quite unlike the shiny suburb of Sunnydale on *Buffy*. Such juxtapositions can seem at once down to earth and charmingly weird. As the *Serenity* drifts through space, it's accompanied by twangy music right out of a Civil War documentary. "I want viewers to equate the past, the present and the future," Whedon explains, "not to think of the future as 'that glowy thing that's distant and far away.'"

And woven into the action, there's a juicy (and prescient) political allegory. At Wesleyan, Whedon was deeply influenced by his professor Richard Slotkin, the creator of the theory of "regeneration through violence": the notion that frontier myths allowed conquerors—including the pioneers of the American West—to rewrite bloody history as heroic fairy tale. *Firefly* is set in just such a postimperialist universe, after China and America have formed a corporate supergovernment, the Alliance. In essence, it's Coca-Cola as the White House. Our heroes are post-Reconstruction crooks scraping by on the serrated edge of the law, and depending on which way you turn the moral prism, they might resemble an antiglobalization cadre or followers of an outer-space jihad. In the show's first episode, Captain Reynolds taunts a drunken Alliance member with the Confederate refrain "We shall rise again," and the implication is clear: these characters may be underdogs, but whether they are heroes (even to themselves) is a loaded question.

But as with Whedon's other shows, *Firefly* is as much a character study as it is an abstract debate. The ensemble includes a courtesan, a thug, a preacher, a rich-boy doctor, a tomboy engineer, and a psychic. They are all archetypes with inner lives. Leading this crew is Mal Reynolds, who is, like Buffy Summers, a singularly thorny pop creation: a mordant, dark-humored fellow with bile boiling just beneath the surface. (Think Han Solo, only with more interiority.) His former enemy is now his government, and frankly, he's not coping well. When Whedon cast Nathan Fillion, he encouraged him to watch John Wayne films, aiming to help him capture elements of Wayne's physical grace as well as his dark undertones.

"Mal's politics are very reactionary and 'Big government is bad' and 'Don't interfere with my life,'" Whedon explains. "And sometimes he's wrong—because sometimes the Alliance is America, this beautiful shining light of democracy. But sometimes the Alliance is America in Vietnam: we have a lot of petty politics, we are way out of our league and we have no right to control these people. And yet! Sometimes the Alliance is America in Nazi Germany. And Mal can't see that, because he was a Vietnamese."

The show's other central concern diverges intriguingly from Buffy's universe, where fate and destiny loom large. "I'm a very hard-line, angry atheist," Whedon says. "Yet I am fascinated by the concept of devotion. And I want to explore that." (His existential revelation arrived during an adolescent viewing of *Close Encounters of the Third Kind*—an experience soon followed by a reading of Sartre's *Nausea*.) Mal tells the preacher who is a passenger on his ship,

"You're welcome on my boat; God ain't." If Buffy is the chosen one, forced to struggle with a responsibility that comes from outside, Mal is defiant in his belief that his fate is meaningless. "This is a man who has learned that when he believed in something it destroyed him," Whedon explains. "So what he believes in is the next job, the next paycheck, and keeping his crew safe." It is a typical Whedonian inversion: much the way Buffy is a demon-killer obsessed with the morality of killing, Mal is a man of action frozen by his conviction that nothing really matters, a man forced to choose his morality at each juncture. "Whatever I may think of him politically, he's a guy who looks into the void and sees nothing but the void—and says there is no moral structure, there is no help, no one's coming, no one gets it, I have to do it."

Can Whedon bring these bleak undercurrents to television intact? If *Buffy* is any indication, the answer is yes—but only if *Firefly* wins an audience. For despite Whedon's clout, the show wasn't easy to get on the air. The original two-hour pilot was idiosyncratic, with slow, John Ford–style pacing that thrilled Whedon but baffled Fox. He agreed to speed things up, but the network wanted other changes, like turning a married couple into flirting singles. He refused. "I wanted a marriage on my show, not 'Melrose Space,'" he says. Such prickly negotiations flashed Whedon back to his earliest experiences in Hollywood—and left him nursing a very Mal-like resentment against the strictures of Fox, his own personal Alliance.

Whedon discusses these frustrations with me one night over dinner. "There were so many times I thought, It's time to retire in rage and confusion," he says. "Some of this was just forgetting how difficult it is getting a pilot on the air. And some of it was hubris." He pauses to sip some chardonnay. "As I learned, pride goeth before a fall season. Or, as my writer Mere Smith put it, 'There are no atheists in Fox shows.'"

But if Whedon is expert at nursing a grudge with the suits, he is also buoyed by the recognition that he commands a deeply loyal audience. His fans have been waiting for *Firefly* with a mix of eagerness and trepidation—and a sometimes unnerving sense of ownership. The previous evening, at a pre-Emmy panel discussion in the lush Academy of Television Arts and Sciences auditorium in North Hollywood, Whedon was pelted with demanding questions: Why was *Buffy*'s last season so dark? ("Oops!" he replied.) Was he spread too thin, cheating on his other shows in favor of his new creation?

But afterward, as he crouched by the stage, these critics turned worshipful, clutching DVDs and Sunnydale High School yearbooks, their faces dented with the desire to say one smart thing to the guy who created their favorite show. "In the season finale, Xander's crayon speech—did you mean that to have Christian imagery?" a middle-aged man inquired. A nine-year-old girl told him that she wanted to join the *Buffy* cast. And then a dewy young woman leaned forward and gripped his hand between hers, pulling him in for enforced eye contact: "I just want you to know—we trust you. We know you know what you're doing. We know it will be great."

Such damp effusions are the kind of thing that many television creators would shy away from. But Whedon loves it down there in the geek trenches. "That's the only reason I'm alive!" he says, placing his palms flat on the table-cloth. "We're paying homage to the same thing: the storytelling. I wanted to create a fiction that would affect people's lives. And this has affected people's lives. It's affected my life. Without it my life is meaningless."

Atheist though he may be, Joss Whedon has a kind of faith—in narrative passion, the kind that creates lasting loyalties. "Every time people say, 'You've transcended the genre,' I'm like: No! I believe in genre." For Whedon, fantasy inspires a visceral response that realism can't match. "*Law and Order* is the most enjoyable thing in the world!" He laughs. "But I do not go through life imagining myself as Sam Waterston, breakin' a case, prosecutin' a guy."

There are other, more ambitious TV shows that he admires, *The West Wing* among them. But Whedon is clearly not tempted to create that kind of "grown-up" show—no matter how many Emmys he'd win. "I'm not an adult!" he says, shaking his head. "I don't want to create responsible shows with lawyers in them. I want to invade people's dreams."

The Man Behind the Slayer

LAURA MILLER/2003

Not many people can create a cult phenomenon, and few of those set out to do it from the start, so fans of Joss Whedon's *Buffy the Vampire Slayer* may be forgiven for suspecting the writer/director of possessing superpowers rivaling those of his famous heroine. It would be exaggerating to say that his statements are studied like the utterances of the Oracle of Delphi, but let's just say that after seven years as the genius behind the *Buffy* universe, Whedon has learned to measure his words carefully.

Salon reached Whedon at his office in Los Angeles a few days before the May 20 broadcast of the final *Buffy* episode. We wanted him to answer a few of our own lingering questions about *Buffy* and perhaps to spill a few hints about the future—for the *Buffy* characters and for Whedon himself.

Miller: How do you think longtime fans of the show will feel about the final episode on May 20?
Whedon: It will make some people happy, it will make some of them angry, and if people aren't crying at least a couple of times during it, we won't have done our job.

Miller: Buffy started out seven years ago as a new kind of hero, one that broke the traditional masculine mold. Instead of deciding that her destiny sets her apart from regular people even though she devotes herself to protecting them, she was always determined to have a life. But lately, she's been acting a lot more like an old-fashioned male hero.
Whedon: This last season has been about that, taking the idea of how the Slayer is different from other people and really exploring it. The last episode is in fact about that very issue. Part of that has to do with where we want to go with the message of the season, which is really contained in the last episode, deal with the idea of separateness. And honestly, some of that comes from the

actors. Ultimately there always had been some separation between the star and the ensemble. You find that bleeds into your storytelling. The way that Giles got hipper and Willow got sexier. Because that's who [the actors] were. You live with these people and interact with them for the past seven years and that starts to creep in. The whole "I'm a stalwart hero who does the job" sort of came from Sarah [Michelle Gellar] a bit.

It also came from "I've come back from the dead!" This is no small thing, no coming out of the shower. You don't buy that back cheaply. Whereas last year Buffy went to a place of dark questioning, which is very much not Sarah, this year was about "OK, I have this power that sort of separates me from the rest of the world," which in a weird way is the life of a star.

Miller: She's also dealing with authority, too, how hard it is to be in charge.
Whedon: That's just me. Everybody has been in a similar position in one way or another, but a lot of that [groaning] "Hey, being in charge is really hard!" is me, whining.

Miller: Was being in charge harder than you thought it was going to be back when, as a screenwriter and script doctor working on movies like *Speed* and *Toy Story*, you weren't in charge?
Whedon: No, actually, it was a little easier. When you're in charge you really get to do things your way, and ultimately it's better than the other thing. But having said that, it is not a small amount of responsibility, and sometimes the weight of it . . . the weight of "I need this to be as good as it can be and I need it to send the message I want to send and serve as what the fans want and need, and I need to do that twenty-two times a year—no, wait, forty-four times a year," there is a great pressure that nobody else is feeling. At the same time, nobody else is feeling the total grand plan. Everybody sees a portion of it. But ultimately most of it has to be seen by me, the panorama, and that changes your relationships. And that's something we explored with Faith. When Faith became the leader of Buffy's group, she had to *become* the leader. It's different from, "Hey, I'll just run things for a while."

That said, everything in my power is done to show off other people as much as possible and to share power—and to get out of things.

Miller: You're known for having that master plan, for having mapped out the whole arc of the story, not just within a season, but also from season to season. But there must have been changes to that plan over the years, stuff you couldn't help or that you realized as you went along would be better if you did it another way. What were some of the big changes from your master plan?
Whedon: The master plan does not have a master plan. Television ultimately finds itself, and after it finds itself, it finds itself changing. I'd have a year

plotted out, maybe two years in advance. And I had the major points that I knew I needed to hit and they would serve as anchors and we'd get from one to the next, and that was great. But the rest you deliberately don't have a master plan for, because you don't know what's going to happen. Apparently people seem to be responding to this Boreanaz fellow [David, the actor who plays Angel]. Apparently Seth [Green, who plays Oz] is gone. Apparently this villain isn't working out and this one's popping like crazy. You need to improvise, you always need to.

TV's like whitewater rafting: Without rocks, there wouldn't be rapids, and it wouldn't be as much fun. Rolling with it gave us Tara and Willow coming out. It gave us Spike falling in love with Buffy. Rolling with it found out that Anya and Andrew were comic geniuses. You plan your ideas and themes, and then you let the rest form naturally, and then it feels real. It doesn't feel like you're imposing something on everybody. Ultimately, the staff—who are the biggest fan-geeks in the world, and I'm including myself—when they watch an episode have to feel the way the audience does, and more importantly the characters have to feel the way the audience does. If the audience doesn't buy that Buffy's brought back from the dead, then Buffy can't buy it. They've got to go, "I can't believe this has happened. It's horrible." If the audience is feeling the loss of Angel and feeling that she can't have a relationship with Riley, she's got to feel the same way. You feel that out.

Miller: But sometimes you push back against some of the things the fan base, which is so possessive, wants.
Whedon: Sure, yeah. There's obviously the fact that Angel has his own series now, so what are you gonna do? It's not like we're reading the Internet and go-ing, "OK, Ain't It Cool says blah blah blah." We take our fan base's opinions and concerns very seriously, but at the same time we're the storytellers.

In terms of the *Angel* thing, the truth is that by year four we would have been throwing up our hands going, "How can we possibly make this fresh?" Often what the fan base wants is for two characters to get together romanti-cally, but that often doesn't leave the narrative with anyplace to go. It's Sam and Diane [from *Cheers*]. That's why we had Angel go bad when he and Buffy got together. Because—and I've gotten into so much trouble for this phrase—what people want is not what they need. In narrative, nobody wants to see fat, married Romeo and Juliet, even if fat, married Romeo and Juliet happen to be [Dashiell Hammett's detective couple] Nick and Nora Charles and they're really cool and having a great time in their lovely relationship and really care about each other and have nice, well-adjusted children. Guess what? People don't want to see it.

That was the problem we ran into with Riley. We said, "Let's give Buffy a healthy relationship," and people didn't want it. They did some great work together. But at the same time, when they were happy, it made people crazy. We found this with Willow and Tara, we found it with Gunn and Fred [from *Angel*]. It's fine for a while, but ultimately the course of true love is not allowed to run smooth.

Miller: Were there things you planned to do that you had to abandon? In particular, I know a lot of people who speculate that Buffy and Xander were once intended to get together.

Whedon: That was fluid. The concept was in the air and they both sort of got pulled in different directions storywise and we didn't feel like there was some big point we weren't paying off, so we ended up not doing it. We liked him with Anya, and she had a lot going on, and it didn't really seem to be the thing. The concept was out there, but it was never a mission statement. A lot of concepts were out there, then you sort of wait and see. Besides, Xander got so much goddamn tail. I'm sorry—*that's* a nerd? He went out with Cordelia, he had an affair with Willow, he lost his virginity to Faith. He nearly married Anya. The guy's James fucking Bond over here. It's a lie! It's a lie!

Miller: Anything else?

Whedon: I had a huge arc planned for Oz.

Miller: That was a heartbreaker.

Whedon: It was, and so Willow got her heart broken. I took what we were feeling and put it on-screen, so everybody would be on the same page.

Miller: What was your idea for Oz?

Whedon: I mean the thing with him and Veruca, the female werewolf, and that triangle. That was going to run through a good portion of that season. I really wanted to see where we could go with that. Paige Moss was really cool, she did a great job. But she only did it for a couple of episodes because we lost the boy. But then four episodes later I got to meet Amber Benson [who plays Tara]. So, like I said, you gotta have the rocks.

Sometimes we had guest-star issues. Quite frankly, I had planned to see Tara again later this year and Amber decided against it. I'm not unhappy because we got to make the statement with [Willow's new girlfriend] Kennedy that you can move on and you can live. It's scary, and we've played a couple of episodes about how frightening it was for Willow to enter into another relationship, how it felt like a betrayal—because it felt like that to the audience. That was an interesting place to go. You know what they say, every time a door shuts . . .

Miller: Would Willow have become gay if Oz hadn't left?

Whedon: It's very possible. The idea of exploring somebody's sexuality and that it would probably be Willow was out there. Then Oz left. And we thought, how do you follow Oz? People loved the shit out of him, though they hated him when he first arrived. The one romance that we could give her that would really affect people in a new way would be with a woman. We didn't know how far we were going to go with it.

In the same way, Dawn was the next Riley. When we did Dawn, part of the mission statement was, let's have a really important, intense emotional relationship for Buffy that is not a boyfriend. Because let's not have her be defined by her boyfriend every time out of the bat. So, Season 5, she's as intense as she was in Season 2 with Angelus, but it's about her sister. To me that was really beautiful.

With Willow, we'd talked about the idea [of her becoming gay] and the opportunity was dropped in our lap, so we said, Let's do it as a sort of metaphor with this other witch. It's very physical, it's very romantic, it's very private. Then, we'll see where it takes us, and where it took us was to something more specific. We were pretty much accused of being coy and we had a lot of fun making metaphorical jokes. But we decided, yeah, these two have real chemistry and this is clearly a romantic relationship and there's no reason not to physicalize it because it means we will get a lot of really funny hate e-mail.

Miller: What, you were bored? You weren't getting enough as it was?

Whedon: We weren't getting a lot of hate mail. I kept thinking we were going to [for earlier aspects of the show]. We were shooting one scene in the very first episode, and [executive producer] David Greenwalt was standing next to me saying, "You're going to be murdered." And I'm like, "What?" But ultimately people accepted what we were doing until Willow came out, and then not so much.

But we don't really think about that, any more than we were thinking about the people it would help. Then people came to us and said, "I was able to come out because of your show," and we were like, "Whoa! Well, we meant to do that." We're very conscious of our responsibility, but you can't make stories based on it, because stories are by their nature irresponsible. It's gratifying that we got to do something that really mattered to people. That wasn't why we did it, but it sure was cool.

Miller: This season you've had to come up with the ultimate villain, and the First, being disembodied, presents some challenges. Now you have introduced an evil priest as its main henchman, and I think he could be the scariest bad guy so far.

Whedon: He's pretty creepy, isn't he? I love Nathan [Fillion]. He's an extraordinary actor who would not have been available had a certain door not shut, however temporarily [a reference to Whedon's series *Firefly*, starring Fillion, which was canceled last year]. I want to come down against the patriarchy and there was simply no more potent image. At the same time, I'm not coming down against priests. This guy clearly is not one. He's very bad at it.

Miller: His denomination is kind of unclear.
Whedon: Yeah well, again, it's the image of the thing. I believe that religion has contained within it an enormous amount of misogyny, and that cannot be denied. That's something that I will always bridle against and that image [a priest] is potent because of that. However, I have nothing against religion as a concept, or as people practice it. Religious institutions on the other hand, I believe cause people to fly planes into buildings. It's very dangerous. I do think that he is the creepiest priest. He is the most bald-faced misogynist we've had since, well, since last year, with Warren.

Miller: You've created a world where religion isn't to be trusted but some conventional religious items do have power in it. Crucifixes and holy water are still harmful to vampires.
Whedon: Ultimately, I'm dealing with a vampire myth. It's not any huge secret that I'm an atheist. For me, the most radical thing I ever did was have Riley go to church. I thought that was really cool. It makes him really different from the people in my universe, and somebody who is new to me. I've never met a well-adjusted person. It's weird.

So I am an atheist, but I'm telling a vampire story and everyone knows that vampire stories involve crosses. You haven't seen many of them and we haven't done much with holy water, though we've used it on occasion. We pretty much stick to stakes. That iconography is not something I want to explore. However, I do use Christian mythology. Buffy, resurrected much? She pretty much died for all of us by spreading her arms wide and . . . well, I won't go into it. That's what I was raised with. As much as I learned Greek myths and as much as I read Marvel Comics and watched *The Prisoner*, I grew up around Christianity and Judaism and those are the prevalent myths and mythic structures of my brain.

Every vampire fiction reinvents vampires to its own needs. You take what you want. I took that they have to be invited into the house, which a lot of people apparently didn't know about. I had always grown up thinking this.

Miller: They're sometimes said to not be able to cross running water.
Whedon: Yeah, I didn't use that one, although I've never had anyone jump over a stream. The idea of them looking like monsters and then looking like people, that was in *Lost Boys*, and that was very useful for us. You could have somebody fool you, or someone like Angel seem like he's not a vampire and then he is one. You make up rules that you need and jettison the ones you don't. I had to jettison one of the rules from the movie, which was that Buffy

had sort of a cramping every time she was around a vampire. In a series I didn't want her to always know when she was around a vampire. And that's too bad in a way because it was a very primal, feminist concept that she literally feels it in her womb, as it were. But I had seven years and she needed to be surprised.

Miller: Were there any other final notes you wanted to strike before the conclusion and couldn't, besides having Tara come back?
Whedon: We also talked about bringing Oz back, and quite frankly we didn't have the money. We had a whole cool idea and we just didn't have a dime.

Miller: What's next on the agenda for you? You made an allusion to the demise of *Firefly* being only temporary.
Whedon: I have hopes that there may be another venue for *Firefly*, although I don't have any proof yet. But I've been fighting to find a place to do a version of that because I like the story so well and the actors so well.

Miller: Was that a big change to do a show that was centered on a grown man instead of a young woman?
Whedon: It's so funny, because I have a lot of movie ideas and they all tend to revolve around young adolescent female superheroes. But not *Firefly*. This one is about Joe Schmo, everyday life, and then of course I introduce River, the young female superhero. Let's face it, I'm just addicted. But it was nice to have a show that was about different perspectives and to really get to explore all of them. I was excited that I was going to have a happily married couple that was not boring. Because that's just so rare in fiction and it's such an important thing in life. And yet apart from [Dashiell Hammett's] *Thin Man* series, I think it's never really been adequately represented. And I had a preacher on board, to explore the concept of faith, people who don't have it and people who do. And of course the captain was the me figure because he's very tall and handsome, but cranky and also slim.

Miller: Are there going to be any all-new projects?
Whedon: Yes, I think there are. What they are I can't say, obviously. I still have a deal with Fox, and I'll be running *Angel* and I believe there will be some development down the line. I definitely want to make a movie of some kind in the next couple of years. I have a number of ideas that are vying for my attention, sort of like a horse race. They're all at the starting gate and it'll be interesting to see which pulls ahead.

Miller: Both TV and movies?
Whedon: Yeah, but I'm letting it be a void right now because I'm so fucking

exhausted. It doesn't hit you until you let it. I used to get sick every season at the end of the season. My body said, OK, can I? After seven years I have to admit I'm kind of reeling. Now, I also have a four-month-old child, so: double reel.

Miller: Is it going to be hard not to have *Buffy the Vampire Slayer* in your life? After all, that's what you've been doing for seven years.
Whedon: You know, no. Because it really was time to stop. Like, I loved going to college, but I was happy to graduate. It was an extraordinary thing and there will never be anything like it again. Ultimately, I wasn't going on set as much, wasn't directing as many episodes. I was still very much involved, but the physicality of being there was less. The people on the show that I'm pals with I see anyway. I had a great crew, and hopefully I'll get to work with them again. I'll miss them, but I won't miss having to turn out twenty -two stories about Buffy in a year. I feel like we did the best we could for a long damn time and it's time to tell the next story. Even if it's about Willow.

Miller: Is that a hint?
Whedon: No. If there turns out to be a spinoff with any of the characters, I'll be interested. It'll happen because we have something to say and not because we have an actor ready. But we won't have anything to say until we catch our breath.

Miller: A last question: Can you tell us about some of your favorite *Buffy* moments or stories from the past seven years?
Whedon: Here are a few of my favorite things that also represent larger things. The scene where Angel has become Angelus but is pretending he's not and that he's just had a one-night stand with Buffy and that destroys her. When he came to her and said, "Why are you making a big thing out of it?" When he acted like a guy. I wrote that scene and thought, "I might be a worse person than I ever imagined because I am able to write this scene. I think I just tapped into somebody really horrible and it came rather easily." Ugh.

I would have to say the moment Amber and Tony started singing together [in the musical episode "Once More with Feeling."] That made my hair stand on end. That makes me so happy. First of all, it was the first counterpoint I've ever written. It was beautiful voices raised in song about really depressing emotions. My two favorite things put together.

Off the top of my head, Willow licking Willow. Just having double Willows, just the absurdity. That whole thing was such a romp. As a director, I didn't do too many of the romps. It was always, [in an agonized voice] "Oh, Angel, we can't ever be together!" Ally [Hannigan, who plays Willow] was like, "Your shows are always about Buffy," so I said, "I'll write one for you. In fact, there'll be two of you, what do you think about that?" God, some of the funniest stuff we ever did was in that episode, but also the scene where they find out that Willow is alive and everybody, everybody, is so goddamn funny. It's Giles, Xander, Willow, and Buffy, the fearsome foursome.

JoBlo.com Visits the Set of *Serenity*

THOMAS LEUPP/2004

From JoBlo.com, November 8, 2004. © JoBlo Media Inc. Reprinted by permission.

With his latest project *Serenity*, prolific writer/director Joss Whedon looks to prove he can achieve success outside the world of *Buffy the Vampire Slayer*. Of course, *Buffy* isn't exactly the easiest act to follow. Adored by both critics and audiences alike, the show became the WB Network's centerpiece, made Sarah Michelle Gellar a star, and spawned a popular spin-off.

Whedon's next project, the sci-fi/western hybrid *Firefly*, didn't fare as well, lasting only eleven episodes before Fox pulled the plug. When a defiant Whedon announced his intention to take *Firefly* to the big screen, even his most ardent fans couldn't help but be skeptical about the show's feature film prospects.

He found a believer in Universal. Encouraged by the show's strong DVD sales, the studio wrested the rights from Fox, gave Whedon the greenlight and *Serenity* was born. The film follows the same basic storyline as the series: five hundred years in the future, the crew of a small but nimble spaceship travels through the universe, transporting dangerous cargo and not asking questions.

Recently, Universal invited JoBlo.com down to their studio lot to visit the set of *Serenity* and meet with the filmmakers. The scene being shot was a brief fight sequence in which female lead River Tam (played by Summer Glau) sweeps the leg a la The Karate Kid, knocking some unfortunate fool on his ass. Following that was another brief fight sequence set inside a bar, in which Summer, this time aided by some fancy wire work, takes out a few more guys.

Though not featured in any of the day's scenes, lead actor Nathan Fillion was on-hand in case Joss needed him for the occasional background shot. In the meantime, he demonstrated a skill that most working actors develop after spending many a month on a movie set: the ability to catch a nap amidst the noise and chaos.

In between camera setups, Whedon took a break to talk with us about his feature film directorial debut. Though tired and hoarse, he spoke at great length about his experience, providing glimpses of the trademark wit that distinguished his television work.

Leupp: What are the challenges of adapting a TV series for the big screen?
Whedon: It's incredibly hard, building a story that doesn't repeat or contradict what we've already done, that satisfies the fans and yet is really made for people who've never seen the show. There's pitfalls everywhere. It's the hardest story I've ever had to structure. Writing these people is the easiest thing in the world because I know them so well. The other thing is the TV show is built around slow development of character; movies are built around momentum. They're very different things. So you have to sort of take things that you . . . you have to let some things drop and you have to speed some things up and you sort of have to know which ones are which.

Leupp: Will you be providing some back-story for those who are unfamiliar with the series?
Whedon: Yes, to an extent. It has a different way of telling the same story. We do River's troubles with the Alliance and her integration into the group. We don't repeat the first time they meet or anything like that, but we get the information in a new way. Again, like I said, that's the trickiest part.

Leupp: As a screenwriter, you've been known to have issues with the way directors have turned your words into film.
Whedon: Well, after *Alien Resurrection*, I said, "The next person who ruins one of my scripts is going to be me." And I think I'm doing a fine job of it. Actually, I think the director on occasion could have used a little more imagination and the writer could have shut up occasionally. We fight, but we're still getting along better than I usually do. [Laughs.] It's been great, 'cause unlike TV I have the time to really explore what it is I'm doing and go back and reassess every day. Every time you shoot a scene it affects fifty other scenes. It's constantly shifting, hopefully not so much that it doesn't know where it's going.

Leupp: What's the most important thing you want to add to make this feel "cinematic"?
Whedon: Money. [Laughs]. You know—scope, breadth, a sense that this is not a story either visually or even dramatically that we could have told in an hour on TV.

Leupp: How does directing action sequences for film differ from doing them for TV?
Whedon: It's much less of a chore because you have more than half a day to do it. You can actually really set things up and you can train, you can actually

break things, and all kinds of things that we can't afford to do on TV. That's a big part of making it more cinematic, letting the action have a lot more scope. It's not just "Set up two cameras, what do ya got?" which unfortunately on the shows ends up being a lot of the time.

Leupp: What are the particular challenges of the action sequence you're shooting today?

Whedon: The particular challenges are just keeping it real. It's a scene that can easily become over-the-top and I'm trying very hard to stay away from a Matrixy kind of aesthetic. So I don't want anybody doing anything that people can't do. I mean to an extent. Fighting is a little more precise, but I'm trying to dirty it up as much as possible so that it feels real. And that's very hard to do. Your stuntmen have to be so precise about their timing; it's very hard to say, "And now also you have to make it look really really ugly." That's the biggest challenge.

Leupp: What are some of the influences on the Western aspect of the show?

Whedon: It's weird because I just read a thing with M. Night where he said *McCabe & Mrs. Miller* was a big influence on *The Village* and I'm like, "*McCabe & Mrs. Miller* is influencing a lot of really weird films." That was a big one. *Ulzana's Raid* was a huge influence. And *The Searchers* too, both because they're so uncompromising.

Leupp: I know you had issues with how Fox marketed *Firefly*, so how involved are you with the marketing campaign for this?

Whedon: Very involved. We've worked together only on the little Comic-Con thing we did, but I've met with all of their divisions and everybody here wants to be on the same page. They're incredibly supportive. Companies talk about "synergy" and the left hand doesn't know what the right hand is doing and he's actually kind of angry about it. And these guys have really sort of worked as a holistic whole, which is really nice. So, I think that should work out better.

Leupp: How hard was it to get Universal to sign off on this film?

Whedon: I've gotta tell you—I'd like to brag about how well I sold it, but Mary Parent and Universal liked *Firefly* and the words she used was, "This is a no-brainer." She has been supportive of this project since before I'd made up the story. And although it's taken a lot out of me to get it to where it is . . . it's been a real struggle, the support they've shown has been constant.

Leupp: Any truth to the rumors that you might be directing *X-Men 3*? How is your relationship with Fox?

Whedon: Nobody has approached me about the *X-Men* franchise. My relationship with the film division . . . I haven't really worked with them in a long while. My relationship with the network? Not so great. But my deal is with the Television Production . . . so we've had a good relationship for years. We did *Buffy*, *Angel*, and *Firefly* together, and that seems fine. I don't really have a relationship besides the Television Production . . .

Leupp: Is film more stressful than television?
Whedon: Well, it's been as stressful. I thought it would be less stressful. I thought I'd be golfing in between takes and writing sonnets. Two things have not worked in my favor. One is, although I don't have three shows to run—and believe me, nothing will ever be as hard as that was—the movie takes up your attention in a way that three shows do. All of the creative energy that you're usually pouring into telling twenty to forty stories a year, you're pouring into one. And you find you need it. You wake up in the middle of the night and you go, "His pants are too baggy!" And it's important. You have to watch everything so carefully because every mistake you make is gonna be forty feet high. Whenever you think, "Well, maybe that's good enough," I say to myself, "Cinerama Dome."

Leupp: What's the status of the *Buffy* animated series?
Whedon: A presentation is being made. It hasn't been bought anyway, but it's still in the creating stages. So it's still possible . . .

Leupp: At Comic-Con you said that it would be difficult to take *Firefly* back to the small screen. Do you feel that you would have a hard time going back to television in general? And would you like to maybe direct the *X-Men* franchise if it was offered to you?
Whedon: Would I like to make an *X-Men* movie? That'd be bitchin'. You know I actually really like those actors and really like those characters and I think there's a lot that could be done (with them). But I'm not setting my sights on that. I have my sights set on exactly one thing, which is this. I am totally prepared to go back to TV. Not 24/7 as I did in the first years of *Buffy*, but now I've learned enough about surrounding yourself with the right people and delegating that I can actually run a show without ruining my life. TV is a medium that I love in a very different way than I love movies. The things that I can't do in this movie, the smaller moments, the long protracted interaction, watching people change over the years. I've waited my whole life to make movies, but movies don't do that.

Leupp: What is the status of The Buffyverse TV movie?
Whedon: We haven't really heard anything. Obviously there's been a regime change at the WB. The fans are interested. I'm interested. I don't think either

Sarah or David would want to do it, but I think there's ten other characters I could name who would be totally worthy of movies, and I'm just waiting for somebody to say yay or nay.

Leupp: Would you write or direct them?
Whedon: I would certainly be involved. I would never let one of those stories be told without overseeing things.

Leupp: Do you intend for *Serenity* to be a stand-alone project? Or part of a trilogy?
Whedon: I look at it as a stand-alone. You can't help but—especially because it comes from the series—think about all the things you want to do. But everybody says, "Is this going to be a trilogy?" They don't even say, "Is there gonna be a sequel?" It's trilogy—they go straight to trilogy. And "Are you gonna shoot the second and third back-to-back?" Umm, movie might suck. Let's start at point A. I think of this as an absolute one-shot. Could it sustain more stories? Well, obviously I designed their world and these characters in this ensemble to sustain ten years' worth. So yeah, there could be more. We'd love to do more. We have to make this one good enough to deserve that. That is the only thing that I'm thinking about.

Serenity Now!

JIM KOZAK/2005

From *In Focus*, August 2005. Reprinted by permission.

"If we'd done this and we'd heard crickets chirping, it would have been very depressing," admits *Buffy the Vampire Slayer* creator Joss Whedon.

The veteran screenwriter is speaking of this summer's "Can't Stop the Signal" hit-and-run public screenings of *Serenity*, the almost-finished sci-fi actioner that marks his feature directorial debut. Whedon, in fact, is hurtling toward Riverside, California, for one of the thirty-five Signal screenings being held that evening in thirty-five cities throughout the United States and Canada.

The crickets' odds of being heard are not the greatest. All thirty-five of the June 23 *Serenity* screenings sold out in the space of hours; some in minutes. Many of the tickets that disappeared from the Movietickets.com and Fandango websites quickly resurfaced on eBay, where scalpers began successfully hawking them for hundreds of dollars.

A third-generation sitcom writer (his earliest post-college job was turning out teleplays for the Nielsen juggernaut *Roseanne*), Whedon immediately demonstrated a highly marketable faculty for resonant comic storytelling, one by turns edgy and disarming. He soon evolved into one of Hollywood's most sought-after script doctors, earning alluring sums to cure expensive projects like *Speed* (1994), *Toy Story* (1995), and *Twister* (1996)—but was often denied screen credit for his considerable labors.

A 1997 return to television brought him markedly more control and recognition. Based on his much-admired feature screenplay (which had already been made into a less-admired 1992 movie directed by Fran Rubel Kuzui), the TV version of *Buffy* became one of the most critically acclaimed series in television history, and provided Whedon a means by which he could hone his filmmaking skills with an eye toward directing for the big screen.

While *Buffy* lasted seven seasons, a subsequent Whedon-created series, *Firefly*, aired only ten episodes before Fox put the axe to it in 2002. Set centuries in the future—in a solar system far, far away—it followed the adventures of a

Solo-esque interplanetary smuggler and raised scores of fascinating narrative questions Whedon never got to answer.

Universal's decision to greenlight *Serenity*, the big-screen sequel to *Firefly*, was said to have been influenced by *Firefly*'s phenomenal post-cancellation DVD sales. An extraordinary two hundred thousand copies of the "Complete Series" were purchased in the first four months of its release. On July 6 of this year, more than eighteen months after the DVD set's release, it would rise (again) to the number-two spot on Amazon.com's daily "top seller" list.

The finished version of *Serenity* is due in cinemas September 30. *In Focus* interviewed Whedon on the occasion of his forty-first birthday, as he journeyed from Universal City to the June 23 Signal screening of *Serenity* at Regal Entertainment Group's Jurupa 14-plex.

I. HAN SOLO AND MAL REYNOLDS

Kozak: Happy birthday.
Whedon: Thank you!

Kozak: How did you celebrate? Was there a spaceship-shaped cake?
Whedon: There was a cake. It was normal shape. We were scoring, so we got to hear a full orchestra play me "Happy Birthday." It was pretty intensely cool.

Kozak: Was it cooler than what you did for your birthday last year, when you were still shooting *Serenity*?
Whedon: Yes. Last year we were shooting the vent shaft and the vault heist and they were both really cramped and there was a carrot cake involved. It wasn't pretty.

Kozak: Fans and the media have grown fond of comparing *Serenity*'s hero, Mal Reynolds, to *Star Wars*' Han Solo—and when *SFX Magazine* once asked you, "Which movie would you love to have written?" you replied, "*Return of the Jedi*!" Had you been given the reins of *Jedi*, where would you have driven it? Would you have given Captain Solo more to do? Would Leia not turn out to be Luke's sister? Would the "another" Yoda spoke of late in *The Empire Strikes Back* turn out to be not-Leia?
Whedon: Well, first of all, I believe that my actual answer was the movie that I would have liked to have made was actually *Revenge of the Jedi*. Because that's what it was originally called.

Kozak: An important distinction.

Whedon: It really is. And when they changed it I was very worried. Of course they got their "Revenge" later on, but at the time I didn't know that.

Everything you said was right on the money. The *Millennium Falcon* would not be piloted in the climactic scene by Lando Calrissian and a frog. It would have been Han, getting it done. The "other" to whom Yoda referred would of course have been a young, female, badass Jedi, because where else would I go with that? It would have not been revealed in the first five minutes that Darth Vader was going to be redeemed. And, yeah, there would have been a little less incest.

Kozak: I could see you resolving the love triangle perhaps a little more dramatically.

Whedon: Yes, I would have made it a little harder on everybody. Oh, and I would have had some extra lyrics for the Yub Yub song. And I think his father would have been James Earl Jones [who provided Vader's voice], or at least Dave Prowse [who filled Vader's armor].

Kozak: This summer's . . .

Whedon: Wait, I have one more thing. In the trailer, it looked like Luke was going to go all bad. And I definitely would have explored that territory. It looked like his dad was going to win him over. He looked like he was allied with the Dark Side a little bit. And I realize that, now, again, after this latest "Revenge," that's old news. But at the time it was riveting and they didn't play that out at all. That would have been a big deal.

Kozak: Back to *Serenity*, aren't all movies forged from the ashes of failed TV series destined for mammoth success? When you converse with the Universal executives, do *Star Trek* and *Police Squad!* [which spawned Paramount's *Naked Gun* blockbusters] come up a lot?

Whedon: *Star Trek* and *Police Squad!* do not come up.

Kozak: Never once?

Whedon: *Star Trek* has come up, but not really as a phenomenon, because they felt the show had an enormous following, much bigger than the following that *Firefly* has. And it had years to sort of percolate, and grow even stronger. And nobody mentions *Police Squad!* I think because nobody remembers it.

Kozak: So nobody's banking on these precedents?

Whedon: No, but you know, I just hope you're right about that whole "mammoth success" thing.

Kozak: This summer's sold-out hit-and-run public screenings of an almost-finished *Serenity*—I count sixty-five such screenings so far—appear to be wholly unique in the annals of motion picture exhibition. Is it safe to say you're encouraged that so many thousands have been willing to stay out till midnight on a school night for these?

Whedon: I really am. If we'd done this and we'd heard crickets chirping, it would have been very depressing. At the end of the day I'm as worried about the marketing campaign as I would have been had we never done this, because it's the people who don't know what this is about that we need to reach out to. But, yeah, this has been an enormous boon, and it's kept a fire underneath Universal and it's just been exciting for everybody.

Kozak: Is there anybody in particular we should credit for this idea?

Whedon: Their head of marketing is Marc Schmuger and he's a smart guy who knows his job. There's a bunch of guys I deal with and they're interested in trying something different because they've got something different on their hands. Not just the phenomenon, but the movie itself is not cut and dried for them as a marketing game. It's not a simple film. The fact that they're looking to do something odd and make a noise that way I think is actually kind of cool.

Kozak: There are fewer horses and heads of cattle in *Serenity* than in the *Firefly* TV series. Do you suspect perhaps the series was somehow hobbled in the early going by its more overtly "Western" visual elements?

Whedon: Yes and no. I think Fox was terrified of the Western concept. The fact that there are no horses in this movie is only by virtue of the fact I didn't find a place for them. Not by virtue of the fact that I deliberately avoided them. Because the Western element is still a part of the story. It's a frontier story. For example, I did look back at the series and say, "Okay, Mal being thrown through the holographic bar window is maybe a little jokey for the movie." It's a good shorthand for the series but I think for a movie you have to work through the logic just a hair more. But the ship scaring the horses that we used in the credits? The last image of the credits in *Firefly*? That works great. That to me is a timeless image that combines the two just fine.

It just didn't happen in this movie, 'cause, well, a lot of things didn't happen in this movie. Because I had two hours instead of seven seasons.

Kozak: You did not set out to make the movie less "Western."

Whedon: No. I wasn't looking to go less "Western." In fact, I was thinking, "Can't I find a place for a horse in this?" But the answer was no.

Kozak: The budget for *Serenity* is maybe a quarter the size of the one *Batman Begins* employed, yet four times the size of the two-hour *Firefly* pilot, which itself employed big sci-fi sets, big special effects, location shooting and horses. What does that $40 million *Serenity* movie budget buy you?

Whedon: It definitely buys you a giant space battle. And a lot of very carefully shot, worked-out action, and a lot of bigger stunts. It buys you more scale. Some of what it buys you you wouldn't notice because you basically have to make things denser and cooler and the visual effects have to be higher-resolution. Sets have to be more visibly thick material, because everything's being turned up so big. So, to an extent, you get more bang for your buck on the small screen. So you have to compensate for that in a movie budget.

It buys you a great deal. It doesn't buy you the movie we made. Basically knowing what we were going to shoot before we built it and having [veteran Clint Eastwood cinematographer] Jack Green light it as fast and as beautifully as he did is what bought us the movie we made, because it came out looking like we had a lot more money than we did. And, basically, it buys you a bunch of different worlds, 'cause we had to build pretty much every one. Practically every scene in the movie takes place on a different world. So it bought you all of that and, of course, it brought back my ship.

Kozak: Everyone, I believe, enjoys the Chinese cursing. [In the futuristic universe of *Firefly* and *Serenity*, everyone speaks both English and Chinese, but almost all of the cursing is in Chinese.] Is it true your wife speaks Chinese?
Whedon: It is, although she's lost some of it, to her chagrin. She did live in China for a while and teach English there, and is the person who educated me about China. Probably not the language I would have chosen, because you can say something that's paragraphs long in like two syllables, so I kept having to write longer and longer curses, just so people could hear the Chinese. But it does make perfect sense. China is going to be the greatest world power on the planet within this decade.

Kozak: Had you married someone else, might the *Serenity* characters be cursing in French or Japanese?
Whedon: Y'know, it's possible. I would have chosen Japanese myself.

Kozak: The Japanese are a world power.
Whedon: They are, and I love the language and the culture so much. But to be realistic about where we're headed, China is the place. And since there is great love for it in my family I decided to go there.

Kozak: Is it a certainty at this point that Shepherd Book [the mysterious preacher character who haunts both *Firefly* and *Serenity*] once did the bidding of evil men?
Whedon: I would say. Yeah.

Kozak: You think we'll ever see that story?

Whedon: I'm not ruling it out. Obviously, one doesn't like to speak of sequels without carrying nine rabbits' feet, crossing one's self, and knocking on wood, but that is a thread that is not lost to me.

Kozak: In the TV show, there was no sound in space. Will space, as rumored, be noisier in the big-screen version?
Whedon: Yes and no. We've kept space sound-free. But the climactic battle takes place just at the edge of the atmosphere of the satellite moon where Mr. Universe lives, and because it's inside the ion cloud, we don't actually see any stars. They're inside this big cloud formation above the planet. And so, because of the way it was playing, it just started to be more and more apparent that we did need to have a battle going on in there, and we couldn't just hear it when we cut inside the ships. So we sort of—I don't want to say "cheated," because that would sound too true—but since we're not looking at the stars, since we're close to atmosphere, let's just turn this into a big loud scary battle so that we can experience what they're experiencing. And in that sense there has been a slight shift.

Kozak: Well, you certainly had sound in the "atmo," as the characters call it, on the series.
Whedon: We're calling inside the ion cloud "atmo," even though it's a little unclear to me, because there's actually science involved.

Kozak: What do you hear about *Serenity* perhaps moving to late summer?
Whedon: I've not actually heard. It could be released late summer, although I've looked at the weekends and I've sort of tried to work the schedule myself and figure out what's best. I guess I saw something about it on the Internet, but that source hasn't talked to me.

Kozak: So nothing has trickled down to you via official channels?
Whedon: Sometimes it takes a good deal of trickling to get to me. Sometimes I'm right in the loop and sometimes I don't know there's a loop.

II. WINDING *TOY STORY*

Kozak: On the *Toy Story* DVD commentary, I think you're mentioned only once, as the guy who contributed the line, "Wind the frog!" How late in the process came your involvement in that project? Was it just a dialogue polish, or did you shape the story as well?
Whedon: It was [*Toy Story* director] John Lasseter's concept. I had been working at Disney and I was staying at my farm in New York in the summer and

they called and said, "We have this other project, *Toy Story*, which we think is going to be a go, we think it's the next movie. Can we send you the script? Because it needs to be rewritten."

Kozak: Which Disney project were you working on when you got the *Toy Story* call?

Whedon: I was working on, let's see, it was either *Marco Polo* . . . First they wanted to do *Journey to the Center of the Earth* meets *The Man Who Would Be King*, which eventually became *Atlantis*, which is why I'm credited on it. Because I was the first writer on it, even though I had not a shred in it.

Then they said, "No, wait, we want to do *My Fair Lady* with Marco Polo." Which I not only wrote a script for, I actually wrote the lyrics for three songs that [veteran stage composer] Robert Lindsey Nassif wrote the music to.

Kozak: So you were already working on other Disney cartoon projects.
Whedon: Yes.

Kozak: And then you got the *Toy Story* call.
Whedon: And they sent me the script and it was a shambles, but the story that Lasseter had come up with was, you know, the toys are alive and they conflict. The concept was gold. It was just right there. And that's the dream job for a script doctor: a great structure with a script that doesn't work. A script that's pretty good? Where you can't really figure out what's wrong, because there's something structural that's hard to put your finger on? Death. But a good structure that just needs a new body on it is the best. So I was thrilled.

I went up to Pixar [the Northern California–based animation studio which produced *Toy Story*], and stayed there for weeks and wrote for, I think, four months before it got greenlit, and completely overhauled the script. There were some very basic things in there that stayed in there. The characters were pretty much in place except for the dinosaur, which was mine. I took out a lot of extraneous stuff, including the neighbor giving the kid a bad haircut before he leaves. There was a whole lot of extraneous stuff.

And then there was finding the voices. We were still casting. Ironically, Disney put the kibosh on the person they wanted for Buzz Lightyear because he wasn't famous enough, so we couldn't use Jim Carrey. But they had Tom Hanks in place. It was basically finding the voices and sitting with them while they came up with the gags and going over the boards and working with Jeffrey Katzenberg. It was a great, great process because you're sitting around with a bunch of animators who are basically drawing caricatures of each other, getting Sharpie headaches and making a lot of jokes, and they're the sweetest bunch of guys.

Kozak: As you were writing *Toy Story*, did you have any sense that you were involved in launching what would become one of the most lucrative new big-screen genres of all time?

Whedon: I think the thing that's important to remember about it is simply that digital animation was starting to happen, but everyone was using it for the same thing, which was, [Whedon affects a shaky hippie voice] "To blow your mind—by putting the camera through a keyhole and into the ass of a fly and through the stars." Nobody could control themselves.

But John Lasseter was like, "We're telling a story. We're making a cell-animation film. We'll never think of it as anything else. We'll never place CGI just to show what it can do, just to play tricks. This isn't a 3D movie. This is a story." Everything was very old-school in that sense. That's what made it stand out and that's what spawned the generation of movies that came after it. It was simply, "Oh! We already know how to do this; we've just got a slightly new medium to do it in."

Kozak: Did you have any influence on the decision to break with Disney tradition and not have the characters sing?

Whedon: They knew they didn't want to, and I knew they shouldn't. I joined Disney because I wanted to write musicals, because I wanted to do what [*Little Mermaid* and *Aladdin* lyricist] Howard Ashman did. That sort of movie fell by the wayside while I was there. I watched as the musical numbers became more and more beautifully animated and more and more disposable musically. The animated musical died with Howard Ashman.

Toy Story was a different animal. This was never meant to be a musical. These characters were not the kind that would sing and dance. It just didn't have that feeling.

Kozak: So you spent four months on *Toy Story*?

Whedon: I spent about four months on it before we got the green light. When we got the green light and the script was approved and they were putting it together, I walked away, started doing other things, then came back a couple months later. They had shut the movie down. I went up to Pixar, and they actually said, "Listen, we're having to shut down for a while because we're having story problems. Many of you are going to be laid off, and Joss is here to fix the script." And then I was just like, "Why are you pointing at me? What's going on? This is horrible!" I think this was "Black Monday." I don't know if it was a Monday. I think it was a Monday. But it was definitely referred to as "Black."

So we sort of went back into the trenches and made sure we had everything we needed and nothing we didn't. And then, you know, as is always the case with animation, I spent another couple of months on it and then it got reworked somewhat from there. I think one of the last things that was added—certainly it was after my time, and it's the thing I most wish I could take credit for—was the crane-worshippers.

Kozak: The little three-eyed aliens.
Whedon: I think I spent more time explaining that I didn't come up with that than anything else.

Kozak: How much time altogether did you end up investing in the project?
Whedon: More than six months. It was not a polish; it was a rewrite and with animation you're writing with every visual. Every shot is up on a board somewhere, so you're writing in great detail. It's a very fluid and complicated process.

Kozak: Can you point to a specific *Toy* contribution of which you're particularly proud?
Whedon: I think the thing that I can point at and say, "This I am proud of," is really the voice and the sensibility of the characters, keeping them from being that sort of old-school Disney—what my wife would refer to as "old-man humor." Getting a little more voice and a little more edge into the jokes and into the bits, and just helping the structure, seeing it through.

The whole thing with the mutant toys, as we referred to them, forming the skateboard thing to bring them out, that came after Mattel rejected my Barbie-as-Sarah-Connor rescue scene.

Kozak: I remember them talking about that on the DVD. Were you invited to participate on the DVD at all?
Whedon: Uh, no. [Laughter.]

Kozak: Didn't get the phone call?
Whedon: No, I didn't. Somehow Pixar has managed to scrape by without me. I thought *Toy Story 2* was actually beautiful and wonderfully realized and I didn't have anything to do with that. I definitely feel I played a part in *Toy Story*, a substantial one, but it is John Lasseter's movie.

III. THE AGONY OF *RESURRECTION*

Kozak: I thought your original screenplay for *Alien: Resurrection* was brilliant—with its epic final battle on Earth, for Earth—and vastly more engrossing than what ultimately made its way to the screen. I have to assume there were budgetary issues, because I can't imagine another reason anyone would tinker with it.

Well, let me ask you something. This ending that took place on Earth. What happened in it? Where did it take place?

Whedon: It took place in a forest . . .

Yes. Oh wow. That's the first one. There were five. And it was always either "the director had a vision" or they had a budget issue. And as a script doctor I've been called in more than a few times, and the issue is always the same: "We want you to make the third act more exciting and cheaper." And my response inevitably is, "The problem with the third act is the first two acts." This response is never listened to. I usually walk away having gotten one or two jokes into a script and made some money and feeling like I am just bereft of life. It's horrible. The exceptions were *Toy Story* and *Speed*, where they actually let me do something.

In the case of *Alien: Resurrection*, they decided to spend their money in other places than going to Earth. And I just kept saying, "The reason people are here is we're going to do the thing we've never done; we're gonna go to Earth." But there were a lot of things that we hadn't done that we ended up not doing because of a singular lack of vision.

But rather than go into all of the reasons why *Alien: Resurrection* is disappointing to me, I will tell you that, yes, I wrote five endings. The first one was in the forest with the flying threshing machine. The second one was in a futuristic junkyard. The third one was in a maternity ward.

And the fourth one was in the desert. Now at this point this had become about money, and I said, "You know, the desert looks like Mars. That's not Earth; that's not going to give people that juice." But I still wrote them the best ending I could that took place in the desert. And then finally they said, "Y'know, we just don't think we need to go to Earth." So I just gave them dialogue and stuff, but I don't remember writing, "A withered, granny-lookin' Pumkinhead-kinda-thing makes out with Ripley." Pretty sure that stage direction never existed in any of my drafts.

Kozak: Given that you've described your experience on *Alien: Resurrection* as something of a personal Vietnam, is there irony to the fact that your feature directorial debut also centers on a crew of in-over-their-heads space-criminals?

Whedon: Somebody pointed that out to me, the similarity between *Serenity* and the *Betty* [*Alien Resurrection*'s spaceship], and it just stopped me in my tracks. I was like, "Yes, my pony did its trick again!" I really never thought of it until somebody pointed it out to me. But the irony goes further than I could have imagined because we shot it on the same stages at Fox where they shot *Alien: Resurrection*. In fact, *Serenity* was built over the pit that they dug for *Alien: Resurrection* for the underwater sequence.

The history of *Alien: Resurrection* is fairly twisted also because I wrote a thirty-page treatment for a different movie. They wanted to do a movie with a clone of Newt [the little girl from *Aliens*] as their heroine. Because I'd done some action movies and I'd done *Buffy*, they said, "Well, he can write teenage girls and he can write action, so let's give him a shot." The franchise was pretty much dead, and I wrote the treatment and they said, "This is really exciting. We want to get back in this business. But we want Ripley. So throw this out." That one was probably my favorite; I think it was a better-structured story than the one I ultimately wrote.

Kozak: You've created with *Firefly* and *Serenity* another universe in which the spaceships do not travel faster than light, while *Star Wars* and *Star Trek* and *Battlestar Galactica* and virtually every other major spacefaring franchise utilizes faster-than-light travel. Does this betray perhaps a particular fondness for the *Alien* franchise, which also eschewed FTL?
Whedon: Very much so, and I think the roots of it go eons beyond. The science fiction that I love, generally speaking, was very sort of specific. What I loved about spaceships was the idea that they might break. The idea of being in one. The idea of the grittier, realistic, hard-science kind of space that was actually creepy to be in. That's why *Alien* just blew me away. I was like, "These are people who don't even like each other. There's no structure here. They killed the handsome guy. I can't figure this out." It was just a scary place to be. The most important line in *Star Wars*, to me, is the moment Luke looks at the *Millennium Falcon*, the most beautiful ship I've ever seen, and says, "What a piece of junk!"

Kozak: Do you want to go so far as to say that you like the *Alien* movies better than the *Star Trek* and *Star Wars* movies?
Whedon: I like *Star Wars* and *Alien*. I think *Star Wars* and *Alien*, those were the two that formed me the most. The *Star Trek* movies I've enjoyed. I've never been a Trekker. I've taken them for what they're worth but I don't think they're on a par with those other two.

IV. LOSS OF *SPEED*

Kozak: You're said to have written most of the dialogue in *Speed*, and created some of the characters. I'm guessing most of your fans can easily recognize your voice in the dialogue, but which were your characters? Did you create Gigantor, for example?
Whedon: The movie was pretty much cast; in fact it was cast. It was a week before they started shooting when I came in. So I didn't create Gigantor; I did, however, call him that. I had to explain to Keanu what that meant because he had never seen *Gigantor*. The only character I tremendously changed was Alan

Ruck, who was cast as "the asshole." I'm using quote marks. He was cast as that guy you hate. And he was very artificial. He was a lawyer. He was on the phone and he was a bad guy and he died. And I think Alan Ruck is a great comedian and a great actor so I was like, "Why don't we just make him a tourist? A guy, just a nice, totally out-of-his-depth guy?"

Because part of what I did on *Speed* was pare down what they had created, which was kind of artificial. The whole thing about "[The Keanu Reeves character is] a maverick hotshot," I was sort of like, "Well, no, what if he's not? He thinks a little bit laterally for a cop. What if he's just the polite guy trying not to get anybody killed?" Part of that came from Keanu.

Kozak: It's surprising that you were brought in so late in the process.
Whedon: Yeah, they brought in Walter Parkes and Laurie MacDonald to produce it uncredited. I had a relationship with Jorge Saralegui for a long time; he encouraged me to write *Suspension*, the spec that sort of made my bones, and had brought me on to *Alien* and *Speed* and was a huge benefactor and collaborator when he was at Fox. Jorge brought me to Walter and Laurie and we just got along famously.

Kozak: Did your contribution deal mostly with the second act, on the bus, or did you have a lot to do with the first and third as well?
Whedon: It was dialogue straight through. There were a couple of plot things just to make connections.

Kozak: Yes? Which?
Whedon: I don't even know if I can remember, but killing his partner was one of them. How they found certain clues that helped them find him. Why they went to the subway and stuff like that. I said, "I think I have a better gag than 'It hits an airplane and it explodes.'" But they were like, "We bought the airplane. It hits the airplane and explodes. Just get us there." And it was all about finding the emotional reality of the characters and getting them from A to B in a realistic fashion.

Kozak: You own a *Speed* poster on which your writing credit remains.
Whedon: I do.

Kozak: Was it a misprint? Was a teaser poster issued before the Writers Guild arbitrated that credit away?
Whedon: It was "the" poster. And they put it out and then the arbitration happened kind of late. And so they pulled it and changed it.

Kozak: So there are maybe a lot of those floating around out there somewhere?

Whedon: I don't know if they were actually up or if this was just the final mock-up. I just know that I have a copy of it. The arbitration was a great sticking point with me. I've always just disagreed with the WGA's policy that says you can write every line of dialogue for a movie—and they literally say this—and not deserve credit on it. Because I think that makes no sense of any kind. Writers get very protective of themselves. They're worried that some producer will want to add a line so he can put his name on it. But what they can do is throw writers at it forever without putting their names on it because of this rule. So I actually don't think it works for writers. It certainly didn't work for me.

Graham Yost [who received the sole screenplay credit for *Speed*] has always been very polite to me and very sweet but he did say to me, "You would have done the same thing." And all I could say to him at the time was, "Well, I guess we don't know if that's true." Because I'd never been in his situation. Then more than a year later John Lasseter called me and said, "I want to give all the animators who worked on the story credit on *Toy Story*." And I said, "Sure." And there are entire episodes of *Buffy* that I have written every word of that my name is not on. Which is gratifying to me because it means I finally have an answer to that. Which is, "No, I wouldn't."

V. *WONDER WOMAN*: FLIGHT AND HEIGHT

Kozak: I understand you've not yet written a word of the *Wonder Woman* screenplay.
Whedon: Not too many words.

Kozak: Did you tell Warner Bros. you weren't keen to deal with it until *Serenity* enters release?
Whedon: Not release. It's not that I haven't been working on it.

Kozak: You have been working on it?
Whedon: The way I work, I'm like a vulture. I circle and circle and then I dive. I usually don't actually write anything until I know exactly how it's going to turn out. I don't "let the computer take me away." I'm an absolute Nazi about structure. I make outlines. I make charts and graphs with colors.

Kozak: You've done that for *Wonder Woman*?
Whedon: Not for *Wonder Woman*, because I'm still working out the plot. But I'm finding the moments that matter; I'm finding the things that make the story really resonate, the things that I just can't wait to film. I have great big questions to answer, but I'm in that beautiful, free-form poetical place where you just get to think up moments and see if they fit in your movie. And that's

almost more fun than anything. And that work, which is a vital part of what got me interested in doing the job in the first place, is being done.

But I do have to see *Serenity* through. I'll be finished with the movie within a month but I have to make sure it gets taken care of all the way through release. I have, in the past, found that I was able to do more than one thing at a time.

Kozak: Will Diana be able to fly under her own power, or will an invisible plane be involved?
Whedon: I do not believe she will be flying. I think we have a guy who flies. I don't see her flying. She might jump. There could be some hopping. And there may in fact be an invisible plane. But if there is, it will be because it came out really cool. And I have theories about how to make that work.

Kozak: You've said there will be "no star-spangled panties" like the ones Lynda Carter wore in the old TV series. Are you ruling out star-spangled miniskirts?
Whedon: Not exactly. The look that she's sporting in DC Comics right now is closer to where I'd have her than the TV series, or the old look. The color scheme and the silhouette have to remain because they're her. But the American flag is not what she's going to be wearing.

Kozak: So you're not ruling out minis?
Whedon: No. She's still going to look like Wonder Woman. She's not going to look like Trinity. She's going to look like Wonder Woman, but she's just not going to be hokey.

Kozak: In the teaser poster the eagle remains on her chestplate.
Whedon: The eagle is OK with me. Because it's not like we invented them. It's a lot less to swallow than the fact that Jor-El wears a big "S." That bugged me.

Kozak: As you go about casting Diana, do you set a height requirement? How important is it that the Amazon princess be tall?
Whedon: It's important. I'm looking for somebody statuesque, regal, beautiful, who can really act and do a lot of stunts with no elbow or knee pads. I'm asking a lot. So if I happen to find all those qualities in somebody who does not quite meet my height requirement, I will be casting some really short love interest. The height is definitely a part of the package. But the most important part? No. And the fact of the matter is, a woman stands as tall as she makes you think she is. For example, I always thought [*Buffy* writer-producer] Marti Noxon was four inches taller than she actually was. I just found that out last week.

Kozak: *Wonder Woman* producer Joel Silver prides himself on his casting acumen. Has he yet offered any suggestions?

Whedon: No. You know, we talked specifically about that. And the idea was always, "Write the part, and then we'll figure it out."

Kozak: You've also talked about her being very young. Are you thinking college-age? Teenager?
Whedon: I'd say that's a pretty flexible thing because it's her first time setting foot in the world of men. But that doesn't necessarily mean she has to be a teenager. So, yes, they are thinking of a young woman. They're thinking, I expect, of something franchise-able.

Kozak: Will it be appropriate to describe the *Wonder Woman* movie as a fish-out-of-water tale?
Whedon: I would say very much so.

Kozak: Will this be one of the key ways it distinguishes itself from other superhero movies?
Whedon: Yes, I think so. Ultimately, structurally, yes, that's a big distinguishing factor, but I think there will be other elements that are specific to her. But then again, I haven't seen the new *Batman* and I haven't seen the script for *Supes* [Warner Bros.' upcoming *Superman Returns* feature].

Kozak: Will Diana contend with a print-derived supervillain?
Whedon: At this point I'm looking at creating something a little different. I don't think her rogues gallery necessarily offers me what I need. But that's not a final decision, that's just my instinct.

VI. COMIC BOOKS AND COMIC-BOOK MOVIES

Kozak: Fans continue to wonder achingly what a Joss Whedon X-Men movie would look like.
Whedon: I wrote an X-Men movie. I wrote a huge overhaul of the first one. It was based on their structure. It was not used.

It was the same thing: They brought me in for the third act. I said, "The problem starts on page one. Let's talk about the whole movie," While adhering to the structure they had. That's the fun of being a script doctor. And it's actually what prepares you for being an executive producer in terms of script. You're constantly re-writing. It's like, "What does this mean? How does it come together? What's it all about?"

My frustration over *X-Men*, which I think I was a little ungentlemanly about, came as much in the process of my not being informed that my rewrite had been thrown out as it was about the movie itself.

But, basically, I think I had gone a little bit more towards the comic. I had the Danger Room, which was, "Very nice. Lovely. Can't afford it." The Danger Room played a big part in it. And it also ended with Jean Grey sort of holding back and holding back and then doing something extraordinarily powerful, and in the last scene she was dressed like Phoenix. It was fun to do, and I was disappointed that it wasn't used. And the first movie had a lot going for it. It had a lot of integrity, and a lot of love and a lot of cool stuff but I was disheartened.

Look, I'm going to have trouble watching *Batman Begins* because I pitched a Batman movie to them that I fell so in love with that I couldn't get it out of my head. And, no matter what, I'm just going to be going, "Oh, that one scene. Oh, I just wish . . . Oh!" Even if I love every frame, you just don't get over stuff like that.

Kozak: I don't recall ever hearing about you pitching a Batman movie.

Whedon: It was right when they first starting talking about making another *Batman* movie, and there was no director attached. And I can tell you exactly when I pitched it because—funny little story—my agent said, "You know, I wouldn't call you. I know you don't want to do other people's stuff, but it's Batman, and I figured I'd mention it. They want to do something." I'm like, "Well, I guess you'd have to 'Year-One' it because, I mean, you can't go any further in the direction they've gone." He's like, "Well, y'know, whatever." I'm like, "Y'know, I'm not going to think about it." And then I talked to my wife, and she's like, "Dude." And she doesn't even like comic books. She was like, "No. Are you kidding? It's Batman!"

And, you know, I started to think about it and I did come up with an origin movie and I just got completely overwhelmed by how much I loved the idea. I was just like, "Oh my God! This is really . . . I'm going in to pitch! What the hell!" And I was clearly not on the same wavelength as the people I was pitching to. I was talking about personal epiphanies and they were talking about an '05 slot. So the meeting was just kind of a non-starter. I was talking about a smaller film, they were really looking for a big franchise thing. So I got in my car and headed back to the office and I literally said to myself, "How many more times do I need to be told that the machine doesn't care. The machine is not aware of what is in your heart as a storyteller." I got back to the office and they cancelled *Firefly*. So I was like, "Oh! So, uh, just once more. OK!" That was not a happy day.

But, again, I don't want to be speaking ill of the *X-Men* people or of Warner Bros., because they had a perfectly valid agenda that I just wasn't really aware of.

Lauren [Shuler Donner, who produces the *X-Men* movies] has always been a big supporter, and so has Avi [Arad, CEO of Marvel Studios], and we talked about *X3* but the schedule totally didn't work out. But had I done an X-Men movie—and obviously it would have been *X3*, the first one I that I could have done—I just feel like I would have pared it down character-wise. They were talking about all the new characters they were going to bring out, and I was like, "I think you have all these great actors in your movie already. [laughs] Why don't we, y'know, stick with them?'"

But *X3* was definitely a Phoenix story because I think Famke Janssen is really underrated as an actress anyway, and because it's Phoenix, for Christ's sake.

Kozak: Have you used anything in *Astonishing X-Men* [the best-selling Marvel comic book Whedon has been writing] that you had originally been thinking about for the first *X-Men* movie?

Whedon: Nothing from the movie script is even remotely connected to the comic book. I can't really do that. I can't really take something and then stick it somewhere else. If I could it would probably make life easier, 'cause I often think up chunks of stuff that I then can't use. But the fact is you have to come at everything as if there had been nothing before and there will be nothing after.

I mean, if I'd had a great idea that was a great idea for a comic book for the X-Men as they were when Grant Morrison left them [Morrison was writing the comic-book adventures of Cyclops and Wolverine immediately prior to Whedon's run] that happened to have been something I wrote for the movie that had been taken out, I might have considered it. But that wasn't the case.

Kozak: You've been critical of the first *X-Men* feature's script. What did you perceive as its chief deficiencies?

Whedon: Eh, I don't feel like ragging on somebody else's work. In private I'm just as catty as anybody, but that's not something I would really do in an interview. The movie is never going to be satisfying to somebody who wrote a script that wasn't used. Whether or not the script was better or worse, that person is always going to have a skewed perception of the movie.

Kozak: Were you surprised at how well the first *X-Men* film was received?

Whedon: I think I was a little surprised. But, like I said, it had an integrity to it, and it had some moments and it had a feel that was a little bit fresh. And superhero movies were notoriously bad, and it sort of stuck its head above the pack a bit.

Kozak: Leaving aside for the moment *Wonder Woman* and *Batman* and *X-Men*, is there a comic-book franchise you'd be especially keen to bring to screen?

Whedon: The only time I ever read a comic and said, "Jesus, that should be on the screen," I found out that somebody else was already developing it, and it was *Global Frequency*. It should be a TV show. I adore it. [*Global Frequency* creator] Warren Ellis is like a God to me. I met him by chance years ago. I walk into [the Hollywood comic-shop] Golden Apple, which is not my usual store because I don't live there. And he was there doing a signing and they're like, "Oh, it's so good you came out for this." And I was like, "For what?" I had no idea he was even in the country. And he was so sweet because I was just about to start *Fray* [a Whedon-authored comic-book series set centuries after the events of *Buffy*], and I had never written a comic. And he said, "Well, have you seen any scripts?" And I was like, "Uh, they sent me an Alan Moore script." He's like, "Oh my God, you poor thing!" I'm like, "He does describe things . . . a lot." And he said, "Yeah, yeah, he'll do three pages on one panel. I'll send you a script and you can see how little you can get away with."

Kozak: I'd love to see a *Global Frequency* series come to be.
Whedon: And I heard good things about the pilot and the script from a bunch of my comic-writer friends and my TV-slash-comic-writer friends. And I don't know what happened. It just made perfect sense as a show.

Kozak: Given how you seem to embrace ensembles, does Marvel's *Avengers* project over at Paramount offer any particular appeal?
Whedon: Y'know, the thing about the X-Men is they have a coherent core. The Avengers to me is tough. I wouldn't approach The Avengers, I wouldn't approach the Fantastic Four. The X-Men are all born of pain, and pain is where I hang my hat.

Kozak: Weren't you once approached by New Line about an *Iron Man* project?
Whedon: Yes, well, is there anybody in more pain than [Iron Man alter-ego Tony] Stark? I wrote an entire treatment, pitched the thing, it was approved. I really enjoyed the people at New Line and then I suddenly—I was doing a lot of work on TV—and I suddenly went, "I can't . . . develop . . . a script."

Kozak: You were too busy?
Whedon: It wasn't even that I was too busy, because I'm always busy. I just can't be in development. And I loved the story and I felt very bad about having led them down the garden path because I was on it for a while, working the story out. And I just said, "You know what? I can't just sort of write a script and have them spend eight years. . . ." You know, I remember running into [*Seven* screenwriter] Andrew Kevin Walker eight years before *X-Men* came out. He said, "I'm writing the X-Men movie!" [Walker's script was one of the many not used for *X-Men*.—Ed.] I just couldn't go through that. And I didn't

have the power at that time not to, so I just backed away. But I really liked the story. I really like the character because he's full of self-loathing—and that, my friend, I can write.

Kozak: Did Tony still have shrapnel in his chest?
Whedon: It wasn't a shrapnel thing. It was just a weak heart that was not helped by his constant drinking.

Kozak: So you're still reading comic books at age forty-one?
Whedon: Yes, at age forty-one I go to a comic-book shop every Wednesday.

Kozak: Anything besides *Global Frequency* you'd care to recommend?
Whedon: *Runaways*. I picked up the first issue and every single one of them has been a gem. *Powers*, of course, I think everybody already knows about. I think *Plastic Man* doesn't get the props that it should.

Kozak: Kyle Baker's version?
Whedon: Yeah, that's some funny stuff. That's like some old-school *Mad* magazine Will Elder stuff. I think it's pretty great.

Kozak: Any particular comic-shop people can find you in on a Wednesday?
Whedon: Well, I live near Hi-De-Ho. I work near House of Secrets. And there's a good pizza near Golden Apple, so it's kind of a toss-up. The trouble with doing as much work as I do is I also have to send my assistant to the comic-book store; how lame am I?

　　I'm trying to think if there's any other comics that I'm missing. And of course, that's one of those questions; list questions always leave you terrified and blank.

VII. TV, WITH AND WITHOUT WHEDON

Kozak: Were you more invested in polishing up the early *Buffy* scripts than the early *Angel* scripts?
Whedon: Yes. The early *Buffy*s, I was writing half a script, a whole script, re-breaking stories. I was in it up to my eyeballs because we really didn't have the staff put together yet. And I had [early *Angel* showrunner] David Greenwalt, thank God, or I would not be alive today.

Kozak: Was it David who did most of the *Angel* polishing during its first three seasons?
Whedon: We shared that. But what I would do with *Angel* was more break the

story and then take a polish pass, as opposed to take the script and completely rework it. Because I had David at the helm, he could be the guy who had to do the all-night frantic version and I could just sort of help.

Kozak: Does it surprise you that at least some fans hear a lot more of your voice in *Buffy*'s first five seasons than they do in the first four seasons of *Angel*?
Whedon: We would try to do something a little bit different with *Angel*. People have the tendency to think that I either abandoned *Buffy* or didn't do anything on *Angel*, and I was thickly in both of them. The difference was, once *Angel* started I couldn't be on set. I was literally on set for three years on *Buffy*. And then all of the sudden I couldn't be on either set that much.

Kozak: Being on set is important for the writing?
Whedon: It really is. Just because once you've written something you have to make sure it's actually shot the way it's written. Because with TV directors there's a lot of hit-and-miss. You can get a terrible hack or you can get a really great guy who just missed one really important point.

Kozak: Do you think that's true of most TV series? Writers are typically on set to keep an eye on things?
Whedon: Oh yeah. The executive producer is basically the director. What I learned from my film sets is that a director doesn't have to create anything, but he is responsible for everything. And the same thing goes for executive producer on a TV series.

Kozak: They teach you this in film school?
Whedon: They taught me that about directors in movies. I learned it about executive producers in TV the old fashioned way. I had a TV director once say to me, "One of these days I'm going to stand over your shoulder and tell you what to do." And I actually took him up to my office and said, "Let me explain this. It is my job is to stand over your shoulder and tell you what to do. It is not your job to stand over mine."

Kozak: When you visit the Internet, are you shocked how little fans know about this process?
Whedon: Sometimes it's a little dispiriting when you see, "Well, Joss had nothing to do with that." Well, there's nothing that goes on screen that I had nothing to do with.

Kozak: I think there's a lot of confusion also about how different a director's role is on a TV set versus a feature set.
Whedon: It's a grueling medium. It's a tough thing to do, to be an itinerate

director. I was talking to David Semel, who was one of our best directors—he did a lot of great episodes—and he was going off to *Dawson's Creek*, and I said, "That would be fun, to get away and do a completely different show where you're handed this script," and he said, "Y'know, you go onto a show where everybody's been doing it for a couple of years, they all know each other, they all know how they like to play their part and what they want to do and how they like to be treated and they all know the drill and they have an executive producer that they answer to, and you're going to go there every day and pretend that you're going to tell them what to do and that they're going to listen to you." It's tough.

I had directors who I conflicted with and I just flat-out thought they were not getting it done. I've had conflict. No regime is without it. But good work on my show always stayed on screen. If somebody wrote something, and it was right, I'd never change it, because I am too lazy. There are producers who need to control everything and I needed to control exactly what needed controlling, and if somebody could get it done, I would walk away faster than you could see me. Like I was Bugs Bunny. There would just be smoke in the shape of where I was. Because that's not what it was about. It was about, "Is the work being serviced?"

Kozak: You're obviously better at this than most. You've made a lot of really good shows.

Whedon: Well, I had a lot of really good people. And I think part of running a show is having a vision for the show, and there's a lot of different talents that you need. The tough thing about directing, and this goes for executive producing too, is nothing prepares you for it. I had editors who got a shot at directing. One fell on his face. One did brilliantly. I had cinematographers. I had actors. I had writers. Everybody wants a shot, and nobody is prepared. Because directing is almost like an alchemy. There're so many different factors, so many different skills involved, the most important being communication and some visual sense.

Everybody who works for me did their best work because they knew everything that was good enough was going to get on screen. And that's how I was able to do one show, and then two and then three at a time. Because I kept surrounding myself with smart people who knew they were in an environment where there really wasn't any competition. There was just the story. And they all busted their butts to do their best work because they knew they were going to be honored for it.

Kozak: Just not by the television academy.

Whedon: No, the television academy would ignore them and in fact make fun of them.

Kozak: When we spoke on the *Serenity* set last summer, you mentioned you weren't watching any TV save *Law & Order: SVU*, and you've subsequently admitted to a fondness for *Without a Trace*. Will these inspire you, perhaps, to create your own TV police procedural?

Whedon: I have no immediate plans to do a series right now. I do, however, have an idea for a procedural. I can't believe that I do. But I'm not going to realize it for some time. Because I need to take things at a different speed for a while. I had a notion. I went, "Oh my God, I can't believe I just found a procedural." That's the last thing I ever thought I would make.

Kozak: I'd guess you would start it as a procedural and turn it into something else.

Whedon: That's usually the way it is.

Kozak: Have you added any other season-passes to your TiVo of late?

Whedon: *House.* I adore *House.* I've loved Hugh Laurie forever, but I love that character. I actually choke up at the thought of how powerfully noble and beautiful his total misanthropy is. He touches something very special in me because he's just so mean.

Kozak: Anything else?

Whedon: *Numbers. Cold Case. Veronica Mars.*

Kozak: You watch *Veronica Mars*?

Whedon: I'm a latecomer. We just started.

Kozak: You know what they call *Veronica Mars*?

Whedon: "The New Buffy."

Kozak: "The New Buffy" is what they call it.

Whedon: Well, the pilot was pretty damn good. So, yeah, I just demanded the tapes so we could catch up.

Kozak: Is there zero chance you'll be pitching pilots for the 2006–2007 TV season?

Whedon: Yeah, I'm not going to be pitching a pilot this season. I have other things. I'm very tired.

The CulturePulp Q&A: Joss Whedon

MIKE RUSSELL/2005

From CulturePulp.com, September 24, 2005. Reprinted by permission.

Buffy the Vampire Slayer creator Joss Whedon always wanted to write and direct feature films—but even he admits that *Serenity* was a strange choice for his big-screen debut.

"A lot of people told me that—repeatedly," he says, "because [*Serenity's*] a story and not a *premise* movie—like 'Oh! He sees dead people!' or 'He's old and he looks like Tom Hanks now!'"

It's true: *Serenity*, which opens Friday, September 30, is hard to sum up in pithy sentences. But let's give it a shot:

In broad strokes, the film tells the story of space pirate Mal Reynolds (Nathan Fillion)—a cynical, Han Solo–style mercenary whose thieving days are interrupted when the government sends an assassin (Chiwetel Ejiofor) to kill the psychic on his crew (Summer Glau) after she mentally eavesdrops on some alarming state secrets.

There are chases. There is banter. Things explode.

But try to describe *Serenity* in greater detail, and things get complicated in a hurry.

For starters, the movie's actually a sequel to a cancelled TV show called *Firefly*—which Fox unceremoniously dumped in 2002, after airing eleven of fourteen produced episodes out of order.

Whedon—in a move that hasn't been seen since the Zuckers turned TV's *Police Squad!* into the *Naked Gun* franchise—refused to take that cancellation lying down.

"I loved the characters," he says. "I loved the people who played them. And I just thought, 'Their story's not told yet.'" So he convinced Universal to take a risk on a relatively low-budget ($40 million) film after a small but rabid group of fans calling themselves Browncoats snapped up somewhere north of two hundred thousand copies of a DVD set collecting the series.

It's easy to see why *Firefly* became a cult fixation: Its universe is richly textured in a way you don't see much in mainstream sci-fi. Set five hundred years hence—in a new solar system mankind is colonizing, frontier-style—the film juggles a large, diverse crew that includes Gina Torres, Alan Tudyk, Adam Baldwin, and Ron Glass. And it mixes culture and language in some unexpected ways: Our heroes bicker in Old West cowboy-speak and curse in Chinese, and every set-piece and costume-scrap is a crazy mash-up of East/West motifs.

Whedon helps sell all this by shooting *Serenity* in a naturalistic, handheld style, with the considerable help of Clint Eastwood cinematographer Jack Green. (In the book *Serenity: The Official Visual Companion*, Whedon describes the look of one fight scene as "Robert Altman's *The Matrix*"; this is, incredibly, a fairly accurate assessment.)

We talked with Whedon for over an hour about *Serenity*, *Firefly*, rabid fans, the personal politics of his solar system, the *Serenity* mix tape, bizarro marketing strategies, the joys of studio non-interference and quality bootlegging, the dangers of becoming a cult icon, why touring a spaceship in a single take is a really good idea, and much, much, *much* more.

I. AN EXPLANATION FOR THE NEWBIES

Russell: So if you were going to pitch *Firefly*'s basic premise in terms that a novice would understand, how would you put it? The popular take seems to be that it's Han Solo's story—if Greedo still shot first.
Whedon: Which I believe I, myself, said.

Russell: Well, there you go.
Whedon: Or if Han had come into the bar five minutes later and never met that old man. But you asked how I would pitch *Firefly*, which is different from *Serenity*. So which one am I pitching?

Russell: I'm sorry—*Serenity* is the one we'd want to talk about.
Whedon: I mean, of course, some people are thinking of both. . . . But if I was going to pitch *Serenity*, I'd say it's a space adventure that involves the lowliest of people in the most mundane of circumstances getting caught up in something giant and epic—without lasers, aliens, or force-fields to protect them.

Russell: It strikes me that any one *Firefly* character, taken alone, would be a premise character. But you have nine of them interacting.
Whedon: Well, that's kind of the point. And that's part of what makes it difficult to sell and balance—and what makes it worth doing.

What I started out with was these characters, because I had done the show

Firefly, and I *loved* these guys—I loved the characters, I loved the people who played them, I loved the *way* they played them. And I just thought, "These people, their story's not told yet. They're ready for it to be told on a much grander scale than perhaps anybody had anticipated."

And that is a strange way to come at trying to build a film. It's not the way I usually do it. Usually it *is* about a premise, and I build a character from that. But I knew this universe was exciting and fresh and textured and very real to me, and I had these people—and I knew that they were in a world of trouble, in terms of where I was going with the series.

I did know that I had something that was worthy of a movie. An easily told movie? Not necessarily. But a movie that would have more than just a premise. It would really get into their lives and tell the big, epic story—with the big chases and the big trouble and the fights and all the glory that we go to the movies for. But at the same time, it would be about the people in it—as opposed to the things you can accomplish with CGI.

Russell: Speaking of which, I saw the film last night [September 1] in a screening that wasn't an all-Browncoat screening. And it played very well. Which, as a big fan of the *Firefly* TV series, I was a bit concerned about. And I have to salute the climactic space battle in its final form: A lot of newbies—people who'd never seen the show—were saying that it was thrilling in a way that certain *Star Wars* dogfights haven't been in a long time.

Whedon: That's very impressive, considering how beautifully done those dog-fights are. So much money! The money! All that money!

I think our dogfight works because you get a sense of their situation, which is: They're really little and they have no guns!

Russell: Well the way it's storyboarded and assembled to have a documentary feel is also fascinating—there's a "shaky-cam" look to the effects that *Firefly* sort of pioneered.

Whedon: Well, it looked like that for a reason. *Buffy* was made because there was a character I wanted to see that I wasn't seeing. And *Firefly* was made because I was missing something in televised science fiction, and also in the movies: a gritty realism that wasn't an *Alien* ripoff.

The template I was working from was *NYPD Blue*—it was "you are there." It was, "We just happened to have a camera, and then this happened." Obviously, these were larger-than-life stories, and obviously [in *Serenity*] there was some arch and manipulative camera work, because much the way Mal realizes he's a hero, the movie realizes, "I'm a movie!" But we always tried to keep that presence: We're there, the cameraman might fall over, everyone might die, and none of us is safe.

II. BUILDING THE 'VERSE (AND TALKING LIKE A MAN NAMED MARION)

Russell: *Firefly* and *Serenity*'s political and cultural underpinnings are unusually well thought-out. You've obviously developed a whole system of planets, a Sino-American political system, a mix of languages. How long did the concept fester in your head before you started writing?

Whedon: It festered for a while. It was probably two or three years after I came up with the idea that I made the TV show, a year-and-a-half doing that, and then a couple of years to write the movie. So it's had time to bake.

And people are always like, "They're fighting an evil empire!" And I'm like, "Well, it's not really an evil empire." The trick was always to create something that was complex enough that you could bring some debate to it—that it wasn't black-and-white. It wasn't, "If we hit this porthole in the Death Star, everything will be fine!" It was messier than that, and the *messiest* thing is that the government is basically benign. It's the most advanced culturally. . . .

Russell: And [the government-sponsored assassin] The Operative has an honorable point of view—in his way.

Whedon: Oh, he *totally* does. Mal is somebody that I knew, as I created him, I would not get along with. I don't think we have the same politics. But that's sort of the point. I mean, if the movie's about anything, it's about the right to be wrong. It's about the messiness of people. And if you try to eradicate that, you eradicate them.

Russell: And on a sheer love-of-language level, it's about the clash of dialects. Several of the characters speak in an old-timey-Western-paperback patois. Why did you choose to make the connections between the Old West and the future so overt?

Whedon: Because that's where it came from. It came from my love of frontier stories—in the movies and in actual, historical frontier stories. And also because if you *are* Han Solo—if you are living hand-to-mouth—you're dealing with a very classic frontier paradigm, which is that life is really hard out here. The law is, at best, obtuse and often useless—and occasionally dangerous. And the *lack* of law is troublesome, too. And you learn to make your own, and work on your own terms, in order to survive.

Right now, we live in an age of extraordinary convenience—where you can have an entire group of friends and social gatherings and all your food and all your movies without ever leaving the house. And so I'm more and more fascinated by the physical—by people who "make their own fun," as it were. As David Mamet so perfectly put it, "Everybody makes their own fun. If you don't make it yourself, it ain't fun—it's entertainment."

Russell: Thank you. I still think *State and Main* is one of Mamet's best movies.

Whedon: I really do. . . . I mean, you can look at the people in *Serenity* as people who are living in a Third-World country—because other people with the best of intentions are trying to, uh, "help" them, but they're kind of out of reach, or nobody knows how the system works well enough to do any good.

The frontier, to me, was fascinating because it *is* so extreme. And at some point, almost everyone is confronted with that kind of extremity. And it's extraordinary how it changes us. It's what makes disaster movies fascinating to me—because they take people like us and say, "Whoa! Well! Who comes up to the mark? How do you change? Who's in charge? How does the system—how does, you know, society—dissolve when the walls are not existentially but *literally* broken down?"

And obviously, you don't want a disaster to happen to anybody. But this movie is about people . . . who are used to a certain level of peril and extremity in their lives that most people in this country aren't. Or weren't.

Russell: Getting back to the question of language: I was wondering how the hell you found actors who make all that old-timey dialogue seem effortless. Because that's a hell of a coup.

Whedon: It is. And with Nathan, he got so completely comfortable with it that we actually had to have him talk slower, because he could rattle it off so fast, people couldn't understand a word he was saying.

Russell: And when he posts to the message boards on the fan-sites, he kind of writes that way, too.

Whedon: He gets a little Mal on. . . . The dialogue is built out of a number of things: my own desire to make up silly slang, because I love the liquidness of language. . . . It's largely Western. It's also Elizabethan. There's some Indian stuff. There's some turn-of-the-century Pennsylvania Dutch. Irish. . . . There's absolutely anything that fits. But I think [the cast] will all band together and kill me because of the Chinese.

And there's some John Wayne—which is different than just "Western." *Nobody* talked like John Wayne; John had his own thing that was so lyrical. The way he talked and the way he moved were both way too graceful for a man who was supposed to be that tough.

Russell: [laughs] I know.

Whedon: Then again, his name *was* Marion.

Russell: Hey, John Ford cast him in a movie where he went to Ireland.

Whedon: Yeah. He had an extraordinary individualism. And that's in there, too.

See, with Nathan, I just got incredibly lucky, and for everyone else, it just works in different ways. When you start to work with actors, you start to write to their different strengths—you start to know what's going to trip them up and what's going to play to their different strengths.

III. THE GENIUS OF JAYNE, AND THE DIFFERENCE BETWEEN POLITICS AND PARTISANSHIP

Russell: I'd like to go out of my way to praise Adam Baldwin's work in the film. I really expect him to get some more work out of this; he knocked every single line out of the park.
Whedon: Adam is quite large to be a secret weapon. [laughs] He really is. It's great fun to take someone like Summer, who's never done a film—except for a small bit—and really get to show her to people. It's just as much fun with a guy who's been working for twenty years. Because he's so funny, and so vital. His love of that role, and what he brings to it. . . . Yeah, he does. He knocks every single line straight out of the park. Adam really is bigger than life.

Russell: Now, I know his political views may not be your own. And one of the things that strikes me about the show is that, in terms of both gender and personal politics, *Firefly* and *Serenity* have one of the more diverse fan bases I've ever seen. The show's been written up in progressive and conservative journals. . . .
Whedon: Yeah. I would say about the movie that it is very political, but it's not *partisan*. And I think the curse, right now, of the politics of our nation is that a line has been drawn down the middle of our country—and that's not actually how the human mind works.

Russell: Well, the problems are hugely complicated infrastructural problems, and we're trying to solve them with bloodsport. David Foster Wallace said that.
Whedon: Yeah. It's not useful. The political statement that *Serenity* makes is very blatant—but it can be embraced by someone who's extremely conservative or someone who's extremely liberal. That's not the point. The point is: It's a *personal* statement.

What *Serenity* and *Firefly* were both about is how politics affect people personally. And the *personal* politics are the only politics that really interest me. I'm not going to make this big, didactic polemic—I'm just going to say, "When there are shifts in a planet, those tiny little guys are the ones who are affected. So let's hang out with them—not the Federation heads or the Jedi Council."

Russell: [laughs] Right.

Whedon: And with the show, the idea was to have as many points of view as possible. The reason I made the Alliance a generally benign, enlightened society was so that I could engage these people in a debate about it.

Now, in the film, obviously, there's more chasing and guns than debating—

Russell: Plus explosions—

Whedon: You know, people don't love a great debate flick.

Russell: And when people try and make them, and critics praise them as great "message movies," no one goes to see them.

Whedon: Yeah. Including myself. But if you let the points of view exist, then it does the work for you. In the show, that was always the idea: Nine different people see the same thing and have nine different reactions to it, based on who they are and where they've been. And that's what made for the drama. And, uh, most of the comedy.

Russell: I'm a vague acquaintance of your colleague Brian Michael Bendis, who lives here in town—and one thing that strikes me about his work and yours is that you're guys who aren't ashamed about coding up all your messages in a genre structure.

Whedon: Well, I have always been a fan of his. I love genre. I love fantasy. I love science fiction. I love horror. I love musicals. I love finding a different way to express what I want to say. And I think, ultimately, it works best for me—because otherwise, it would be boring and didactic and I wouldn't know what the hell I was doing. Genre helps me with structure, and structure helps me get through the day.

IV. THE PROBLEM WITH NICELY CARPETED SPACESHIPS AND THE MAD SKILLZ OF JACK GREEN

Russell: The show and film are also fascinating in that they have no aliens, or dorks in jumpsuits with prosthetics on their nose-ridges. Nor does the spaceship in any way resemble a flying Sheraton Hotel.

Whedon: [laughs] The thing I love about science fiction—future stuff, particularly—is the sense of being there. It's very important. And I'd seen a lot of shows with ships where they all tend to look like that—

Russell: Nicely carpeted spaceships.

Whedon: Exactly. That's why there's a toilet [on *Serenity*]. That's why there are ladders. That's why I'm obsessed with vertical space. I'm obsessed with the *messiness* of it.

As much as *Star Wars* and *Star Trek* are old, weird uncles of this movie—and one of them may be the father, but we haven't gotten back the DNA test yet—*Alien*, particularly the first one, also has significance. Because it gave a real sense of, "We live here. And this is where we eat, and this is where we sleep, and we climb up from here to here, and the vents run here."

And that sense of the physical is another reason why I was doing the camerawork the way I did it—so you were not in that remove of, "AND NOW WE WILL ENACT THE DRAMA THAT EXISTS IN MY BIG JAR OF DRA-MA." It was, you know, "Everything here is beat-up and real and crappy, and you go up and you go down." Apart from the artificial gravity that one must inevitably have—because one doesn't want to make a floaty movie—the textured reality is there. I want to *be* on that ship, and I never felt like I was *on* those other ships. They were big, giant Sheratons.

Russell: And you don't see a lot of science-fiction films lit by Clint Eastwood's cinematographer.

Whedon: You know, how cool is Jack Green?

Russell: How did you explain this to him?

Whedon: I didn't really have to. He read the script; he got it; we talked; he got it. He knew there was a Western thing going on, but he also knew I wasn't looking to ape the Western—I was just looking for something that felt real and cobbled together with a lot of different palates.

And the thing about Jack is: He can actually do any damned thing. You ask Jack for a certain thing, and he's got it in his repertoire. His druthers is to stay out of the way.

Russell: He's probably the secret weapon that allows Eastwood to deliver all his movies on-time and under-budget.

Whedon: Certainly. He's the reason we got to make a movie that looks—I think—a good deal more expensive than it was. He moves *so* fast, and he makes frames that I think are just as gorgeous as anything. But he doesn't announce, "JACK GREEN IN THE HOUSE!"—either on set or on film. He stays out of the way, and then he gives you stuff like that Shepherd Book/Mal scene—which, with *three lights*, is one of the prettiest things I've ever seen. He's not afraid of blacks, and neither am I, and that's a really important thing to me. He's not afraid of losing things, of keeping it a little sloppy. At the same time, he's very precise. And he moves faster than a lot of guys who are in TV. I can't say enough about Jack.

And he's perfect for this because he's got a Western background, but he's done everything—and he's not turning this into a big-hat pastiche. Because when you say "space Western," a lot of people are gonna go, "RUN!!! JUST RUNNN!!!" To me, it is that to an extent, but it's more just a space adventure.

I remember my father being *very* angry when people said that *Star Wars* was a Western. He'd say, "It's not a Western! It's a WWII flying-ace movie!"

Russell: Mm-hm. It's *The Dambusters*.

Whedon: And of course it's a hundred different things—as is anything that feels new. But to me, it's perfectly logical, because you're out there in what is termed "the final frontier," and you're in the same situation that people were in when the final frontier was California: "We've got exactly this much cured meat, we've got exactly this many bullets, and we have no idea where we're heading." So it's not so much a question of genre, it's a question of the reality of the thing—and the fact that the Western was always an immigrant story, and you get to mish-mash all those cultures together. That's how we made this country, and that's how we're going to make every country from now on.

So Jack is perfect for all of that, because he understands it all—he makes it all real. You still get your sci-fi jollies, but none of it feels like, you know, like there's a Theremin playing.

V. BETA-TESTING A MARKETING PLAN (AND STICKING A PEN IN YOUR NECK)

Russell: Now, Marc Schmuger and his Universal marketing team have really been using your film to beta-test a new way of marketing movies. Obviously, they can afford to do these sorts of experiments on your film. I'd love to hear your take on the specifics of that.

Whedon: To me, the whole thing is fairly impressive. On the one hand, it's really nice, because I realized that they were saying, "The best thing we have to advertise your film is your film." And I thought, "Well, that's better than, 'We have to hide it until it opens and then run like bunnies.'"

But at the beginning, when they first talked about showing it to the fans in a number of preview screenings that was, you know, pretty big—

Russell: I think it was sixty-five, wasn't it?

Whedon: And that's not including the festivals. I think it'll end up having been shown about seventy-five times before it opens. I and a lot of people were a little scared: "What if we ring the dinner bell and the fans are all full?"

Russell: Well, that and the movie heaps these Kobayashi Maru levels of abuse on the characters. I mean, fans are gonna go binary on that.

Whedon: Some people might go, "Hey! Wait a minute! He took the sky! Where's my sky?" But, at the end of the day, what they [Universal] were trying to do. . . . They felt the fans—based on their experience of seeing them see the movie—weren't going to go, "Yawn! Well, we got our jollies and we're going to move on." They wanted to build the momentum with the idea that, "Oh, this is really something. And the noise that you guys are making could be heard elsewhere." And that was the thing.

The fan base has been very loyal—and, I think, *unprecedentedly* involved. But it was really about the people who have no idea what *Serenity* is—or who could give a rat's ass—hearing these waves in the distance sort of heading towards them and going, "What is that?" And that was thinking two steps ahead of where I was thinking.

And it seems to have worked. We've gotten some coverage in a lot of places that would not have given us the time of day. But it's still hard. I mean, the job that they were given—to sell a movie with a title that sounds vaguely Buddhist; that doesn't have an easily sellable premise; that doesn't have a single bankable star, unless you're a huge Alan Tudyk or Adam Baldwin fan like I am [laughs]—it was a hell of a thing for them to take on. And so they just said, "Well, *we* love it. *They* love it. Let's work with 'love.'"

Russell: [laughs] What a novel idea for a marketing department.
Whedon: Oh, yeah. I tell you, I've been pretty impressed. And they were always looking for things to do that were different. You know, the little Internet River bits.

Russell: Yes! How *did* you enjoy gurgling with a pen in your neck?
Whedon: You know? Uh, good times. And I'll be able to explain it all more when it's done. But that came not from Universal saying, "We have a marketing idea"; that came from Universal going, "What's weird? What's fresh? What's fun?" And me going, "I have a silly notion. . . ."

It was a chance to say, "We're gonna throw everything up there. We're just gonna keep coming at people from different angles." Because that's kind of what the movie does, and that's kind of what makes it interesting. So we're just gonna keep spreading out the mythos that this thing is built upon, so that even if somebody has no idea who anybody is, they know there's some *body* there—not something they *missed*, hopefully, but something that they can rely on—something that's been thought out, something with some *weight*.

VI. FLASHBACKS AND 'ONE-ERS'

Whedon: You said you've seen it with—

Russell: I've seen it with the fans and the non-fans now.

Whedon: You know, we spent a *long* time with this movie, in editing, getting it to a place where non-fans would be able to enjoy it. It was the hardest thing about it.

Russell: I actually wanted to ask you about that. In the first ten minutes of *Serenity*, you manage to explain the entire premise of the show in three folding flashbacks and a long, single take that takes us on a tour of the entire ship and introduces all the characters. I just want to say: That must have been *murderously* hard to write.

Whedon: Actually, not the hardest part. It was hard to *structure*. I sat down and said, "Now: I have to tell a story that I haven't told before, and explain it to people and not contradict stuff." Yeah, the task that I put before myself is one I hope *never* to put before myself again. [laughs] But once I figured out what I wanted to do, it made such incredibly perfect logical sense to do a narration that turns out to be a lecture that turns out to be a dream that turns out to be a holographic flashback, you know?

Russell: Possibly the first time we've seen that many things fold into themselves in a movie in a while.

Whedon: It was a lot. But it was twofold: It was a way to include a great deal of exposition without becoming the most boring film ever. My other idea was to have Anthony Hopkins talk for twenty-five minutes at the beginning. . . . But Oliver Stone stole it from me. But the other thing is, it worked because what I'm basically doing is a story about Mal as told by River. So where we start is in River's mind—and River's mind is completely fractured. So to tell something that is constantly re-adjusting—that is constantly pulling the rug out from under you—is to basically experience the world the way she's experiencing it.

When we go to *Serenity*, it's very deliberate that it's an endlessly long take. For one thing, you get to see all the characters, the whole ship and the way they interact—and to do it in a one-er feels very fluid. But it's also to stop that disassociative River mind, and to put you in Mal's and *Serenity*'s space—which is, no matter how much you protest about being a villain, a completely safe and understandable space. So it was a deliberate contrast to what had come before, to do that long take. And it made perfect sense to me, because I already knew what that ship looked like and where everybody in the ship would be and how they worked and how they'd interact. It actually came very quickly.

Russell: Well, and there's that wonderful handoff moment where Mal says, "Do you know your part in this?" and River replies, "Do you?"

Whedon: You know, that was the only re-shoot we did. There is that bunch of crates in the back of the cargo bay—and I remembered that bunch of crates in the back of the cargo bay when I said, "I need half a day; I know what's missing from the movie. Um, besides excitement and coherence." And it's the handoff. I was like, "I thought the one-er would be the handoff, but it's not." I thought people would know to identify with Mal—but there are so many people and so much going on, that nobody understands. This is something we were getting showing it to audiences who hadn't seen [*Firefly*]: Nobody understands that this is the guy they're supposed to watch, and by the time they figure it out, we're too far into the movie. So I said, "Give me those crates." And they literally piled them—Jack Green was shooting *40-Year-Old Virgin*, so this is basically Jack's year—

Russell: Yeah, no kidding.
Whedon:—so we basically brought the crates onto the set of *40-Year-Old Virgin* on a Sunday, piled them all up, and we shot that and a couple of little inserts and things.

And "Do you know your purpose?" "Do you?" was basically my way of telling the audience, "River is watching this guy—so you should, too." And it completely changed the way people felt about everything that went after: They had their eye on Mal. And it made things flow a lot better.

Russell: There are other little handoffs like that in the movie that I think only fans of the TV show might get. One of the ones I've seen discussed online, which I love, is the handoff of the Blue Sun liquor bottle from Jayne to Simon.
Whedon: Mm-hm.

Russell: Given their relationship, it's a big moment.
Whedon: That was a scene where, you know, Mal gives his St. Crispian's Day speech, God bless 'im—and I originally wrote a scene where everyone chimes in and says, "I'm in." And I just thought, "If Jayne says he's in, there's no way nobody else *isn't* in."

Russell: Right. If he's in, everybody is.
Whedon: But then, when I was shooting it, I was like, "Because he and Simon . . ." And that's more in the series than it is in the film that the two of them combat, but they're still total opposites: Simon is the total idealist and Jayne is the total pragmatist and completely selfish. If there were an angel and a devil sitting on Mal's shoulders, *that's* what they'd look like. It's maybe the hoariest thing in the movie, but by God, it says what needs to be said: You pass the bottle to Simon, and they're a team.

Russell: It's no hoarier than having Dean Martin and Ricky Nelson singin' a song together in *Rio Bravo*—
Whedon:—with Walter Brennan—

Russell: With Walter Brennan. You know, and that worked.

Whedon: Some dulcet pipes in that number.

VII. DEADHEADS AND BROWNCOATS

Russell: You've also done an absolutely smashing job of ignoring the massive amounts of bootleg *Firefly* fan merchandise. I'm thinking specifically of Blue-SunShirts.com. . . .

Whedon: I'm a Deadhead, and where I come from, bootlegging's a good thing.

Russell: If the movie's a hit, and more official merchandise starts coming out, do you think there's going to be a crackdown?

Whedon: I have no idea. I never have a piece of merchandising; I haven't reached a place in the Hollywood DNA chain where I can actually ask for that. So it's not like *I'm* losing money.

But even if I was? You know, I'm doin' fine. I have a job. I'm doing just fine. And the fact that people are making this stuff? You can call it "bootlegging" or you can call it "free advertising."

Russell: Let's hope they keep calling it the latter.

Whedon: You can also call it "the fact that people are taking it to their hearts." It's no different than fan fiction or any of these online communities. It's important to them and they *wear* it—and that makes me proud. And I don't give a good goddamn who's makin' money off it.

Russell: Now, do you have a favorite piece of fan—I'm sorry, "free advertising"?

Whedon: [laughs] A favorite. . . . You know, I have to admit, when I first saw the Blue Sun t-shirts, I thought they were pretty cool—because it didn't announce itself, and I think it had a really good logo. And I hope if I ever get to make another one of these, I get to pay off some Blue Sun action, because that was one of the things in the movie that I was sad to drop.

But a favorite? Um . . . hard to say. The best thing I've ever seen a little off the beaten track was at a Browncoat booth—it was their raffle-drawing postcard for Equality Now. And it had a big picture of River—it was beautifully done—and it had pictures of Buffy and Zoe and Kitty Pryde, and even Wonder Woman and Fray, and all of these heroines I'd created. And I looked at it, and I swear to God, I got all misty: I was like, "Oh my God! It's almost like my work *means* something!" And seeing that, and knowing that these people were raising money for Equality Now, which is really important to me, was gi-normous. I had the biggest rush imaginable when I saw that. And I picked up, like, forty of those postcards.

VIII. JOSS'S *SERENITY* MIX TAPE (PART 1)

Russell: I have a friend who's a big film-score geek, and I told him I was interviewing you. He told me you wax philosophic and rhapsodic about the score to this film for like three pages in the new companion book that just came out—
Whedon: It's actually five pages.

Russell: Oh. Sorry.
Whedon: No, I mean it was five pages when I typed it. That was written before we'd *hired* a composer. All those memos [in *Serenity: The Official Visual Companion*] were [written] before we made the movie; they were pre-production memos. I gave David Newman that memo; I also gave him a mix tape with everything on my iPod that might be useful.

Russell: And this is actually what my score-geek friend wanted to know: What were those songs?
Whedon: There were a couple of songs from Nickel Creek, whom I adore—I love them with a fiery vengeance. There was some movie stuff: *Angela's Ashes*, Elmer Bernstein's theme from *Far from Heaven*—not because they were necessarily the right idiom, but because the themes were so incredibly indelible within the first twenty seconds, which is about as much time as I usually gave David. [laughs] They had to become indelible before there was too much going on for anybody to hear anything.
    I'm gonna forget a bunch of stuff. Definitely important was "For the Turnstiles" by Neil Young, off *Decade*—because it has this very sort of dampened banjo in it. And I played this for him particularly when we were going over it, just to say, "Look at how he's taking all the reverb off of this, and making just as sort of personal as possible." And I referred to this—in a phrase that sort of came back to me over and over again in my discussions of scores—as follows: What Neil Young was saying in that song was, "Fuck all y'all—I'm on my back porch." You know, in the seventies, when a lot of stuff was getting really symphonic . . . he was going, "Fuck all y'all—I'm on my back porch."

Russell: That actually sums up the sensibilities of a few *Firefly* characters.
Whedon: Yeah. It really does. And that was definitely the big one. I'm actually looking for the CD itself. . . . I might have it in one sec. . . . I'll see if I happen on it or if it's too late. . . . [rummaging noises] Okay . . . last chance . . . everybody in the pool. . . . Bupkis. Oh, well. No joy.

Russell: That's okay. I think the fan base is going to have a lot to chew on just from what you told me.

Whedon: Well, there was a lot of different stuff. I think there was the third movement of the Mendelssohn concerto that Sarah Chang played? It was either Mendelssohn or Sibelius—I'm don't know which one I used. Because, you know, I love me some violins. Although, at the end of the day, it all became about cellos. The whole movie is CelloFest 2005. *Be there!*

If I remember another, I'll shout it out.

Russell: Yeah, just shout it out randomly while we're talking about other stuff.

Whedon: It happens every now and then. My brain works that way. I stop thinking about something and I remember.

Russell: Musical Tourette's. It will be good. Now, the plot—

Whedon: Oh. I know one. It was "Poems" from *Pacific Overtures* by Stephen Sondheim.

Russell: Oh, Sondheim. Of course.

Whedon: Just because of the Asian thing and the simplicity of this entire song written in haiku.

Russell: Mm-hm. Yeah, I'm a Sondheim fan myself.

Whedon: Yeah. He's my guy.

Russell: I'm still dying to see someone make the great film of *Sweeney Todd* that needs to be made.

Whedon: You know, they're talking about it. But I don't get to make it, so. . . .

IX. MR. UNIVERSE, THE *ANGEL* TV MOVIE, AND JOSS'S *SERENITY* MIX TAPE (PART 2)

Russell: Now, I've written about this elsewhere, and I wanted to ask you about it: The film's plot feels more than a little like an overt metaphor for the story of the *Firefly* series itself: The crew has to get a message out, and they need the help of a guy—Mr. Universe, whom I'd argue is a stand-in for the fans—who lives alone with his bank of computers. Was that in any way a conscious decision?

Whedon: It absolutely was not.

Russell: Really.

Whedon: But I read it, and I think I read it in your article—and I was like, "God damn! You're right!"

Russell: And that was a totally unconscious thing.

Whedon: It was totally unconscious. I created Mr. Universe because I needed a place for the final battle—and getting the message out was a way to have a final victory that wasn't, you know, "Hey, we blew up the bad guys! *Yub-yub!*"

Russell: "Yub-yub!" [cackles]

Whedon: Oh, believe me—we spoke much of "the Yub" in editing. But no—I wasn't thinking of that at all.

It's funny, because recently I was talking about the last season of *Angel*, and the non-cliffhanger that people gave me so much flak for. And I'd always said, "The whole point of the thing was that the fight wasn't over yet." And then it occurred to me that you could do the same thing there [with *Angel*] and say, "Well, the circumstance of the thing was also a way of saying, 'The show isn't over yet, *fucker!*'" But I never thought of that at the time. But it really lays itself out that way—as to say, "We're not finished. We've got a lot to say. So we're not going to finish saying it."

Russell: Well, now, Tim Minear's doing a Spike TV-movie, right?

Whedon: That's the hope. I haven't put anything together yet; I'm just trying to line people up.

Russell: I think *Buffy*verse fans are waiting with baited breath to find out exactly how that battle in *Angel*'s finale went. Will the TV movie tell us?

Whedon: Uh, if there's—I believe yes. You will finally find out what happened—who lived, who died, who lost one arm or two legs, who was supposed to be the Chosen One but went over to the Dark Side. All that stuff.

Russell: Fantastic.

Whedon: And I actually did find the CD. So let's see what else is on here that's of interest: Jill Sobule, some Hans Zimmer, Ian Ritchie, Tracy Chapman, some Indigo Girls—oh, and "God's Song" by Randy Newman. And then it ends with "Black Peter" by the Grateful Dead.

And so you're thinking, "Hm, that's some seventies vibe there."

Russell: [laughs] There is a strong seventies vibe.

Whedon: The early seventies, too. And a lot of earthy girl-rock, because I'm me. But it is a very kind of homey and huge seventies-Western influence. And to take a few really dense orchestral pieces and take something sort of down-homey—"I'm on my back porch!"—and put the two of them together was really sort of the mission statement for David. Which I think he accomplished in kind of an amazing way.

Russell: Yeah, Newman pulled it off really well.

Whedon: He really did. He can make with the pretty and with the eerie—and he can be as specific as the old school. I mean, so many of the new school [produce] that sort of Zimmer "wall of sound"—which is great for writing, because you just put it on and you emote for the entire track; it's not a specific emotion, it's just all very portentous. And David can write stuff that is as specific to the moment as the stuff that John Williams does, or some of the old-school composers—but without calling attention to himself.

Russell: And he rolled in a lot of Eastern flavors without it sounding like yet another "Fifth Element" pastiche.

Whedon: Exactly. And it's tough. You've got to do the East without the tourist's bazaar we've all visited.

Russell: Right. Without the vibe.

Whedon: And you've got to do the West without sounding like "Sons of the Pioneers" or some dreadful pastiche. And there's not a lot of precedent for mixing the two that fluidly—like, without just *announcing* it. The closest we came when looking for temp scores? "Shanghai Noon." And that was making a point of "This is the West! This is the East! This is the West! This is the East!"—where we were trying to say, "This is all just happening." But, because I'm obsessed with the frontier thing, all the instruments being the ones they can carry. That's why I want to keep the mandolins and the guitar and the cello and the more sort of spare, old-fashioned instruments without falling into goofy-hood.

X. *SERENITY'S* FUTURE AND JOSS'S COMMANDMENTS

Russell: Now, let's suppose that *Serenity* finds its audience and there's a chance to make another film or, God forbid, return to television. Would it be a prequel, as I heard Chris Buchanan hint at one of the fan screenings, or would it continue the story from where we left off?

Whedon: I would tend to continue from where I left off. That doesn't mean. . . . I think what Chris Buchanan was probably saying was that, you know, we would get everybody—and I obviously don't want to get all spoiler-y—

Russell: Right. I know.

Whedon: But things that seemed irrevocable, uh, well, *are*—but the movie itself already has a bit of a flashback structure, and the show had it, as well. And I think there's ways to weave in important character pieces without ruining the momentum of a sequel that would, in fact, pick up from where this left off.

I'm not a prequel buff. I don't want to see "Mal and Zoe: The Early Years" with William Katt and Tom Berenger. I mean, I do. But I'm more interested in the consequences of what has come. Because the audience has experienced it. And for me, the audience experience is the other experience—if the people in the movie aren't going through what the audience is going through, then I'm doing something wrong. And the audience—assuming you have a sequel—has seen the first one. So they've lived through it. And if the characters haven't, there's a disassociation that I don't think you can ever buy back.

Russell: Absolutely. Now, I'm sure you've seen that shirt that says "Joss Whedon Is My Master Now" in a *Star Wars* font. So let's say you *are* their master. What are your marching orders?
Whedon: I'm thinking that I'd like them to sit . . . and possibly roll over. This shirt's just hilarious. My marching orders do not exist. If I start pretending that I am in charge of anybody, then madness will surely follow—or, perhaps I should say, make itself more visible.

I would love to say, "Everybody run and tell everybody about the movie!"— but I think they get that I want them to do that. That's already done. And I don't want to say it ad nauseam, because I don't think I am actually anybody's "master." I am the fan that gets to have the most fun. I get to walk the set every day. I totally get to be there when the story's broken. I get to do all of the fun bits. Every day is fan day for me. That's who I am. I'm the fan that got the closest. And I don't think about a master relationship.

Russell: Well, and the danger with genre creators, particularly because they tend to develop very rabid fans, is that you get so into managing your fiefdom—and I'm *certainly* not talking about John Byrne at all—that you lose touch with whatever made what you were working on special to begin with.
Whedon: Yeah. I mean, it's the finest line you ever have to walk—because you spend your entire artistic life trying to get to a place where you have absolute control over your work and can say exactly what you're trying to say the way you want to say it. And in order to do that, you have to get through so much oppression and nonsense and pain. But once you do it, you're *instantly* in danger of becoming hermetically sealed and cut off from anyone around you. And so you have to walk this incredibly fine line where you get as much control as you possibly can and then always know that while you have it, you have to be in the world, listening to the people around you and learning from the experiences you're having—and not just sort of swimming around in your power.

And it's hard. I mean, you see a lot of great artists who finally realize their dream and. . . . You know, I think it's no coincidence that very often, when a person makes their most personal film—you know, the one they got in movies to make—it's their worst. It's like you have to serve a master of your own—and that's the audience.

And the way I work is through connection with the audience. The way I work is through the audience going, "That's me! I'm doing that! I feel that!" And so if I lose that, then I'm useless.

And I think at some point I may become useless, anyway: The things I have to say will no longer be things that people need to hear—either because I've accomplished what I set out to accomplish and created a new genre paradigm with characters—where people go, "Okay—now we accept the strong women, and the morals click, and you're just sort of doing this over and over again." I might become the old guy. But I hope that if I do, I become the old guy who . . . realizes it. [laughs]

Russell: Well, you have a couple of different media you can retreat into if that happens. I mean, you may be the first director to have the latest issue of his comic book come out the same week as his feature-film debut.
Whedon: It's pretty cool. It's pretty cool. I ain't lyin'.

XI. "EXCLUSION BOTHERS ME"

Russell: You did something very gutsy with *Serenity*—you actually tried to make, without apology, a movie that will satisfy fans and newbies. Most film-makers in your situation will either dilute their film shamelessly or proudly (and sort of suicidally) declare that they don't care about pleasing anyone but their core audience.
Whedon: Well, if I didn't care about pleasing anyone but their core audience. . . . First of all, Universal would have run like bunnies. [laughs] And wisely.

I mean, the trick, the difficulty of the thing, was pleasing and honoring the fans. That was very important to me. But at the end of the day, if I'm not making a movie for everybody, then I don't get it. I don't like clubs with exclusive rooms, okay? They bother me. Exclusion bothers me on a very, very primal level. And if I'm making a movie that deliberately isn't talking to *anybody* who walks into it, then "I've lost the mission, bro," as we used to say.

So inevitably, what I'm trying to do is please and excite and delight people, and *possibly* make them think—but not so much that their heads hurt. I slip in something that makes them go, "Because I understand this experience, and I enjoyed it, and I identified with it, here are the things I'm trying to say or I'm interested in. Something more than a ride happened here. I felt like I went through something." That's really important. But it's gotta be for everybody, or it really just. . . .

It's like jazz. Jazz is really fun when it's live. But I will never listen to jazz on my iPod or anything. Because jazz is really for musicians. I'm enough of a wannabe that I can go to a jazz club and listen to it and have a great time—but it's music about music. It was the thing that I hated about the eighties—when everything became movies about movies. In the seventies and eighties, movies were using, as their point of reference, movies. It's one of the reasons that I was so in love with Peter Weir back in the day, because his movies evoked something very natural—they could evoke just this *overwhelming* sense of being lost inside of nature and water and wheat and whatever that he seemed to have a command of that nobody else had. And he was using film to do it. And everybody else—even Scorsese, whom I worship—seemed to be using film to talk about film. And that led to things like *New York, New York*, which is one of my favorite movies—but it also led to a lot of self-referential bullshit, and a lot of loss of reality and humanity.

Even *Star Wars*—the other day, I was talking about this—really was the first movie that I can think of where it was based entirely on existing movie structures. It was one step removed. It was a story about stories. And obviously, they *all* are, to an extent. But I feel like, to me, that's kind of distancing; that's not what I want to be doing. What I want to be doing is just using the medium to communicate.

Russell: Well, you see that happening all the time in writing now. Tom Wolfe has gone off on the fact that he thinks people should leave their Graduate Writing Programs and do some reporting when they write their novels.
Whedon: That makes sense. It's tough. And it's tough for me, too, because I'm known as Mr. Pop Culture Reference; at the same time, that's the last person I want to be. It's one reason that I created *Firefly*—so I no longer would be able to make any.

Russell: [laughs] Right. You have to invent Fruity Oaty Bars.
Whedon: Exactly. Which is probably the closest thing I have to a contemporary concept in the movie. And everybody does it. Shakespeare did it; there's plenty of references we're not getting. But the other stuff seems to outweigh that in his work, I've noticed. [laughs]

XII. THE COMIC BOOK AND THE RELAXED STUDIO

Russell: Now, you've said you had at least a hundred stories to tell with these characters. And I know you've said the film compressed two or three years of a *Firefly* story arc. But what are a couple of the cool side stories we never got to see?
Whedon: I'm not gonna tell you! Because God willin' and the creek don't rise, I might get a chance to tell some of them. . . . I have plenty of ideas as to which ones they might be. Some of them will never be told, because it's too painful that I could never tell them, because they really belonged to the series. Some

of them may find themselves being told in a sequel. So mum's the word from me. You'll have to take my word for it.

Russell: Well, the *Serenity* comic resurrected what I presume was an idea for the TV series—where you brought back Agent Dobson from the pilot episode, and he's got one eye and he's psychotic.
Whedon: Yeah. I would have done that on the series. I love Carlos [Jacott, who played Dobson in the TV episode].

Russell: He's always got this great look of wounded dignity to him.
Whedon: He's one of the guys I can always count on—and just about the funniest man on the planet.

Russell: Now, that comic has been a surprise blockbuster.
Whedon: It's done well.

Russell: I know it's on its third order at my local comic-book shop.
Whedon: I felt like it was kind of an event, and I worked really hard on the story, we got really good people working on it, and we got all the best artists in the business to do all these covers. I wanted it to be more than a comic—I wanted it to be a collector's item. But then people were really happy about the story and the contents as well.

Dark Horse told me they underestimated the first printing—but now, here we are with a third? That's pretty sweet. If you think of the number of fans of the DVD, comic-book numbers are smaller. They work on a different scale. So I don't think it's totally shocking that we managed to make a splash—it's very gratifying—but at the end of the day, comic books are a smaller pond. So we have become, if not a whale, then a shark.

Russell: When Chris Buchanan was here for a *Serenity* preview screening, he seemed pretty gee-whiz about the whole production experience. In fact, he told a story about your stage being right next to the executive offices, and executives just walking by and saying, "Hey! Let us know if you need anything!"
Whedon: Yeah.

Russell: Did you ever feel like you were getting away with murder?
Whedon: No. It felt like we were getting away with a movie—which, in this town. . . .

You know, I've murdered lots of people, and really? Nobody cares. But trying to actually make a movie? People really get upset, and they want to get involved, and they want to mess it up. And not only did [Universal] *not* mess it up, but they were incredibly helpful. Like, when we were in the testing process, they had level heads, they had good ideas, they understood where the audience was not getting what we needed. And yes—when we were shooting, they were like, "We love your dailies. You're making your days." They literally came by and said, "We're just resting on our way to another movie." And I think they stopped by twice.

As a youth, what I wanted to do with my life was make summer movies for a studio. In this case, I'm *near* my goal—I'm making early-fall movies for a studio. I want to make movies that please people, that are exciting, that are meaningful and visceral, and that studios can be proud of. I didn't want to make highbrow think pieces. So all I've ever asked is that [the studios] let me do for them what I wanted—what I think will be best for them.

So many times, I've run up against people who are like, "Well, we've got another agenda." And I'm like, "My agenda will make you *richer*! I want to reach more people with this thing that will be better!" And I don't mean to sound like I'm all that, but I've dealt with some pretty amazingly stupid situations. And so for a studio to just go, "Yeah, we believe in your story, and you're doing it for the budget; godspeed!"—shouldn't be an amazing experience. But it sure was.

Interview with Joss Whedon

DANIEL ROBERT EPSTEIN/2005

From *Suicide Girls*, September 30, 2005.

Genre fans, rejoice! Joss Whedon has finally directed for the big screen and he's bringing some of his TV pals along with him. His television series *Firefly* was cancelled before its time by the Fox network and now the company that owns NBC, Universal Studios, is continuing the adventures of Captain Mal Reynolds and his band of outlaws in the movie, *Serenity*. Whedon has all the elements that made his television works great, such as hot, ass-kicking females, humor with a sly wink, and well thought-out scripts, but now it's backed by a $40 million budget. . . .

Epstein: Before this all got started, someone at Universal sat down and figured out that if *Serenity* makes this certain amount of money and they sell this many DVDs according to how the *Firefly* DVDs sold, they should give you a certain budget. Are you privy to that kind of information?
Whedon: I'm privy to the essentials. Ultimately how good the DVDs sold certainly helped. But nobody ever said to me "Ok we need a number on the DVDs before we greenlight the movie." I was already into the script, I was giving it to them, the timing was fortuitous, and if nobody had bought the DVDs, they might well have gone, "Well gee I don't know." At the same time, everybody knew that nobody saw the show so we didn't really know what a big fanbase there was.

I don't think Universal gets enough credit. People assume they decided to do it after the DVD sales. But they'd been in it for almost a year before that. Based on the shows, the cast, and the world, they said "Yeah there's a movie in there."

Epstein: One can't be as successful as you have been without being able to navigate through the business side of things. How much does that impact what you are doing?

Whedon: We knew that this movie was going to be made for a certain budget, and we had a pretty good idea what that budget was going to be. It was not going to include giant star salaries, but it was not going to be a tentpole movie budget. Now I'll write something where the universe explodes and turns into a butterfly, but at the end of the day I'll pick my battles. In the case of *Serenity*, I had to literally pick my battles because I could only afford to film one or two of them and tailor it to whatever I can get. I like the parameters. If it's $100 million, $50 million, $2 million, or if it's $100,000 I'm telling you the same basic story. I'm talking about people and it's just how grand can I make it. So we came to a budget based on the script that was smaller by Universal standards but bigger by mine. Then it was all about being extremely responsible with that money, to make sure it showed up on the screen and making sure I didn't spend anything I didn't have. Every season of every show that I did, and that's twelve and a half seasons, came in under budget.

Epstein: Wow.

Whedon: And sometimes those were some expensive-looking shows. I believe in being responsible with other people's money. When you do that, it gives the studio an enormous amount of confidence and it gives you a little leeway in case the unexpected happens, which it always does. So yeah, I think about money, but I think about it like a producer and not like an executive.

Epstein: In *Serenity*, watching the outerspace battle scenes and even watching the hand to hand combat scenes, I felt it all had kind of an anti–*Star Wars* feel to it. I don't mean an anti–*Star Wars* feel in a negative way, but it just didn't look like World War II dogfighting, and you had a lot of interesting angles in the hand-to-hand combat fight scenes. Was that conscious?

Whedon: It was basically the same directive that I had for the entire movie. Which was make it kinetic, make it lived in, make it gritty, and unkempt and real. That's what I thought was missing from sci-fi. In movies and TV everything had gotten so CGI, distant, purposeful, and grand. I felt that life in space isn't going to be that much different than life here. So the action and the rest of the scenes are all done deliberately to be more haphazard. Not studied in a *Star Wars*, isn't this beautiful and perfect, and not studied in a *Matrix*, here comes the slow mo jump over the head way.

Epstein: How much did working with [frequent Clint Eastwood cinematographer] Jack Green and his crew help you up your game?

Whedon: Jack doubled my game. Jack's nuts. He is not only just wildly talented, gives you a very lived-in feel, he lights things very organically but he is also the fastest guy in the west. He doesn't need thirteen lights to show how it's going to look. He can take two lights and know what the film will see them as.

He moves faster than a lot of TV guys that I've worked with. That means we get to shoot and shoot and shoot. I get to work on performance and I'm putting everything we have up on screen because Jack makes it happen so fast.

Epstein: That's pretty amazing. From reading *American Cinematographer* I knew he was fast but I didn't think he was that fast.
Whedon: Yeah, I didn't either. But we did thirty-three setups in one day and the average in TV is probably twenty-five. One of the actors said, "Explain how this is different from TV please."

Epstein: In the past when you were a working screenwriter, some of your scripts were ripped apart in some of the most horrible ways imaginable. Even though you've directed plenty of television, you've now directed a feature film. Did it make you make you understand why those directors and producers might have been so harsh on your screenplays?
Whedon: After *Alien Resurrection* I did put my foot down and literally said, "The next person who ruins one of my scripts is going to be me." Then you get into it as a director and you realize, "Oh I actually missed something that I wrote." I missed it even though I wrote it, like this stage direction or this nuance or I didn't bring enough energy in this scene and you want to club yourself so you can only imagine what it's like for people who aren't you.

Epstein: You, more than anyone, understand about having a rabid fanbase. I think the example I'm going for here is like when John Travolta will go on Oprah and the entire audience will freak out and go nuts. But then no one will go see the movie he's promoting. Does that make you realize that even a rabid fanbase can be fickle?
Whedon: I think ultimately the difference is that what my fanbase is responding to is the work itself. John Travolta fans are responding to his persona and his fame but not necessarily the character that he's playing. When he lands a good project, that's great, but they're rabid for a different reason. For me they're responding to the fiction. It has nothing to do with me. People don't yell when they see me. I'm not sexy. I mean I'm wicked sexy, but only if you're well, me. It doesn't mean they'll all rush out to see the movie or that they'll all love the movie because they love my other work. It does mean that when my fanbase gets rabid it's not about, "Oh my God I saw him walk down the street." It's about, "There's a story that I love hearing and seeing."

Epstein: Were the big changes that happen in the movie *Serenity* there when you first came up with the concept?
Whedon: Some of the plot devices are basically boiled down from where the series was heading. Then obviously there are some changes and there's a toll

on the characters that is tougher, bigger, harder, grittier and more final than it would be for a series, because when you're writing a movie, there is no second movie. There can be sometimes, but if you start writing for them you water yourself down. You have to assume that this is the only statement you're ever going to make with these characters.

Not everything that came from the series is wrapped up in the movie. But the major parts that the series was headed for are dealt with. I had to make the movie absolutely self-contained so that you didn't need to see the series. But this is what I wanted to say with it, just wider.

Epstein: With the makeup effects, how was it working with KNB on the movie as opposed to Almost Human on the series?
Whedon: Oh we never really established what the Reavers looked like exactly. KNB were great and Almost Human did some amazing stuff for me. The truth is, there was a snafu about that whole hiring thing so Almost Human never really got a chance to present. But KNB came in, did really solid stuff and gave us some fine-looking Reavers.

Epstein: When it comes down to actually coming up with what the Reavers actually looked like, did you describe it to an artist or can you draw?
Whedon: I draw minimally but I describe maximally. I leave some space for the artists to see what they come up with. One of the artists that I had working was [Swamp Thing co-creator] Bernie Wrightson. I saw the drawings and I was like, "Jesus, this guy sure likes Bernie Wrightson a lot." They said "Yeah, that's because he is Bernie Wrightson." I'm like, "No way you got him!" But they did and he did some concept drawings for Reavers, which was really cool.

Epstein: Did you use any other comic book creators?
Whedon: I got some comic book guys, Leinil Yu and Josh Middleton to do some ship and wardrobe designs but not for the Reavers.

Epstein: What kind of discussions did you have with Summer Glau about her character of River, because she is the one that is the most different from the series?
Whedon: River is the one character who never really got to blossom on the series. We were only beginning to figure out who she was so her arc is really central to the movie. Everybody else had kind of presented who they were so we dealt with what we knew already and streamlined certain things. But we did have all of that work done for us already, which made directing a lot easier.

Epstein: How was choreographing the fights for Summer different from the fights you had done in the past?

Whedon: The difference is that Summer did it all herself. With the exception of a couple of wire gags, she did every single thing herself so it made shooting the fights actually fun for the first time in my life. It was like watching a dance so we just kept the camera on her, made sure the hits registered and that was it. Having a lot of prep time and having a girl that could do that much brought it to a new level.

Epstein: I saw that a lot of actors in *Firefly* you had worked with before on your previous series, except Adam Baldwin. I'm a fan of his so what made you think of Adam Baldwin for the role of Jayne Cobb?
Whedon: He auditioned for it. That's what Adam Baldwin does; he's a working actor. He auditioned, got the part, and made it unforgettable.

Epstein: In the writing stage for *Serenity*, did you pass the script along to people that you'd worked with on the series like Tim Minear and Ben Edlund for notes?
Whedon: Yeah absolutely. I showed it to Tim and some of the other writers that I'm close with to see what they got out of it. They're always really helpful.

Epstein: How much pressure did you feel while doing this?
Whedon: It wasn't really pressure. The studio was extremely supportive. Their fortunes don't rest upon the success of the film, but they're very invested in it, so that's a good feeling. You want your first film to be, let's say, not sucky, so that pressure will always be there. But ultimately it was about as low-pressure a gig as I could hope to get for my first outing.

Epstein: Is there going to be an extended cut of *Serenity* on the DVD?
Whedon: No; we'll see some deleted scenes but I believe the cut I delivered is the best cut there is. I think everything that I took out of the movie, even stuff that I liked, should have come out.

Epstein: What are some of the deleted scenes?
Whedon: There was a scene of setting up Inara [played by Morena Baccarin] in her world that ultimately slowed down the momentum. What you really needed to know about Inara was that she's the girl Mal [played by Nathan Fillion] left behind. You know what that dynamic is. They love each other but they can't get along. I had a long scene of her talking about her life and stuff that would have worked in a series but in a movie it was bogging things down. You've got momentum to service.

Epstein: I read you were even on the radio in Australia promoting *Serenity*. Has it been bigger than anything you did with like *Buffy* for instance?

Whedon: It's bigger because it's smaller. Here's a movie that doesn't have a title that explains itself simply. It doesn't have big stars so you got to do more legwork. You want to get people to give it a shot because I think if they go to the theaters, they're going to have a great time, but if they don't go into theaters, I'll never know.

Epstein: What would you be happy with for the opening weekend?
Whedon: I can't give you a number exactly. I'm not much of a numbers guy. I would be happy if the people at Universal are happy. Expectations for the opening weekend are not huge. This is a movie that we think depends on word of mouth. What would make me happy would be a small drop-off for the second weekend, the idea that it didn't just burst and then disappear the way most of the bigger movies do.

Epstein: After promoting the movie until the wee hours of Thursday night, what are you going to be doing on Friday?
Whedon: I'm going to go see it with my wife and some of her family. We're going to see it and there might be popcorn. I'm not sure.

Epstein: You've done comic books set in the *Buffy*verse but not with *Buffy*. Do you see doing anything like that with *Serenity*?
Whedon: We did do a three-issue sort of bridge from the TV show to the movie from Dark Horse in comics and that was really fun. It was well received so I think we'll definitely go back there. We're waiting to see the fate of the movie.

Epstein: I read about this new movie you want to do called *Goner*.
Whedon: It's called *Goners*. They got it wrong.

Epstein: What can you tell me about it?
Whedon: Unfortunately, not much more than you read except that there's an "s" on the end. It is a fantasy thriller, it is pretty dark, and it's all me. So people will pretty much know what that means if they look at my body of work. But it's a new universe set in the present day with a new concept for me and a new bunch of characters. It's been a long time since I got to do that, so that's really fun.

Epstein: With the *Wonder Woman* movie, do you see dropping the granny panties?
Whedon: Yeah, don't worry about that. We'll definitely have a nicer look than that. It will be the Wonder Woman silhouette, but the star spangled adult diapers are gone.

Epstein: Since you're working for Joel Silver, is he going to try and force some *Matrix* special effects on you?

Whedon: *Wonder Woman* is going to have major special effects because she's Wonder Woman. Joel and I are very much on the same page about how big this movie is and what kind of movie it is. I'm not worried about any conflict there. But with Joel, he wakes up and there's conflict, but it's the good kind, the kind that makes good movies.

Epstein: You have to be a good yeller when it comes to dealing with Joel.

Whedon: I don't have to. I don't yell, I do the other thing. I lower my voice. It's very scary. You don't want to be there when I lower my voice.

Epstein: Do you have a favorite *Wonder Woman* era from the comics?

Whedon: I don't really have a favorite. [George] Perez did some great work and John Byrne did some cool stuff. I think Greg Rucka is doing some cool stuff now. But ultimately I don't have one that I can pinpoint as canon. That's kind of why I like the project.

Epstein: Do you have any desire to come back to TV?

Whedon: I love TV. I'm not sure it loves me so much lately, but I love that format. I want to come back, but I've got some movies in me first.

Epstein: Why don't you think it loves you lately?

Whedon: Well, when you have both your shows canceled, you go "Maybe they're kicking me out."

Epstein: How many fantasy stories do you have in you?

Whedon: Oh my God, it just doesn't stop. I have so many ideas that it's scary. If I had none it would be scary. But right now it's just a question of which ones I get to tell.

Epstein: Last time we spoke I quizzed you about what's going on with Ben Edlund, so what's going on with Ben Edlund right now?

Whedon: I saw him last night, but I didn't get the chance to talk to him. So I don't know, but he looks good.

Epstein: For your next TV show, would you bring as many of your writers back as you could?

Whedon: Oh yeah. I found some amazing talents when I was working and I miss them a lot. You can make TV and still go home at night when you got guys like that in your stable.

Epstein: Was bringing back Colossus in your run on *Astonishing X-Men* something you wanted to do? Or they were like ready to bring him back because he might be in the next movie?

Whedon: Marvel asked "Can you bring him back?" I was like, "Hell yeah" because he's cool and I thought I had a way to do it that'll be sweet.

Epstein: He's one of the few popular *X-Men* characters that's never gotten his own series or miniseries. I believe he had a storyline in *Marvel Comics Presents* but that's it. Would you want to do something like that with him?

Whedon: If I can just get the damn comic out once a month I think I'm a hero. So I haven't really given a lot of thought to expanding any one character.

Epstein: What's the process between you and John Cassaday?

Whedon: Cassaday is Jack Green and Nathan Fillion rolled into one. I basically have to do very little with him. I give less direction to him than anyone I've worked with because he just knows how it should look.

Epstein: I got to speak to Grant Morrison not too long ago. Even though Cassaday draws them beautifully, he thinks costumes are dumb. But Marvel told him they wanted the costumes back because of marketing. What's your opinion on costumes?

Whedon: I don't think they looked too silly. I think they looked good and Kitty's looked fabulous. John draws clothes, which separates him from a lot of comic book artists, and he draws them well. Again, costumes was another thing they asked for. I said "As long as John has a hand in designing them, absolutely." I like costumes. I like the way they look in Grant's run too because ultimately those were costumes too, they were just a different strike.

Epstein: Was it weird for you to have to like turn back a bit what a previous writer did, especially one with the stature of Grant Morrison?

Whedon: Ultimately you're not going to do what the last guy did. Never at Marvel did they say "Please make everything that Grant Morrison did not have happened." I was taking over the book from him because I loved his book and I respected it, but I was going to go my own way. That's how it works. But I wasn't out to destroy the Grant era and my run wasn't a reaction against his. His world had gotten bigger and more baroque as they do in a long run. I just wanted to pare it down to a few central people and just vent my feelings about them.

Epstein: During my visit to the set of *Superman Returns* I asked Bryan Singer this same question. Is there a difference between bringing DC and Marvel characters to the big screen?

Whedon: There really isn't a difference ultimately to me because if you find the humanity in the character, you succeed. If you don't, you don't.

Epstein: What's your impression of *SuicideGirls*?
Whedon: My impression is sort of double-edged. At first I was like, well it seems to be a porny. But it's a kind of a porny that celebrates individuality so I sort of like that.

Epstein: Have you ever seen *Buffy* or *Serenity* tattoos on somebody?
Whedon: I have. In fact, I saw a *Serenity* tattoo last night at the premiere and I saw a couple *Buffy* tats.

Epstein: Do they freak you out?
Whedon: No man. If someone's going to put something on them forever, why shouldn't it be something of mine?

Epstein: Do you have any tattoos?
Whedon: I am tat free. I am as God made me, including the baby fat.

Joss Whedon—About *Buffy*, *Alien*, and *Firefly*: The Shebytches.com Interview

S. F. SAID/2006

From Shebytches.com, May 24, 2006. Reprinted by permission.

Credit where it's due. There would be no Joss Whedon interview here without Pixie, the amazing Shebytches columnist. In fact, I would know nothing about Whedon at all if she hadn't made me watch *Buffy the Vampire Slayer*. I'd been aware that the show existed, and that a lot of women I knew loved it, but I'd never really given it a chance. Until I actually watched some—and then I couldn't get enough.

Same with *Firefly*, Whedon's science-fiction western series, and now with *Serenity*, the brilliant feature film based on that series, which is about to take the world by storm. I saw it at the Edinburgh Film Festival in August, and then saw it a second time, because I couldn't get enough of it either. Like *Buffy*, it delivers non-stop action, laughs, and thrills—but it's also got characters who are complex, substantial, believable. The women and the men alike. And how rare is that?

I think that's central to why I am now consumed by the Whedonverse. There's a sophistication to his take on gender that I find incredibly refreshing. I'd discussed this a lot with Pixie, and we both wanted to know more about where it came from. So when I sat down to interview Whedon, that was where I wanted to start. And it turns out he's got lots to say about his love for she-bytches . . .

Said: Is it surprising to you that so many women love your stuff?
Whedon: No. Everybody knows there is a little girl inside of Joss. I literally grew up wishing that I were a woman. That doesn't necessarily give me any great insight into women—in fact, many women I know have gone, "You're an idiot for wishing that!" But I've always felt a great affinity for women on various levels. In particular, I think, a level of sensibility, in that I was raised by a very strong, smart, delightful, extraordinary woman.

Said: Was she a single mum?

Whedon: No. My father and my step-mother, they lived in Los Angeles; I lived with my mother and my step-father in New York. And my step-father and my father are both very dear to me, but my mother was—it was a matriarchal household, and she was a very powerful person. She was a teacher, and affected a lot of her students enormously. And I had older brothers who were kind of merciless—charming, but merciless—and I was very afraid of my father, who is an incredibly dear man, but was not necessarily great with kids. And I was also very tiny, and was very often mistaken for a girl.

Said: I was too! People always thought I was a girl when I was a kid!

Whedon: Well, I had lovely long red hair—less and less of which I have every day—and delicate features. I was quite cute! Something went horribly wrong somewhere, but that's OK. But there was a sense of oppression, of not being taken seriously, of physical fear; there were certain things that I had in common—I was very close to my step-sister as well, she was the best friend I had in my family growing up. Plus, I'm super-gay, something my wife has come to accept and even enjoy. It's just something that has always been a part of me. And so I have, I think, a kind of a feminine sensibility.

Again, I would not take bragging rights to understanding the female experience, and there were often times in *Buffy* when I would say to [writer/producer] Marti Noxon, "OK, what did you go through? What would this be like?" I'm pretty good at getting into the heads of people that I'm not, I think that's probably the one talent I really have, but there'd be times when I'd be, "OK, this is foreign territory to me, I am a fella." So anyway, short answer: no, it doesn't surprise me. It's more than anything else who I'm writing for—or as; I'm writing in drag.

Said: I'm interested in ideas of masculinity and femininity in your stuff. Partly because I don't recognize myself in notions of manhood that are current in our society; and I don't particularly recognize myself in notions of womanhood, either.

Whedon: Yes, I'm also a hideous hermaphrodite like yourself. Oh, the shame! No—nothing against hermaphrodites. But it is difficult, and these are roles that are constantly redefining themselves and re-entrenching. And you do come to a realization, as you get older, that men and women actually do have not just cultural but biological differences, and that some of those clichés about how different they are, are actually true. And while I spend my entire career trying to subvert our notions of masculinity and femininity, I also have to have some grounding in the fact that some of them are based in reality—but some of them are also based in sociology, and those are the ones that have to be done away with, because they are nonsense. There is so much misogyny that is just unspoken or even unknown, among the most civilized.

Even on the drive up here, the driver was telling us about the history of the place, and he says, "In this square, this is where people were hanged, and the women were burned at the stake—they would burn a woman at the stake in the sixteenth century just for saying no to a man—wouldn't it be great if we could do that today?" And instead of just thinking it, I said, "Actually, no, it wouldn't, and it's a little bit creepy that you just said that."

So I think a great deal of work has to be done until there is enough equality that we can actually start to define our roles as either men or women, without the baggage of either oppression or misogyny, confusion or enforced masculinity. Gender, like sexuality, is kind of a spectrum; I think all of sexuality is a spectrum, and to say that there's the one thing and the other is to oversimplify. I do not think we will in our lifetimes get to a place where we can say, "OK, we've weeded out cultural prejudices, now let's talk biology, what's male and what's female, where do they meet and how do we get them together?"

Said: Was it part of the idea with *Buffy* to invert that? I read somewhere that you were sick of seeing the blonde girl getting killed in horror movies—
Whedon: It was very specific, I was tired of seeing that. I want the disenfranchised to have a voice. And people choose particular areas of that; for me it's been women. I had a girlfriend in college, and she was very smart, and I remember when Orson Welles died and I was terribly sad, and terribly drunk, and I said, "This man had so much to say and society conspired to keep him from saying it for so long." And she said, "Yeah, it's interesting that you feel that way about him—I feel that about the entire history of my entire gender!" And I was just like, "Well put." And *Buffy* was very much an attempt to create an icon—to do it subtly, I didn't expect people to catch wind of what I was doing, I expected her to become an underground icon—but in fact she lived above ground, and could eat roots and berries . . .

Said: So you were trying to create an icon?
Whedon: Yes. It was supposed to be something that, you know, little girls would play with Barbie dolls that had Kung-Fu grip. It was supposed to subvert our notions of what a hero is, very specifically. At the same time, it was supposed to do it in a fun disarming fashion. As I've said before, I wasn't trying to make Buffy the Lesbian Separatist, because I didn't think anyone would show up.

Said: How about the way you use metaphor? *Firefly* doesn't have monsters and demons, but even when you did in *Buffy*, they always seemed like ways of talking about emotional realities.

Whedon: When I was writing *Alien: Resurrection*, I began to understand, on a level that I hadn't before, what I was trying to do. Before it was even metaphor, it was simply, "What experience are these people going through that people can relate to? What is the thing that's going to make people say, 'I am Ripley,' not just, 'There's Ripley'?" And I was particularly dealing with this because she was coming back from the dead, and people had to accept that. So I realized, "I have to make it difficult for Ripley to have come back from the dead, because it's going to be difficult for the audience to accept it—but if it's difficult for her to accept it too, they will identify with her, that will be the in." And then that got me to a bigger place of, "Well, what is she going through? What does she feel about herself? Does she really feel human? She's partially alien, what's going on with that? And she's dealing with this robot . . ."

And the moment in the movie—and I loathe the movie, and have said so publicly many times, often when I shouldn't—but I look at it now, and I see the germ of everything I've tried to do in my career. It's the moment when Winona Ryder, who is such a porcelain beauty, looks at herself and says, "Look at me, I'm disgusting." And that's when I said, "OK, now I understand what I'm doing with my writing."

Buffy came right after that. They said, "Do you want to do a show?" And I thought, "High school as a horror movie." And it really was. And so the metaphor that I had begun to strike at in *Alien: Resurrection* became the central concept behind *Buffy*, and that's how I sold it, and that's what they bought, and they got it, and they let me do it—and after that, everything was about it.

And then we came to *Firefly*, and *Serenity*, where I took away the metaphorical aspect—but science-fiction always opens you up to every element of history that you want, because the future is just the past in a blender. And so rather than a straight-on metaphor, it was more an idea of, "I can take anything from the human experience that I've read about or felt or seen—like, what is it like after a war? And it doesn't matter which war or which country—what is it like for the people who lost?"

It's always about people. The idea behind the show was to take nine people and say, "Nine people look out into the blackness of space and see nine different things." That is the show. With the movie, obviously, you can't just say something that vague; I had to make the movie more specific. It's about freedom and about how much you can take, and how much you can control people, even for their own good, before you lose them.

Said: What can you tell us about *Wonder Woman*, the film you're making next?

Whedon: I've just started writing it, so there's not much I can say. It was a bit of a surprise to me, because I've never been a fan of the show or the comic book, but the character, she's the kind of character who doesn't take no for an answer—not even from me.

Said: She's another young female superhero—like Buffy; like River Tam in *Serenity.*
Whedon: Exactly—she's sort of the icon that existed before I came around, so it's an honor to be working with her.

The Onion A.V. Club Interview with Joss Whedon (2)

TASHA ROBINSON/2007

Joss Whedon has had a long and storied history in Hollywood as a screen-writer, on television as the writer-creator of *Buffy the Vampire Slayer*, *Angel*, and *Firefly*, and back in Hollywood as the writer-director of *Serenity*. As an enthusiastic, unabashed fan of all things smart and geeky, it was inevitable that he'd find his way into comics, where (among other things) he's written the far-future *Buffy* spin-off *Fray*, a well-received run on *Astonishing X-Men*, and the *Firefly* miniseries *Serenity: Those Left Behind*. Currently, he's wrapping up his *X-Men* run, taking over writing duties for Brian K. Vaughan on *Runaways*, and scripting future issues of *Buffy the Vampire Slayer: Season Eight*, the official comics continuation of his beloved first show.

Recently, Whedon took the spotlight at the San Diego Comic-Con, where he announced that he's in negotiations to bring the Buffy spin-off *Ripper* to the BBC, showcased his online Dark Horse comic *Sugarshock*, and took five charity auction-winners to dinner, raising more than sixty thousand dollars for the worldwide women's-rights organization Equality Now. Just before heading to San Diego, Whedon spoke with *The A.V. Club* about his current and upcoming comics projects, his film project *Goners*, the status of *Serenity*, why spoilers are ruining our culture, and his much-publicized work on—and break from—the *Wonder Woman* film project.

Robinson: Do you intend for *Buffy: Season Eight* to be completely open-end-ed, or do you have a specific arc in mind?
Whedon: It has a specific arc and an ending. It will be open-ended in the sense that there could be a *Buffy: Season Nine*.

Robinson: In comics, or on television?
Whedon: In comics. There's not going to be a *Buffy* season nine on television. I don't think Sarah [Michelle Gellar] has the slightest interest in doing that,

and quite frankly, I don't think it's a good idea for me, either. I do have to prove at some point that I can do other things.

Robinson: Are there things you can do with the comic that you couldn't have done with the show, and vice-versa?

Whedon: Yeah, absolutely. The thing with the comics is that you have license to go down every alley your brain can think of. Willow's been on a mystical walkabout, you can actually show that. Instead of, "Well, she can talk about it in the magic shop for seven pages, because that's the money we got." You can pursue every thread, emotionally and visually, in a way that you just can't on TV. But on TV, you're on TV. There's actors, the people who created the characters with you, that everybody loves. Oh, and also, the paychecks don't make your family laugh.

The hard part about writing comics is creating juice. Let's say I'm trying to create a love interest for Buffy. People are like, "It's Angel!" "It's Spike!" Some people are saying it's Riley, possibly. Not many. I think that's above Andrew, actually, in the poll. But to create somebody in the comic who has anything like the juice of somebody who was on the show, that's an insane challenge. It's going to be really tough. That goes for the Big Bad, as well. A villain that people care about, who they've only seen as a drawing, is, again, a challenge.

Robinson: So is the temptation to stick to established characters?

Whedon: Well, as much as it serves you. We don't want to just do, "Oh my God, it's this guy! Oh my God, it's *this* guy! Hey, it's that guy on the left from twelve years ago, he's in it!" Eventually, you have to let go and move on, and let the comic-book world be the comic-book world. I think after time, people will come to accept some of the characters, if we paint them vividly enough.

Robinson: What's the status of the *Angel* season-six comic-book concept?

Whedon: Well, we're not calling it season six, because I don't want to people to confuse it with the *Buffy* comic. But it does take place after the end of the show. Brian Lynch has delivered a basic arc outline, and he's doing all the heavy lifting. We sat down and talked about where everybody was, and what kind of world it was, and what we were planning to do, and what we could never have done, and wanted to do. He's sort of taking it from there. I think the first issue is slated to come out later this year. Late, late, late, late this year.

Robinson: Did the show getting cancelled affect the plotline you had in mind?

Whedon: I never would have killed Wesley if we hadn't been cancelled. [Laughs.] I decided how I wanted to end the season before we were cancelled, and I wanted to end it exactly that way while it was still in question. Which was, we're going out in mid-battle, because if we come back, we have something to come back from. If we *don't* come back, then this is how I want it.

With *Buffy*, I needed closure, because she, poor girl, had earned it. *Buffy* is about growing up. *Angel* is really about already having grown up, dealing with what you've done, and redemption. Redemption is something you fight for every day, so I wanted him to go out fighting. People kept calling it a cliffhanger. I was like, "Are you mad, sir? Don't you see that that is the final statement?" And then they would say "Shut up."

It didn't affect, with the exception of the untimely death of young Wesley, where we were going with it. But we did have an idea. The miniseries is called *Angel: After the Fall.* It is much huger in scope, and Brian has brought a lot of new ideas to the table. It is oddly more like what we had planned for season six than *Buffy: Season Eight* is.

Robinson: Why did the TV series ending mandate killing off Wesley?
Whedon: Because it was *awesome.* The writers pitched it, with Illyria turning into Fred, and I was like, "Uh, okay, we have to do that, really, *now.*" You squeeze all the juice out that you can. That was one of my favorite moments that we shot. If you're going to go out, go out hard. If you just go, "Well, off to another mystery. Here we are, arm in arm," that ain't an ending.

Robinson: Do you regret making that decision, since you're planning to continue the series after all?
Whedon: Most people in my universe get more work after they're dead. Look at Harmony. If we had suddenly been given a reprieve, there would not have been a single episode without Wesley in it, dead or not. He'd have been given an eleventh-hour stay of execution. That has to do with my love of Wesley, and let's face it, my love of Alexis Denisof, who is, apart from being a dream to work with, staggeringly versatile.

Robinson: Did you ever feel that the ending was painting yourself into a corner if you did want to continue the series?
Whedon: No, had we had a season six, it would have picked up right where season five ended, because I knew what I planned to have happen right after that battle. If nobody ever found out what I had planned, then we were going out with the statement that life is a battle. And love, sidebar, is a battlefield. But had they given us an eleventh-hour reprieve, we absolutely would have picked up right there. *After the Fall* should give you a glimpse into what we were planning to do about that battle. But no, we didn't paint ourselves into a corner, we were right where we wanted to be. Except for the fact that we were cancelled.

Robinson: Is your *Wonder Woman* film adaptation irrevocably dead, or is there any possibility of going back?

Whedon: I loved what I was doing. I mean, it was really hard. It took me a long time to break the story structurally to my satisfaction. When I did that, it was in an outline, and not in a draft, and they didn't like it. So I never got to write a draft where I got to work out exactly what I wanted to do. In terms of the meaning, the feeling, the look, the emotion, the character, the relationship with Steve Trevor, all of that stuff, I never wavered for a second. I knew exactly what I wanted to do. It was really just a question of housing it. I would go back in a heartbeat if I believed that anybody believed in what I was doing. The lack of enthusiasm was overwhelming. It was almost staggering, and that was kind of from the beginning. I just don't think my take on Wonder Woman was ever to their liking.

I wasn't getting them to feel what they wanted to feel. They couldn't describe what that was to me. We're talking about a huge investment. To ask somebody to jump on that, what is going to be a few hundred million dollars these days, if they just don't have that feeling . . . I had that feeling. I got chills when I think of some of this stuff, but apparently I was the only one who was chilly. Everybody was very gracious about it. It was a blind date, and everybody thought we'd get married, but let's just leave it at the door.

Robinson: What would you do on a set with $100 million dollars, having never worked with a budget like that before?

Whedon: It's the exact same job. The money has never mattered. If you have $100 million, if you have $100,000, you're trying to hit someone in the gut with an emotional moment. If you can back that up with an awesome visual, that's really neat. If you can back that up with a visual that's not awesome, but at least gets it done, tells them what they need to know to hit them in the gut emotionally, that's neat too. If the characters can only talk about it in a room, then the emotional moment has to be really, really good, but it's still neat. That's never really worried me. I've always thought way too big, and then people have gone, "Great. Now you have to scale this way back." In this case, I didn't have to scale it way back, I just had to stop doing it.

Robinson: Can you say anything about the plot you had in mind for your version of the film?

Whedon: Well, I'll tell you one thing that sort of exemplifies my feelings. The idea was always that she's awesome, she's fabulous, she's strong, she's beautiful, she's well-intentioned, she thinks she's a great big hero, and it's Steve Trevor's job to go, "You don't understand human weakness, therefore you are not a hero, and you never will be until you're as helpless as we are. Fight through that, and then I'll be impressed. Until then, I'm just going to give you shit in a romantic-comedy kind of way."

There was talk about what city she was in and stuff, but by the end, she had never actually set foot in America. Wonder Woman isn't Spider-man or Batman. She doesn't have a town, she has a world. That was more interesting to me than a kind of contained, rote superhero franchise. I think ultimately the best way I can describe the kind of movie I was wanting to make—it was a fun adventure, not gritty, or insanely political, or anything like that. There was meat to the idea of, "Well, why aren't you guys better? What's up with that?" Her lack of understanding of how this world has come to this pass.

My favorite thing was the bracelets. I mean, the bracelets are cool, but how do I make that work? In the original comic book, they needed them because they fire guns on Paradise Island. I don't think I'm going there. So, I thought about it for a while, and I realized, "Oh, right, this is how this works." So in my version, she left Paradise Island with Steve, who was a world-relief guy bringing medical supplies to refugees, which is why he was so desperate to get off the island. She goes with him, and the moment she sets foot on land outside of Paradise Island, somebody shoots her in the chest. And it *hurts*. [Laughs.] She's just so appalled. And obviously, she heals within a few hours. She pulls the bullet out herself, and kind of looks at it like, "What the hell is this?" She heals, but she's appalled and humiliated, and the next time someone shoots at her, she puts her bracelet in the way because she's terrified of getting shot. It's just a reflexive thing. She has these bands that they all wear, just a piece of armor, and she puts it up. And then she gets good at it. By the end, it's kind of her thing, but it's because she got shot one time and didn't think that it was awesome. I think that is probably not the feeling the producers wanted to have. Though honestly, that could have been their favorite thing. I don't know, because when I asked Joel Silver, point blank, "Well, if they don't want what I'm doing, what do they want?" he said, "They don't know."

Robinson: In movies and comics, an awful lot of female characters still fall into eye-candy/ damsel-in-distress fantasy-object roles, even the supposedly strong heroine types. You've taken a strong stance toward a more empowering kind of feminism in your work—was that ever an issue?

Whedon: I have no idea. Obviously, nobody ever said "Don't be a feminist." And nobody ever said "Don't be political." The politics of the movie were all more or less moral, it wasn't like we picked somebody to root against, it's just more like everybody either steps up or they don't, and this is their opportunity to do that. I think that's part of how I got the gig. They wanted her to be strong. It wasn't like Buffy was a crone. It wasn't like anybody thought I wasn't going to make Wonder Woman extraordinarily beautiful. That's part of her thing, that she's so beautiful that men can hardly bear it. I'm all about that, and power just makes her sexier. I certainly wasn't turning my back on her hottie-ness, just because of my politics. I think that's a common misconception about feminism in general.

Robinson: Most of your experience working on films seems awful: development hell, and processes that take forever, and having your work second-guessed, dumbed down, or bowdlerized. Have you ever considered giving up on film?

Whedon: Yes. Yes. When I was a script doctor, I was wealthy and miserable. I never had less fun succeeding at a job in my life. Then I got to do TV, and for the first time in my life, people just let me do the thing. That was amazing. Then, when I made *Serenity*, they let me do the thing. They helped me, they guided me through it. It was my first movie, and the people at Universal were amazingly supportive at the same time as being instructive, but at the end of the day, I did my thing. Once you've done that, it's hard to go back to the other, to not being able to do your thing. To putting up with, "Gee, these guys had a bad weekend because of such and such," or "Now they're looking at this actress," whatever it is. And the appalling things that happened to *Firefly*. I could just live inside my rage. I did for a while. Ultimately, it ain't that tasty, and I've learned to sort of put it in a box. I've had more luck than any ten guys I know. I've been able to tell my story more than a few times, and that's the greatest gift. If I'm never given that gift again, I still will have had it, and I'm grateful for that. My gratitude has finally exceeded my rage by a good, long margin, and when I wake up in the morning with my work and my family, gratitude is the thing that guides me, not rage.

Robinson: Do people still try to get you to do script punch-ups?

Whedon: Every now and then. Now that I've actually directed *une filme du Joss Whedon*, it more tends to fall into the, "There's a script that needs work, and you might shoot it as well." I've looked at a couple of those, and I'm interested in that, because I'd like to do that. I actually enjoy the process of script-doctoring very much; it's just like being an executive producer, finding out what's wrong with a story and fixing it, finding out what makes it mean something. That's fun. But then if they don't shoot it, or they shoot it in a way that's counter to what you had hoped for, it becomes frustrating. The fact that I am now the director that might shoot the things that I might rewrite means that that's kind of a different animal. But you never know which project is actually going to go, and which projects they're talking about really fast so you think it's going to go. It's part of their job, but they had me so completely convinced that *Wonder Woman* was *so* going to happen instantly. Every time I'm convinced of that, I'm wrong. You'd think that I would learn, but here's the funny twist, the M. Night Shyamalan moment: I'm a moron. I'm a complete dweeb. I don't get it, I never get it. Every time, I think everybody's lovely, and it's all going to work out, and I've never been right. For some reason, I can't get that right, can't figure that out. I think I'm getting better. I think I'm mean now. You're going to see a whole meaner person, now.

Robinson: With that in mind, what can you say about *Goners*, the horror-fantasy film you're developing?

Whedon: Well, there may be some female empowerment in it at some point. [Laughs.] I *don't* know who put *that* there. It's the same brew that I tend to brew, which is a combination of horror, and heroes, and people crying, and female empowerment. It's been the thing that's made my career, but it's also the thing that's come the closest to killing it: Whenever I write anything, I want to stuff every genre in that I possibly can. And then people are like, "Well, we don't know how to market that, and if we don't know how to market it . . ." [Whispers.] "We're not going to make it." [Laughs.] Although Universal's been great, and they understand exactly what I want, what the movie's about. In eighteen months of working on *Wonder Woman*, nobody asked me what the movie was about, whereas at Universal, I've never had that problem. They really get it. Obviously, *Goners* is about human connection, and loneliness, and responsibility, and power, and the things that I inevitably end up writing about, because they're the only things that interest me. Besides sex, and there's not a lot of sex in it. I'll probably have to change that in my next rewrite.

Robinson: What's its current status?

Whedon: I'm rewriting it. Rather more often than I'd hoped. [Laughs.] It's pretty much where it was, which is bought by Universal, but not greenlit.

Robinson: Do you intend it as a stand-alone project, or a new franchise?

Whedon: Yes. Yes, it has the potential to be the f-word, franchise. That can sometimes kill you, because when people start seeing that, sometimes they stop seeing the movie. It killed me with *Serenity*, because everybody was left with a bad taste in their mouth. We kind of failed. The movie did not make scads at the box office; it barely broke even. But it made oodles of money on DVD; it's doing just fine. But everyone was like, "Wow, we didn't get to make the trilogy." There was never a trilogy! In this sense, this movie is very much a journey. It's not just a classic superhero movie—set up a premise, and here are some cool people, here are the rules, and let's go. It's very much this woman's journey, and it's a very painful, strange, hellish journey. I have to concentrate on that, not the fact that there may be dolls. But, unfortunately, once the word "franchise" comes up, people look at the structure of the script you've given them differently. That's just going to happen. The word "franchise" has almost killed my career. If people don't stop using it, I'm going to get very twitchy.

Robinson: So were all the claims that there were two more *Serenity* movies planned just false rumors?

Whedon: People were like, [French accent.] "Eet's a three-picture deal." I was doing a lot of press in Europe. I was like, "No, it's *a* picture deal." And then, you know, [French accent.] "How do you feel about ze French?" I was like, "Guys, nobody's gone to see the movie yet. We haven't finished making it. Stop calling it a franchise." Almost every question was about, "Are there plans for more?" I get that it came from a TV series, so it already sort of had a built-in fan base that made it feel like a franchise. I understand why I was plagued with the question, but it really did turn into a plague. The fans themselves went to the theatre, saw the movie, and were like, "Oh, I guess he isn't going to get to make any more, the theater wasn't that full." But the *movie*, we *made the movie*. Believe me, I will take my rage about the death of *Firefly* to the grave, but we still pulled off something kind of miraculous. It got buried by the franchise concept. That is not to say that if somebody said, "Hey, you want to do another one of those?" I wouldn't jump on it in a heartbeat, because I would. But it does sort of tend to overwhelm everything else.

Robinson: Does Fox still own the rights to *Firefly?*
Whedon: It's a situation that could not be untangled by me, but yes, they own the rights to *Firefly*, Universal has the rights to *Serenity*, and how that all works out is very strange to me.

Robinson: What do you think it would take to get another *Serenity* movie made?
Whedon: Profit. They're putting out the Collector's Edition DVD, because the DVD is selling so very well. That's something that maybe, some time from now, someone will look at the numbers and go, "Well, that was worth it. Let's do that again. Let's do it smaller, let's do it different." I'd do it on radio. As long as I could write dialogue for those actors, I'd be in a happy place.

Robinson: A while back, a group of fans started to try and organize a "fan fund" to get a second season of the show made. Do you think that model could ever work?
Whedon: You know, I've had the model described, and I believe there is a way in which it could work, but I don't think that the way entertainment is structured right now, that people are ready for it to work that way. I do think that the level of fan involvement in getting things put on will start to extend well beyond letter-writing campaigns. I've very intrigued by the concept of involving the fans at ground level. Saying, "This is what we want to do. Anyone want to see it?" Instead of saying that to a bunch of guys in a room, saying it to the world. I think that could be very fascinating.

Robinson: What's the latest on further *Serenity* comics?
Whedon: There is one coming out later this year. I'm just going over the second-issue script, by Brett Matthews. It'll be another three-issue piece like the last one.

Robinson: Getting back to *Goners* . . . You've been very secretive about the plot, just as you've always been close-mouthed about your projects in advance. Which makes a lot of sense when people are trying to get you to admit how you're going to resolve some big cliffhanger on one of your shows, but it seems a little odder when you're talking about an unknown project.

Whedon: The fact of the matter is, I'm not trying to sell it. In fact, I'm trying to keep it from being sold, because if everybody gets sold on it, and it doesn't happen for two and a half years, they'll feel like they already bought it. The people to whom I must sell it have bought it. [Laughs.] That's good. They got to read the whole script. There's no way everybody who wants to can find everything they want to know about the movie before it comes out. That is one of the worst things in our culture. I believe it's destroying storytelling. Now, I can't stop it, but I'm certainly not going to lay out the entire story when I haven't even got a green light on production, because then, people already feel like they've lived with a character, and not in a good way. It's not intelligent marketing, and it's not intelligent storytelling. I understand there's a limit. There's a point at which you have to talk about it. I struggled with this while doing the promos for *Buffy*, when people were like, "This act-two twist is what makes people come see the show. You absolutely have to put it in the preview." The entire world has turned into the opening credits from *Battlestar Galactica* and that just can't be. My wife and I always shut our eyes during those.

Robinson: Is there a conscious philosophy to avoiding spoilers rather than seeking them out? There are fanatics on both sides of that divide.

Whedon: You know, I had older brothers, and I don't think there's anything worse than an older brother. They pretty much told me the end of everything they got to see before I did. It occurred to me very early on, "This would have been a lot more fun if I hadn't known everything that was going to happen before it happened." I got a little neurotic about it, and people were like, "What up?" So I sat down and I really thought about it, and realized that there is a philosophy behind it, one that I've talked about before, and I won't bore you with. It's the idea of surprise being the point of storytelling, and the most honest emotion, because it's truly humbling. Surprise means you have to reassess what you thought. It means that you were wrong about the way things were structured, and that's exciting, and really important. It also makes for a good story. I mean, *The Sixth Sense* is fine the second time around, but honestly, the first time around, it's dazzling. When it matters, when it makes a difference, letting a story happen to you, letting a narrative take place instead of just waiting for placeholders is a better experience, and it feeds you. We need narrative, it feeds us in a particular way, and deconstructing it completely before you've actually experienced it, I think it leaves us unfed.

Robinson: Do you get tired of fans demanding spoilers? All your online and in-person Q&As seem to revolve around people wanting to know how you're going to resolve this twist or that cliffhanger.

Whedon: I only get tired of having to respond in a way that I know will displease four thousand people all at once. "Uh, no, I can't tell you that, but thanks for your interest." I wish no one wanted to be spoiled, but I get it. I love trailers, by the way. A good trailer is an awesome thing, and I tend to write trailers in my head before I write scripts, and then cull ideas from the trailers. I know what I want to feel, and to encapsulate that is useful as a storyteller, and fun. But I think the need has just gotten overwhelming. It's also just really tough now, because the questions aren't, "Is Spike going to get together with Buffy?" The questions are, "Are you ever going to do anything?" [Laughs.] I'm like, "I can't spoil that."

Robinson: What do you mean when you say you write trailers before you write projects?

Whedon: I'll have an idea, and then I'll start to think about what's behind that, and what would be the big emotional moment, what would be the catch, what would be the thing I'd love to see. It's usually easier in a situation with a known quantity. For example, *Wonder Woman*. Like, how do you introduce Wonder Woman? "Oh, that's cool." I did *Aliens 4*. When I first wrote it, it was a thirty-page treatment that was completely different from what they shot. It didn't have Ripley in it. Somebody just said, "We're interested. Would you write a treatment on spec?" I was like, "It's *Alien*. Are you kidding? I'll carve one on my forehead." That hurt, so I stopped and used paper. [Laughs.] Paper has worked out great for me since, really. But, I thought to myself, "Okay, I've seen three *Alien* movies. *Alien* is one of the most important franchises in my mythic history. What haven't I seen? What are the moments that I go, 'Okay, that's new, that's worse, that's good, give me that'?"

It's easy doing that with a script for a TV show. You can feel the characters, you can get to the emotional moment. With a new thing, it's still part of the process. The most obvious example, and I've used it before, is Buffy in the alley. I really thought about it: [Trailer narration voice.] "It's a bad town to be in, especially at night." There's the girl in the alley. "Especially if you're alone." And then the monster attacks her and she kills it. "And *especially* if you're a vampire." It was that turnaround, which I hadn't seen, and which has obviously been seen a million times now, but this was twenty years ago. I wrote that, and it's in the actual movie. They didn't use it for the trailer, and the scene isn't shot exactly how I imagined it. But when I'm thinking of a trailer moment, I'm not just thinking of how I can grab people. That's my whole philosophy. My entire career is in that trailer moment: The emotional highs of the movie, and the thing you haven't seen, and the thing you're longing for. They should all be connected.

Robinson: You said in a very recent interview that you're going to find out in the next few weeks whether you're going to be able to do *Goners* this year. If that doesn't work out, is it likely to be scheduled for next year?

Whedon: Well, if it doesn't go through this year, a) that'll suck. [Laughs.] And b) something else will. That's part of the idea of putting together small projects. I gotta roll. I gotta roll. I gotta feed the beast, as they say. I love to shoot. And I love the comics, and I'm having the time of my life, and when this comes out, there will have been a new comic unveiled, and it's great, but that's not enough for me, and it's not enough for the fans, either. I need to film some people. [Laughs.] So if it's not *Goners*, it'll be something.

Robinson: You have a lot of comics projects going on right now. You're hitting the end of your run on *Astonishing X-Men*, aren't you?

Whedon: Yes, we are. It seems to have started a long time ago. Since they decided to make us bi-monthly, when I start a new script, I have to go back and look up what happened in the last one. But it's coming along. We're headed toward the thing I pitched to John Cassaday when we were halfway through our first arc, when I said, "Hey, instead of twelve, what if we did this!" We have two more issues, and then the giant-sized annual, and then we are out of there, baby.

Robinson: Where are you with *Runaways*?

Whedon: I'm into the last two issues of my six-issue arc. I'm actually having the time of my life. We got to create the entire Marvel universe circa 1907, and that's really fun.

Robinson: How did the trade with Brian K. Vaughan come about, with him writing *Buffy* and you writing *Runaways*?

Whedon: Really, it was sort of a coincidence. I had been talking to Brian for a while about doing *Buffy*. You know, originally there had been the idea of doing *Buffy* movies that Fox was going to possibly finance, and then we realized that wasn't going to work out, financially. Brian was the first non-*Buffy*, non-*Angel* person that I brought in. I had been reading his stuff and hanging out with him, and I was just a big fan and a friend, and I thought he really got it. He had some ideas about Faith, and we sat down to dinner, me, him, Tim Minear, and Drew Goddard. He threw out these ideas about Faith, and we were all like, "Dang, he's kicking it. He's really going to bring something to the table." Literally, because we were at a table.

When the comic came around, I was like, "You know that idea you had about Faith? Can we play around with that? People really want to see her, and you've got a great bead on her." The idea was always to bring in other writers. His involvement in that has been gradual and almost inevitable. But *Runaways*, you know, he was leaving, and Marvel brought it up, and I was like,

"Please! Can't you see that I'm terribly busy?" But of course, I lost sleep for an entire night, thinking that they were so cute and I loved them so much. So that happened rather suddenly. But the fact that the exchange timed out so close, that's just a big twist of fate.

Robinson: Does working with the Runaways or the X-Men make you want to explore other company-owned characters, or do you sort of scratch that itch and move on?
Whedon: Well, I think I pretty much scratched the Marvel itch until it bled. Marvel is in such flux, character-wise. There's so much going on, I don't really have any ground to stand on. I love working with other people's characters if they're characters that I care about. I've been reading *Runaways* from issue one. It was delicious fun for me to dive in and see what I would do with them. Since I am an insane fan of *The Office*, it was really fun for me to direct an episode, because I had very strong opinions about what everyone was going to be doing in the background, based on all of their history. It's helpful when you're a geek. *Alien*, same deal. Everything where you have something to build off of that you love, it's fun. There are restrictions, *X-Men* particularly because it has such a long history, but it also brings resonance that you can only get from a comic book, or a TV show, or a franchise, something that's gone on for a long time. You say something, and it calls back somebody's entire childhood. That's an opportunity that I adore. By the same token, the moment that you've written one episode of a TV show, you're doing the same thing. You're working with characters that already exist, and are working around them. Most of my career has been doing that. Creating something completely new out of whole cloth is liberating as hell, but you have to create resonance where there is none. It's a different kind of fun.

Robinson: How did your episode of *The Office* come about?
Whedon: I knew Greg Daniels a little bit, because he's married to Susanne Daniels, who is largely responsible for *Buffy* ever being on the WB. And I know Jenna Fischer because she's married to James Gunn, who briefly worked for me, and is a friend and an awesome guy. I saw him at a con, saw his wife, and said, "What do you do?" She said, "I'm starring in an NBC sitcom." I felt really dumb. So I rushed off and watched it. As it happened, I also took offices, briefly, right next to their writing staff, pre-season, and I became chummy with all of them. It was sort of a giant group of chum. So when somebody suggested it, it was kind of like, "Well, the comfort factor is pretty high, because I already know the writing staff and a bunch of the cast, and I adore the show. This will be a completely new thing for me, a real departure." And then they said, "It's about a bat, and there's a vampire." [Laughs.] I was like, "You have to be fucking kidding me." They were like, "Your stunt meeting is here, and your

CGI meeting is here." I was thinking, "Didn't I just *leave* this party?" That was just coincidence. But that's how that happened. God, it was fun.

Robinson: Did you have any input into the script, or freedom to alter it?

Whedon: I wouldn't say freedom to do things with it, because that sounds disrespectful. [Laughs.] But way more input was asked for than I would have ever anticipated. They wanted my notes on the draft before they went into the rewrite. There was a lot of physical stuff, especially when the bat appears, that I got to pitch. I got to pitch a ton of stuff. Some of it, they were like, "Great!" Some of it, they were like, "Hmmm . . . try it." The physical stuff made it in pretty well, and there was some stuff where I was like, "We're not going to shoot this, we don't have time, and I know that it's not going to work." They're incredibly open with their actors, and they're shooting improv. There was that thing about Pam's art. I got to the set and saw Pam's art, and I was like, "This is not right." [Laughs.] I held up production for an hour while they frantically made new art. That was the one time when I felt the power of the visiting director. What are they going to do, fire me? Somebody was like, "You're really working to protect your vision." I was like, "No, no, no, no, no. This is in the script. This is Greg and Brent Forrester's vision. They've written down a very beautiful thing about exactly what her art should be like, and that's what I'm going to put on the screen." The fact that they were that open and collaborative, and the fact that I was always completely respectful of their process and their world, I'm just going to do my best. Obviously, as a director on that show, all you want to do is hide. If anybody notices that it was directed, you've kind of failed. They gave me way more freedom than I can remember giving people. Ever. [Laughs.] I'm not going to lie about it.

Robinson: How much freedom do you have working on Marvel characters? Does the company dictate or suggest plot points or directions?

Whedon: Nothing like that, no. They are extremely hands-off. It's only if I try to set a toe in the actual Marvel universe. There's a reason that one of my teams is in outer space, and the other is in 1907. I didn't want to do a *Civil War* tie-in. At the end of my run, I don't want anyone coming to it who's trying to read it, going, "What's this about, this new information?" It should just be a piece in and of itself. It has happened, like for example, with the Kingpin. They were like, "Well, he's out of the country." He's the Kingpin! It's New York! He's iconic! Finally, they were like, "Put in something that says he took a plane trip." [Laughs.] I was like, "Okay, thank you." The universe itself is too tricky. I can't even live there. But as far as what I'm doing, they've always been completely respectful. They know that I'm not going to do anything too crazy, and I do run it by them beforehand.

Robinson: When you write comics, do you tend to work ahead and write up an arc on one title or the other, or are you more month-to-month on everything?

Whedon: Kind of month-to-month. I have on occasion gotten ahead. On *Buffy*, I delivered like three scripts in three weeks. I just couldn't stop writing, but that's a different animal. Usually, I have my schedule, and after I've written one, I'll try to rush through an outline for the next one based on the momentum of excitement. But trying to get the next script out is tough, so usually I'll wait. I'll write something else, and then later on, I'll try a bite of that and a bite of that. That works out pretty well. It seems like it's going terribly slowly for various reasons, which has been my fault occasionally, but not so much. It seems like it's a long time between bites, especially for the fans, but I do know exactly where I'm going, which is nice.

Robinson: Do you ever have scheduling issues where you really want to be off on a tear on *Buffy*, but you've got a deadline on *Runaways* or whatever?

Whedon: All the time. You never want to be writing the thing you're writing, unless you're actually in it, unless it's just flowing, and you're typing, and you're laughing, and you're crying, and everything's giddy, and you're in the moment. That's the beauty of it. All the rest of the time, all you want to think about is whatever it is you're not supposed to be thinking about. Having said that, most of my best ideas have come while I was procrastinating about something else I was supposed to be writing. So I respect that. If my brain is saying, "You know what? You're supposed to be working on *Runaways*, but you're in an *X* mood," I go there, because if that's where the muse is hovering, I'm gonna go visit her. Sometimes you've got to bite the bullet, and be a man, and say, "Just write the script. Come on, find the inspiration. Bring that muse over here." But if I have a little leeway, and it's clearly going one way and not the other, that's what I'm going to follow.

Robinson: You've talked a lot in interviews about how the best thing about your job is getting to be alone with a good story. But if that was enough, wouldn't you be less frustrated over the difficulties in getting those stories out to the public?

Whedon: The thing is, you can never turn your back on the idea that you may one day tell that story. Three years down the road, I'm doing a *Buffy* comic. Now we're telling that story about Angel in a comic. I got to make *Serenity*. I got to make a TV series out of *Buffy*, which, as you know, did not do that great as a film. If there's one thing I've learned, and this is ever-increasing, obviously, with the Internet and all of the cross-pollination, is that there's always a way to tell the story. There's novelizations. That's why I resolutely will not tell anybody what happened in Shepherd Book's past, because I'm still clinging to the notion that I one day may be able to. There's been talk of doing that inside a multiplayer game, having his past buried somewhere in that game. That's another great way to create narrative. I'm all about that, assuming that ever gets off the ground. Telling somebody at a dinner party or at a convention is never as cool as doing it. So, yeah, I can protect something to the grave. I'll tell my writers, or the person I hope will write it, if I'm not. I told fans my big Tara moment, because the opportunity had come and gone. I still feel like I shouldn't have. I still feel like it's almost disrespectful to what I did, to tell them what I was going to do with her.

Robinson: You've had more luck getting comics going lately. Could you see yourself just doing comics for a career?

Whedon: I would like my children to eat solid food, and possibly go to grade school, let alone college, so not so much. I love comics, very much, and I love being alone, but I also love the other part. I love actors, and I love filmed entertainment, and that is not something I plan to turn my back on. The comic world has its own limitations, as everything does. I adore it, I respect it, but it's not going to take over all of me.

Robinson: What do you think about the current wave of comic-book movies?

Whedon: After *Spider-man* finally got it right, they've improved. I still take issue with most of them, not just as a comic-book geek, but as a storyteller. Every now and then, I see something that I really like, and I think we're out of the time when it was a bunch of old men in suits, going [Old-timey businessman voice.] "Kids like the comic books. He's bitten by a spider. Does it have to be a spider? Nobody likes spiders, they don't test well." Now, the guys in those jobs grew up reading those comic books, and they finally figured out the formula. "Oh, just do what they did in the comic book, and it will be good," as opposed to changing everything. With the exception of *Superman*, nobody had ever really come close to getting it right. Now that there's a different generation and comic books have a different kind of weight in our culture, the movies have gotten better. Not all of them, but a few of them, and that's nice. That aesthetic has infused, à la *The Matrix*, movies that are not comic-book movies, and that's fun, too.

Robinson: If you had carte blanche to make your own movie version of any comic-book property out there, would it be *Wonder Woman* or something else?

Whedon: Well, I've already written *Wonder Woman*, so I'd probably go with that one. If I could do absolutely anything . . . You know, I don't really think about it, because most of the things that I would love to do . . . I pitched a

Batman before they made *Batman Begins*, basically a different version of *Batman Begins*. I still have as much grief about not being able to tell that story as I do about my script for *Wonder Woman*. I fell so in love with just my three-minute pitch. I'd like to do all the greats. You know, Spidey, and the Bats, they've been done. And the X-Men. There's not that much left. Although, you know, Kitty Pryde. First of all, she's got a great power, walking through walls, and stuff like that, and they already have Ellen Page playing her, so that would be cool.

Robinson: Last time we talked to you, there were a couple of things on your plate that have long since stopped coming up in interviews. One of them was the *Iron Man* movie.

Whedon: The *Iron Man* movie is already in production by Jon Favreau. It has nothing to do with my script whatsoever. All I did was write an outline, and what happened with that wasn't them going, "No, we don't like it." Everybody said "We love it," but I just didn't want to be in production, in development with a studio. I had the TV shows going, and I just thought, "This is not the time for this." I really like New Line, and everything was going along fine. I loved the story, but I just suddenly had a flash of, "This is going to be a long period of development. This is not going to happen." Why I didn't figure that out about *Wonder Woman*, I cannot say.

Robinson: So you pulled out?

Whedon: Yes, I just pulled right out. I said, "You know what? This has been fun, but I realize this is a mistake for me right now, career-wise."

Robinson: What about your *Alien 5* concept?

Whedon: Well, they did *Alien Vs. Predator*, so that already happened. And once he's versed a Predator, it's hard to get people juiced to go back. Not impossible, by the way, and I even kind of liked *Alien Vs. Predator*. But that's already kind of been capped by others.

Robinson: Are there other back-burner projects that you'd theoretically like to get back to someday?

Whedon: There are so many that it's almost appalling. I make a list of the things that I'm working on, wish to be working on, or could one day think about working on, and it fills a page. I have twelve clipboards stuck to my wall with projects that I am working on, just to remind me where I am with each of them. I can pull one down at any moment and go, "Okay, here's the outline for the next issues," or "Here's the phone call I need to make to talk about funding for this concept." I've been writing music for a short, for a ballet that I want to film, a little short film with Summer Glau, for a while. It's very hard for me to write music, especially without lyrics, because I cannot play the instruments so well. So it takes me longer than it takes other people. It's a short, obviously, it's not a giant career move, but it's something I've been dying to do. But Summer's going to be very busy terminating people, isn't she? But, yeah, there's a ton of things. I never lack for things to occupy my time. I just lack for, at this point, it feels like traction.

Robinson: Did the success of the *Buffy* musical episode "Once More, With Feeling" prompt you to want to write more musicals?
Whedon: Musicals were my absolute bread and butter. My father wrote Off-Off-Broadway musical lyrics, so did his father, before they both worked in TV. I was raised on a steady diet of Sondheim. That has never changed. I'm absolutely a musicals boy. A lot of people didn't know that, because I love horror movies, and I love other things, but those were the things that you could get off the ground. I made a musical because I was six years into a show, and I knew that nobody was going to stop me. The fact of the matter is, I'm dying to do another musical, more, possibly than any other single thing. The other fact is, nothing is more labor-intensive. Because I have so many things that I want to be doing right now, I'm going to wait before I buckle down and say goodbye to the world for a year or six months. Let's say six months. "Once More, With Feeling" took me four months to write, so let's call it eight.

Robinson: Do you have a story or concept in mind for it?
Whedon: I've had different ideas. Some people have told me I should do *Buffy* for the stage, which I get, and it could obviously be very fun, but I'd like to do something on film. I've got a few different ideas, but I'm still circling them. Although now, my favorite subgenre, thanks to Drew Goddard, is the *Final Fantasy VIII* interstitial videos cut up to music by Evanescence. I think that's the movie I want to make.

Robinson: Do you spend a lot of time on YouTube trolling for that kind of thing?
Whedon: Not a lot of time, but enough. They're awesome.

Robinson: "Once More, With Feeling" has been touring the country as a subtitled sing-along show in movie theaters. Have you been to any of those screenings?
Whedon: I just went to one with [*Buffy* producer] Marti Noxon a few weeks ago. It was really fun, and oddly moving.

Robinson: Did you go incognito, or as part of an event, or what?
Whedon: I snuck in the back, and then at the end, Marti and I came out and waved at everybody. I was actually kind of nervous. I was like, [Vaudeville voice.] "What manner of person would come to a late-night screening of

this episode of television? I don't want to be seen, I'll wear a false mustache."
[Laughs.] But it was a delight. It was really sweet.

Robinson: Are you still doing your in-home Shakespeare readings with
friends?
Whedon: Well, I haven't been in-home. Everybody's been sort of scattered
to the four winds, so we haven't done one for a while. If I could just get my
peeps to all stop going to Canada to do episodes of things, and hang out long
enough . . . I want to get back to it, it's been too long.

Robinson: You've always been a surprisingly candid interview subject, secrecy
about projects aside. When we last interviewed you, you called Donald Sutherland a prick.
Whedon: You know, I *try* to restrain myself.

Robinson: Has that forthrightness ever gotten you in trouble?
Whedon: Oh, yes. Oh God, yes. The fact of the matter is, it's not my natural
bent. Don just pushed, okay? He just pushed. [Laughs.] The fact is, I feel really strongly that one shouldn't be overly candid, one really should follow the
old rule of talking about people as though they were in the room. But I called
Don that, I can't help it. He was mean.

I tend to try to see both sides of everything. The *Wonder Woman* situation
was frustrating for me, I'm sure it was incredibly frustrating for them. It took
me a very long time to write. I was in a very bad place. Having just made a
movie, it was very hard for me to get back into the writer's seat. They wasted
my time, but I wasted a whole lot of theirs. If you come to it always realizing
that the other guy has a perspective, then being candid is all right. If it starts
to sound like a bunch of complaining, then you should shut up, you should
just shut up. That's not the point.

I have stories I like to tell. Sometimes I got to tell them, sometimes I didn't.
Sometimes they came out right, sometimes they didn't. I hope that I'm just as
candid about my own mistakes as I am about grousing, but the fact of the matter is, there are things that I can never say, and I think that goes for absolutely
everyone who works in this town, or any town, or are human. "Yes, darling,
that outfit makes you look fat." Do people say that? No, they do not. Actually,
I would, if anyone did. But they never have. Luckily, I haven't been faced with
that one.

It bit me in particular with *X-Men*, where I was treated sort of shoddily.
I was in England, very tired, and some fanzine asked a question, and I went
kind of off. Well, of course, that fanzine was a web fanzine, I didn't know
about this web thing. I hadn't really gleaned the fact that there wasn't such
a thing as a guy with a photocopier handing out sheets of paper anymore.

Everything I said got to the Fox executives before I went to bed that night. They were pissed, and they were right. That's not what you do. I kind of treat moviemaking and TV like the Army, and I kind of always have. Whoever is in charge, is in charge, and if they're going to march you up a hill and get you all killed, that's what you do. You march up that hill. You have to respect that, you have to respect that chain of command. I've done it under directors I believed in, I've done it under directors I didn't believe in. I've done it with executives and on projects.

Alien broke my heart, and I never said a single word about it until it was out on DVD. I thought, "Okay, now I can start to bitch and moan." Quite frankly, now, because there's always another DVD, or another thing, and everything is reported forever, there really isn't a good venue to cut loose like that, except perhaps the director's commentary. They actually asked me to do an interview about *Alien 4*, and I was like, "Guys, no, you don't want me to do that." It's important to be candid, or else everything sounds like a press release. But it's also important to have perspective, and not to get so up in one's own righteous rage that one forgets that other people are also people.

Robinson: Have any of your experiences changed what you're willing to say in interviews?

Whedon: I've always had a rule. What happened with *X-Men* happened because I was exhausted, and because I had gotten so used to being a muckity-muck in TV that I'd forgotten that in movies, I'm nobody. When you're a rewrite guy in movies, it doesn't matter that you have a successful TV show, you're nobody. They had no obligation to treat me any better than they did, but I had gotten so used to being in a position of respect that I was sort of overly appalled by what happened, because, quite frankly, things just as bad have happened to me a lot, and to other people. It has always been my rule to tell the truth as much as it is useful to the interviewer, so that they are interested and want to call you back someday. [Laughs.] I'm not out there to blow the lid off such-and-such, or get back at so-and-so. I don't have any of that. You can't live with that. It's ungentlemanly, and ultimately self-defeating.

Joss Whedon on Crafts and Craftiness

KIM WERKER/2008

From CrochetMe.com, Interweave Press, LLC., December 6, 2008. Reprinted by permission.

Werker: Ok. We're recording now and I'm here with Joss Whedon. I'm Kim Werker from CrochetMe.com. So, Joss, Captain Hammer—four sweater vests, really?

Whedon: Yeah. Well, four, you know, in that, I mean, he actually has quite a collection.

[Confusion as I interrupt.]

Whedon: Just four at that particular time. He has more than that, obviously. No man can live with only four sweater vests.

Werker: So, the crafty community is dying to know: Are those sweater vests knitted or crocheted?

Whedon: Well. Ok. So this is where we get to the tough questions.

Werker: Yeah.

Whedon: I'm aware of the desperate rivalry between the knitters and the crocheters. And, you know, first of all I have to say: can't there be peace?

Werker: I agree.

Whedon: It's an age-old war. Like the werewolves and the vampires. I think *Underworld* was actually originally about crocheters and knitters, but they thought it would be too controversial, so they changed it to vampires and werewolves. Um, most of them are sadly knitted. However he does have one crocheted, but he did it himself, and it doesn't go very well.

Werker: Doesn't go very well, eh?

Whedon: It tends to come apart. It's not his best effort.

Werker: Well, send him our way and we'll help him bone up on his skills.
Whedon: Good, good.

Werker: So, are you a crafty guy, other than with words?
Whedon: I'm crafty in the sense that I'm duplicitous and evil. But not so much in the sense—I used to knit and crochet. I walked on both sides of that [muffled]. And when I was a kid, because my mom did. But I haven't picked up any needles in a long while except to stab people. My wife does. My wife rocks some seriously crocheting. She started out—she was already a knitter but she started out crocheting hats for a friend who was actually in chemo and suddenly needed a lot of hats. And then, she just sort of went wild with it. She knitted a turtle, and scarves, and a guitar strap for our son. She's pretty fierce.

Werker: That's great. Well, we like to think of ourselves as fierce. Did your mom teach you how to knit or crochet when you were a kid?
Whedon: Yeah.

Werker: Were you about eight years old?
Whedon: I think I was a little bit older than that. I was probably like around twelve, I would say. But my memory for dates is well—obviously I was born with fully-formed grown-up intelligence, so it all sort of blends together for me.

Werker: Yeah, but the motor skills often come after, so.
Whedon: Yes, I'm still waiting on some.

Werker: There was a really significant, like, handmade or crafty element in the sets, especially of *Buffy*. Were you involved with that or was that something that the costume designers and set designers did?
Whedon: That was more them. The crafty part was more—for me was more *Firefly*. Because in *Firefly* we were really trying to evoke the idea of things you make for yourself, of a life that you create with your own two hands. It was all very pioneer spirit, and so it ended up just looking really seventies in the decor, which was not exactly the original intent, but that said, that was very deliberate. On something like *Buffy* it just sort of came to be. I think people tend to fall back on it, you know, to represent something comforting and homey and good. Like, good people in movies and TV have things that are, you know—obviously not sweater vests—but, they have things that are wooly and handmade and very sort of earthy, and evil people live in cold, steel, modernist houses, you know, and wear shiny suits. It's sort of inevitable.

Werker: So, speaking of *Firefly*, you wrote, with Tim Minear, knitters' and crocheters' favorite episode, "The Message," when Jayne gets that knitted hat.
Whedon: Ah, the knitted hat.

Werker: Yeah. Certainly there was that element of homeyness and it really brought a lot of humanity to his character to receive that hat. Did you have any idea that hat would become so iconic?
Whedon: I did not. I did not. My whole thought was that Jayne was your classic bad-guy mercenary type, and I thought this is the one guy who does not have a tortured past, who has a decent, hard-working family, who just, you know, this was his career choice and the idea of him getting a letter from mom that he struggles to read, and the knitted hat, was—it just felt so right. It felt very, very him and very human and then of course I saw the hat with its flaps and its pom pom, and I just couldn't have been happier.

Werker: Was it made—
Whedon: It was made, I believe, for the role, but I could be totally wrong about that. They might've found it somewhere and claimed to make it. I should ask Shawna Trpcic, our costumer; she would know.

Werker: And have you seen them around? I know a lot of people who went to Comic-Con this past summer made some.
Whedon: Oh, I see them constantly. And it fills me with tiny knitted joy.

Werker: Looking ahead to *Dollhouse*, which sort of, from the trailers we've seen, has a bit of a slick look, should crafters be looking forward to any sort of things that will inspire their hands to make something?
Whedon: Hard to say. The, you know, the operation's very sleek, but at the same time, the world they live in is very spa-like, Eastern, and yoga-matty. So, there may be touches in there. I mean it's a little more wicker than actual loom-work. But we were going for a very natural, earthy environment for them inside of a kind of a laboratory feeling. So it's working across surfaces. The viewer will see a little of them in there. I doubt we'll find anything as iconic as the Jayne hat. I can convince Eliza [Dushku] to do a lot of things but that might not be one of them.

Werker: No? But maybe she'll knit or crochet or decoupage in one of the episodes?
Whedon: Obviously decoupaging is too racy for Fox. So, I mean, they couldn't allow that.

Werker: There's whoops and cheers from decoupagers everywhere now.
Whedon: It's just Standards and Practices, they draw the line at this kind of thing.

Werker: We'll let the basket-makers know that they should look ahead to some good wicker.
Whedon: Yes, I think they're going to be both pleased and frightened.

Werker: So, right after, as *Dr. Horrible* hit the internet tubewaves, people started crafting almost immediately. There were people who made their own Wonderflonium boxes and crocheted Dr. Horrible dolls. Did you see that happen as *Dr. Horrible* came out?
Whedon: I think I saw a crocheted Dr. Horrible [muffled]. I'm not wrong about this, am I? You know, anything that inspires people to make their own little version of something be it puppety, be it crafty, be it a high school production of lip syncing, whatever it is, it's the best kind of review you could ever get for any works. It's just cool. I always want things to become plush.

Werker: When can we look forward to the DVDs coming out?
Whedon: We can look forward to the DVD very soon. It should be available on the internet for pre-order before Thanksgiving and definitely for ordering in time for Christmas, oh yeah.

Werker: Excellent. That's really great. We love—
Whedon: You're not fooled.

Werker: No.
Whedon: One of us isn't fooled, but I can't [muffled].

Werker: So, crafty people often feel like they have to let their materials behave and become what they want to be, even if it's not what we had in mind to begin with. Do you feel that's somewhat similar sometimes in how you write characters and plot lines?
Whedon: You're going to need to meet the materials halfway. Yes, you definitely want every skein of yarn to do exactly what you have in mind, but they never will. And that's part of what makes it beautiful. That's part of what makes it not working in a factory. And every actor is going to bring something to the party, and I'm going to embrace what they're bringing as fucking hard as I can as long as it doesn't hurt the narrative, so that it becomes something more than just an idea I had that somebody acted out. You have to remember that if the thing isn't slightly out of control, it ain't art. Or [muffled] craft.

Werker: What do you see as the difference between arts and craft, or do you?
Whedon: Honestly, it really is that little chaos factor. It's when the thing starts talking back to you. When you come up with something that is a little bit more than just a good reproduction of what was in the book, and somehow reflects you in a way that you didn't understand yourself: that's art. If you just manage to reproduce something skillfully as a craft—and it's a beautiful thing and I wish I was better at it—but that's where I [mumbled] for me.

Werker: I read a quote recently, in an article about the resurging DIY movement, that we're "crafting to claim identity, to save the world from soulless junk." Do you see any parallels in people's approach to internet-based video productions versus the big-media productions for television and movies and how people are really taking those media into their own hands right now?
Whedon: Absolutely. I mean, let's face it, in the media there are now eight companies. In any mall you walk into, there are now eight stores: there's gonna be a Gap, there's gonna be a Banana Republic. Everything is becoming consolidated, so where there used to be lots of variety, there are now, like, ten giants and tons of tiny little villagers. And yeah, the villagers are going to start making their own stuff because the materials will be available to all of them, and we can't all just do things the way the giants want, because it does seep something out of your soul. I think it's absolutely true on every level of art that this is the worst of times and, like some guy might have said once, the best of times.

Werker: Do you think, as those eight companies start to really focus on producing online content, do you think the indie vibe, the people who are out to be very creative on their own terms will persist in that atmosphere?
Whedon: I'm sorry, say that again please?

Werker: No worries. As—
Whedon: I thought you said, "No way!"

Werker: [Laughs.] No worries. As those eight companies start to focus their energy into putting content online and possibly—we imagine—to produce it specifically for online distribution, do you think the independently minded people who are right now making content for online distribution will continue? Will they be crowded out?
Whedon: Well, it's a pretty big place to be crowded out of. But if the companies can figure out a way, they will. I mean, they exist by virtue of controlling. Not creating, controlling. And therefore, they will always try to find a way to make sure that nobody else can do what they do. On the other hand, we are now in a situation where everybody can do what they do. And they don't have

that control, which frightens and offends them. So, I will always give them credit for trying to find a way to steal Christmas, but this time they might not be able to. There's always been an independent side to the industry. And for this particular medium, I think it's going to be a lot harder for them to crush it. But they'll try.

Werker: Do you have advice for people in the face of other people trying to crush them?

Whedon: Well, you know, at the end of the day right now, you can create something; what you can't usually do is make a fortune off of it. But if we're talking about the sort of people who are actually checking a crocheting website, we're talking about the sort of people who understand that part of what we're doing is in the process. That it's not about, "I'm going to crochet the most hats! I'm going to be the fastest! I'm going to be the most [mumbled] millionaire without enjoying the process and the product." Ultimately, the artistic expression can't be squelched; it's just they'll try to cut off any avenues for that expression to be, shall we say, monetized in a realistic fashion. Like I'm saying, the sort of people who understand the DIY mentality are more about the doing than the having. So I think that ultimately, my advice is what my advice always is: Make stuff. You know. Right now, because of digital technology, you can make crafty little movies, you can make crafty little things that go up for millions of people to see. You can sort of combine the two ethos-ethoses-ethosees . . . And grab a video camera, tell a story. Be stupid, be something, just . . . It is no longer the time of sitting around and thinking about doing something. If you're going to do that, you can, you know, crochet, and you're already doing it.

Werker: Knitting and crochet are crafts with really strong, obviously, roots in women's history, and there's a really great feminist component to the resurgence right now. Does that surprise you in any way?

Whedon: No, I mean, those things have always been connected. My wife is also a quilter, and that has as much to do with a very strong portion of society as it does with making a warm blanket. These crafts, they represent pockets of interaction that an underclass has always used to gather and to strengthen each other and to . . . what's going on in their communities. So it makes perfect sense that these things would still be connected.

Werker: There were a huge number of people in the online crafts community who helped to spread the word as we were trying to get your attention for this interview. How did you end up finding out about us?

Whedon: You know, I do know that I read something on the internet before my assistant said, "I got the weirdest call." You know, I had made a completely random joke about media attention—but then nothing's perfectly random, is it? Every now and then I'd peek around the corner and there'd be somebody going, "How's that crocheting thing?" And I was like, "I gotta learn to shut up." I was psyched; I was like, "That's right. These people will finally ask me something different."

Werker: It was pretty great. There were a ton of people who blogged about this, and then somebody knew someone who knew someone, and I love the fact that you found out about it before the people who knew someone who knew someone were able to contact your assistant. That makes my heart sing.
Whedon: No, it was out there pretty early on. I apologize for taking so long, but if you knew me you would not be surprised.

Werker: I wasn't surprised, because I know the kind of things you're involved with. I'm thrilled you took the time at all this morning—thank you.
Whedon: You're welcome.

Werker: I've got one final question for you.
Whedon: Alright.

Werker: Do you have a favorite handmade gift you've either given or received, or both? Not that they would be the same gift.
Whedon: It wasn't given to me, but when my son was born, actually, Eliza, a few years ago, gave him a Bishop Tutu doll, which she had gotten in South Africa. It's really cool. He has little glasses, and every now and then Bishop Tutu will suddenly show up again, hanging out with whatever they're playing with. So, I thought that was pretty nifty.

Werker: That is pretty great. Joss Whedon, thank you so much for talking with us today.
Whedon: Thank you. Oh!

Werker: Yeah?
Whedon: You know what?

Werker: What?
Whedon: I've got one other. Dichen. Dichen Lachman is Sierra on our show.

Werker: Yeah?
Whedon: On *Dollhouse*. Her mother sent me—it's not actually very crafty, because it's just a string with a knot in it, but the string was blessed by the

Dalai Lama, and one of his monks tied the knot. She sent it to me as a present of good will because I work at Fox—I mean, in Hollywood. It doesn't really qualify as a craft, tying one knot in it, tying it around my wrist to make a bracelet, but I love it [muffled].

Werker: That's great. I think the love makes it a craft that is special.
Whedon: There you go.

Werker: Great. Thank you so much. Take care and good luck to you.
Whedon: Thank you. You too.

Werker: Thanks.
Whedon: Bye.

Werker: Bye.

New Media Guru: Meet Joss Whedon the Web Slayer

LISA ROSEN/2009

From *Written By*, the magazine of the Writers Guild of America, West, January 2009. Reprinted by permission.

Joss Whedon is wired to write. If he had lived back in Cro-Magnon time, he would have drawn stories on cave walls. (And some Neanderthal would have given him notes.) Fortunately, he has slightly easier formats today, including films, comic books, and the television shows *Buffy the Vampire Slayer*, *Angel*, and *Firefly*. Last summer, Whedon's primal storytelling prowess was applied to the brand-new cave wall known as the Internet, with his self-produced, self-funded, self-you-name-it musical, *Dr. Horrible's Sing-Along Blog*.

A mass of silliness with a tender center, *Dr. Horrible* tells the tale of one young wannabe super villain, the Dr. of the title, who is dying to get into the Evil League of Evil. With equal ardor, he pines for Penny, a do-gooder frequenting his laundromat. His arch nemesis is Captain Hammer, a self-aggrandizing show pony who steals Penny's affections. Dr. Horrible schemes to put an end to Hammer, guaranteeing his entrée into super-evil society, but things go awry in classic Aristotelian fashion. Seriously. Careful what you wish for, wannabes.

The show was a web pioneer, streaming online for free before becoming available for sale on iTunes, where it shot to the top of the charts. It also broke new grounds in its Guild contracts, forged during the writers' strike. Although there's no way to tell where it ranks in terms of online programming, it is certifiably the most successful web musical of all time. Whedon's traits are on display—humor, humanity, musical chops, reversal of expectations, tragic twists—but serving a new medium and no masters. Make that two masters: Whedon and his audience. What make it even more delightful is that it sprung from the mind of a man who is so Internet-unsavvy, he insists, "I'm the guy who can't find the porn."

GETTING ALL INTERNETY

Whedon was inspired by shows he had seen online, like *Star Trek: New Voyages*, a show created by fans that continues the original Star Trek series. "I sat at my counter in my kitchen watching the thing, and so help me God, crying. And I'm not even a Trekkie," he says. *The Guild* (www.watchtheguild.com), a sitcom webisode about a group of online gamers, was another influence. The show's star, Felicia Day, who played a recurring role on the final season of *Buffy*, had created and self-funded it. Whedon ran into Day on the picket line and asked her to explain how the Web works. "She has one of those crazy Rainman brains, she's *sooo* smart, so I sat her down to tell me about monetizing the Internet, and halfway through I was like, *I'm just going to drink my tea and smile and nod and pretend I understand because my God she talks fast.*"

He kicked around the idea of *Dr. Horrible* as an audio podcast. Then he decided to go big, so he could create jobs during the strike. He went to Silicon Valley for funding, but the negotiations took too long. "They're still making the deal," he reports. "So I finally said, 'Let's just do it ourselves,' and my wife was onboard for that."

Brothers Zack and Jed, and Jed's fiancée, Maurissa Tancharoen, had created a YouTube video called *WGA vs. AMPTP* that he loved. So he asked them to work with him on his *Horrible* idea. They thought they'd be playing the roles themselves, until Joss started calling actor friends. Neil Patrick Harris signed on as Dr. H., Nathan Fillion (*Firefly*) as Hammer, and Day as Penny. As Jed puts it, "It wasn't going to be Neil on a webcam."

Pretty much everyone worked for free, with the idea of getting paid if the show ever made money. Two budgets were created, the real one, and the one that paid everyone what they would have cost. The first was just more than $200,000, the second about twice that. Joss and his line producer David Burns went to the WGA and SAG to work out deals. It was especially important during the strike to show how that could be done without screwing people. "For original content for the writers there was no model," Joss says. "The Guild said, 'This is what we would ask per-minute for reuse or repurposing or for a webisode spun off a show.' So that's what we used as our model." They also worked out the DVD fee and are still trying to figure a rate for theatrical showings, so people can have sing-alongs to the *Sing-Along*.

Joss also positioned the writers and three principle actors as profit participants. "There's no reason why there can't be a business model that is completely inclusive in profit participation. I'm the studio. I still get way more than everybody else, after I make back my production costs and everything's paid out. When we're into pure profit, which at this point we are, I win. So—and this was the whole thing during the strike—why try to offer us nothing, when all we're asking for is a percentage? You can't say that 99 percent is ever a bad number."

There was no model for the show itself, and here Joss' ignorance of the Internet came in handy. "Nobody will watch anything over three minutes, nobody will watch anything over six minutes, nobody will watch anything over nine minutes," were admonitions he heard, but his reply was, "They'll watch what they like." He and the writers decided to create the show as a special event, like an old-school miniseries before the days of VCRs (let alone DVRs). People would have to tune in on the same days to see it, for free at least.

Then the strike ended. "We sort of lost the ethos of *let's fight the man*, because I was busy by night getting *Dollhouse* ready," Whedon says. They pulled off the *Horrible* shoot in six days. The whole shebang, from conception to streaming, took five months.

Once the project was completed, a few companies took interest in it. Joss and his cohorts went to a meeting at CAA, "and they were literally like, 'We don't know how to proceed with this,'" at which point Day took the lead. "Felicia was following sites and [explaining that] 'you have to go here, and they don't have a bandwidth, and we always said we were going to stream this for free, and we don't want to let go of that,'" Joss says with wonder. "She was so on top of it, the rest of us were like, 'Yeah, what she said.' It was like a *Buffy* moment—the cute little girl in the room blows everybody out of the water."

So Joss and his crew proceeded to distribute and publicize the show themselves. Except the fans almost beat them to it. Jed was uploading a teaser to see how it looked online before releasing it publicly. He and Tancharoen went to dinner, and an hour later she got an email saying that the teaser had already leaked online. "We hadn't even made our website yet, so we spent days trying to look professional," says Jed.

Joss posted a message on Whedonesque, alerting everyone to the Internet miniseries event. The three acts would air on July 15, 17, and 19, respectively. At midnight on July 20, the free show would be pulled, to be available for paid download after that.

Then Jed hit the button, and the show dropped. In America anyway. "The first response was, 'Why the fuck can't I see this?'" Jed relates. "Angry Australians." Turns out the host site, Hulu, didn't have international capability. They stayed up all night remedying that.

Oh, and there was the crash. "We like to say we broke the Internet, because 'we were too cheap to pay for more bandwidth' doesn't have the same ring to it," notes Joss. The show was getting so many hits—a thousand a second—that the server couldn't handle the traffic. "We broke other things they had streaming nearby and all ancillary sites, like Whedonesque and Felicia's site for *The Guild*, they all went down," Joss says. "So there was this domino effect, people either looking for it or some connection, and that made us feel pretty awesome. We didn't feel bright, but we felt cool."

By day two all was smooth, and the hits kept coming. But when the show went on to iTunes, things really went nuts. The show went to No. 1 and stayed there for five weeks. The soundtrack was No. 2 and also entered the Billboard Top 200 at No. 39, which was incredible considering that it was only available as a download. Joss the Studio isn't talking specific numbers, but he acknowledges that online sales alone have put the show in the black. (Still viewable for free on Hulu, now with commercials, it's had millions of hits.)

Time magazine listed the program in their Top 50 inventions of 2008, at No. 15. "That's the thing I'm most proud of," says brother Jed. For Joss, the high point was probably when the issue of *Variety* came out with the headline, "Scribes Strike Back." "Okay, admittedly five months too late," he admits, but it made him weepy nonetheless. "There was a picture of Dr. Horrible, a picture of me with a picket sign, and nothing else on the front page. Just that article. All of a sudden the politics came back into play, in a good way. People started going, 'Okay, we did accomplish something, we didn't do it during the strike, but we did it and now it means something.' Because it went from this is a political action to this is us making jokes about a horse, to this is a political action again. That was very gratifying."

The DVD was due to come out December 19, after press time. The reason it took so long is that Joss came up with the idea of making *Commentary, the Musical*, a commentary track entirely composed of songs composed by the writers. Almost twice as many songs as the original show, in fact. "It's the most labor-intensive whimsical idea I ever had, especially for poor Jed, who's producing the whole thing," Joss confesses. Pre-orders began on November 28; four days later, it was ranked No. 38 on Amazon. If I may predict the past, I believe that show is going to have stuffed a record number of stockings.

A FASTER FUTURE

Joss went to work on *Dollhouse*, bringing Jed and Tancharoen along on staff. But returning to studio life was jolting. "I came back to Fox and all of a sudden got notes on everything. 'Those are the socks you're going to wear? Hmm, will teenage girls respond to those socks?'" And it's not just the notes. He's impatient with the studio pace now that he's seen how fast things can be done with a digital video and a good idea.

The new series has encountered some familiar difficulties. Originally a fall show, it was rescheduled for midseason. The pilot didn't work, so production was shut down for a few weeks in September for a rewrite. But Joss has said this time it was his idea to rework the first episode, not the network's. While fans are in a panic about the show's Friday slot (at 9 P.M., beginning February 13), he and the staff seem unconcerned.

"*Dollhouse* has had a troubled start, that's not breaking news, and there was a time when I literally was like, *I don't think I can stomach this process anymore*," he admits. "That's not a dig on Fox or the people here, because I'm dealing with a much better class of network people than I was. It really is just the process and all of the other stuff that keeps me from just making the show. I don't feel like in these, my declining years, I have time for that anymore. I need things to happen quickly. I found out that I am a sketch artist, I really am. I was talking to—name drop, Stephen Sondheim—and he said, 'I would not open a show without out-of-town tryouts, I need to mess with it, I need to tweak it.' I'm like okay, *He's Rembrandt, at best I'm Hirschfeld*. I need to put out a drawing every week. That's who I am. That doesn't mean I don't take enormous care with the work. It just means I've got to get it out there."

Joss insists he has no interest in shunting Hollywood aside. In addition to the television show, he's producing a horror film that he co-wrote with Drew Goddard (*Buffy, Angel*) called *Cabin in the Woods*, for MGM-UA. At the same time, "as I've said to Eliza, 'We're running the daycare on the *Death Star*, if you're going to be in the mainstream, it's fairly polluted.'"

He points out that he still has the smoke of the strike rising off of him: "That's the kind of person I am." But he adds that, while the AMPTP's stance during the strike was completely unforgivable, "the fear that generated it was very real and very understandable." The only thing everyone knows about the change that's coming is that nobody knows what it will be.

People have been asking Joss to explain *Dr. Horrible*'s business model, which amuses him no end. "Somebody coming to me for business advice is like somebody asking a guy who makes balloon animals how to pick up women."

Nevertheless, he is a pioneer. But can his success be replicated by others? Or is it only possible for a Joss Whedon, with his fervent fanbase, critical support, and name recognition that's rare for a writer? Maybe, for now. But he's got big ideas that are entirely realizable . . . when he can find the time. "I would like something to be created that isn't beholden to the frost giants, because their need for extreme monetization is antithetical to what this needs to be," he explains. "It needs to be small, modular, to pay off in a respectable but not hysterical fashion. I'm interested in being an Internet Roger Corman. He's responsible for a slew of the greatest directors of the last couple decades, because he was the only B-movie system that there was. Now the whole world can be that system."

Joss Whedon's Plan to Monetize Internet Content (Watch Out, Hollywood)

KNOWLEDGE@WHARTON.COM/2009

TV and movie writer-director Joss Whedon wants to change the way Hollywood does business. While Whedon works inside the studio system on major projects, he also hopes to blaze a trail on the Internet for creating and monetizing independently produced content. In doing so, he is confronting what he terms the "homogenized, globalized, monopolized entertainment system."

One of Whedon's recent projects is *Dr. Horrible's Sing-Along Blog*, an online musical comedy starring Neil Patrick Harris, Nathan Fillion, and Felicia Day, written by Whedon, his brothers Zack and Jed, and Jed's fiancée Maurissa Tancharoen. Conceived during the hundred-day Writers Guild of America strike in late 2007 and early 2008, *Dr. Horrible* was, in part, intended as an experiment to explore options for creative content. The subject of revenues for online content was a timely one, since a major point of contention that spurred the strike involved payment to writers for content distributed online.

Dr. Horrible was released on the web in three parts last July, and Whedon's plan was to remove the free online versions and sell all three episodes as video downloads through Apple's iTunes Store. A week after the series moved to iTunes, it reappeared online on advertising-based sites such as Hulu, a joint venture of NBC Universal and News Corp. In December, a DVD version became available on Amazon.com. With these various distribution channels (and the lack of a traditional advertising budget), *Dr. Horrible* serves as something of a case study for marketing independently produced content.

Joseph Hill ("Joss") Whedon is a third-generation television writer. His grandfather, John Whedon, wrote episodes of such late 1950s and 1960s staples as *Leave It to Beaver*, *The Donna Reed Show*, and *The Andy Griffith Show*. His father, Tom Whedon, wrote installments of *Alice*, *Benson*, and *The Golden Girls*. As Whedon said to Knowledge@Wharton, "I was raised by a tribe of funny people."

After graduating from Wesleyan University with a degree in film studies, Whedon moved to Los Angeles and found early work writing for television programs such as *Roseanne* and editing scripts for feature films. His screenplay for *Buffy the Vampire Slayer* achieved modest success and Whedon received an Academy Award nomination for his screenplay work on *Toy Story*.

Whedon's science-fiction series *Firefly*, produced for Fox television, debuted in 2002. But he tussled with Fox over aspects of *Firefly*: The network insisted on a new pilot episode and aired several episodes out of sequence. The show was cancelled after eleven of its fourteen episodes aired, and Whedon and Fox parted ways. Whedon told Knowledge@Wharton that he was "heartbroken" by the show's demise. Driven by his desire to keep the characters alive—and brisk DVD sales of the original series—Whedon wrote and directed *Serenity* for Universal Studios, a feature film based on the *Firefly* characters and storyline.

Despite the contentious issues with Fox over the network's handling of *Firefly*, Whedon's next television series, *Dollhouse*, a science-fiction thriller starring Eliza Dushku, debuts on Fox television on February 13.

Knowledge@Wharton recently spoke with the forty-five-year-old Whedon about the lessons learned from *Dr. Horrible* and what he believes needs to happen for the Internet to serve as a platform that can sustain original creative content. An edited version of that conversation follows.

Knowledge@Wharton: To what extent was the original impetus behind *Dr. Horrible* to serve as an experiment for how web-based content can generate revenue?

Whedon: It was equal parts that and the love of the silly. The concept originated as an audio podcast that I would do myself because I was hungry to write some songs and I liked the idea of the character.

And then the Writer's Guild went on strike. I tried to make some deals with Silicon Valley companies and song studios to create jobs and put out product. But it took so long trying to make a deal with these companies up north, that I missed my window. So I said, "I'll just do it myself—if that's okay with my wife." And because I could not afford to do a huge, lavish production we did it with a ton of favors.

We were, at the time, very much in the spirit of the strike. By the time we finished writing [*Dr. Horrible*] and had everyone lined up, the strike was over and we all had shows to scramble to do. But we found a window to shoot it. It became us goofing around and just having a great time making a piece of art that we all enjoyed.

Once we finished . . . it was equal parts ethos and capricious glee. We said we were going to roll it out for free and then put it on iTunes. We just steamrolled past everybody's idea of how you market and of how long it takes to do these things. We had people [drawing up] contracts in days that usually take months, because we were tired of people sitting around.

Ultimately, though, we were still in the mind of: This is a bit of a lark. The strike was over and so we wanted to do right by everybody, but we weren't thinking it would be a grand statement. We thought it was going to be cool.

Knowledge@Wharton: Several numbers have been quoted regarding the overall cost of *Dr. Horrible*—"low six-figures"; "around $200,000"—can you set the record straight?

Whedon: We got so much of this done through people doing us favors—department heads and people who have access to things. But you've got to pay your day-to-day crew. The actors all did it for nothing. And we all did it for nothing. So, the production costs alone—the basic costs of filming the thing, and getting the locations, props, and everything—ran a little over $200,000.

We had a secondary budget drawn up in case of a profit, wherein we were trying to find rates for Internet materials. In some cases they didn't exist. We used models that had been created by the guild for repurposed, or reused, material that we used for original [content], because this had never come up before.

We didn't want to leave a sour taste and say, "Well, we made some money off of you guys being kind." It was like: No, everybody has to benefit from what they've done, obviously not enormously—it's Internet money we're talking about—but as soon as we got in the black, we paid everybody off.

So that budget was probably about twice what the original budget was.

Knowledge@Wharton: You've now earned more than twice the original cost?

Whedon: Yes.

Knowledge@Wharton: Which members of the production shared in the profits on the backend?

Whedon: The crew that got paid, got paid. [Those] who didn't get paid [included people like] department heads who had jobs and could afford to do this as a lark.

As we go forward into profit, there are also residual schedules and payment schedules for all of the creative people. We're trying to figure out how that works.

From the start I also laid down a gross participation scheme for my three key actors and the other three writers. While the guild was negotiating for one-tenth of a yen, I said, "How about we just get into some percentages." It was an opportunity to say to the guilds, "Guess how much better we can do"—which, in the case of the Internet, is the only way for the guilds to survive.

We can't accept anything remotely like [our current situation] with the studios.

When the studios talk about the difficulty of monetizing the Internet, they're not lying. There are a lot of paradigms wherein you aren't making that much money. But it's all pure money for them because they have these libraries they can just put on. They're really not interested in putting on original stuff because they can just throw the libraries on and make free money off of that. None of us is in that position.

For [the studios] not to offer the creative community a percentage of what they make—they say, "oh, it's too difficult" and "we're not going to make any money"—is disingenuous to the point of criminality. What they're making is pure profit. For them to shut out the people who actually created the content is something that should be looked into by a federal investigatory committee.

Knowledge@Wharton: It sounds like you want what you've done with *Dr. Horrible* to serve as a model for similar original content.
Whedon: I do.

Knowledge@Wharton: What do you think the likelihood of that is?
Whedon: That largely depends on a number of people—one of whom, sadly, is me. This could just stand out as Camelot and disappear. Or it can be a model that is built on. And I'm one of the people who needs to be building on it. That's something I'm looking into right now.

I'm not a business man. I'm also not a techie. My ideas on how to monetize the Internet for independent productions are ideas that other people have already had. But I am in a position to try to take advantage of them in such a way that we get a toehold in this medium and [establish] a system of creating some original content before the giant companies sweep in and fence it all off.

The movies, TV—everything is melding, everything is shifting. If you saw it on a movie screen, it's going to be on your phone. That territory is moving . . . now in a destructive way because we're losing residuals. But eventually it's just going to be an inevitability that . . . the studios are going to have to rethink how they monetize [content]. Obviously TiVo makes their relationship with advertisers different. And that's going to become more and more the case. A lot of it can't be predicted—at least, not by me.

But if somebody isn't out there creating a system wherein independent production can thrive, it will wither.

We are now in such a homogenized, globalized, monopolized entertainment system where studios are swallowing all independent producers and productions. And they're swallowing each other. Eventually there will just be Gap films and McDonald's films. And that will be it.

The worst thing that's happened in this community is the death of the independent television producer. We have to make sure that that doesn't happen on what is, right now, a public forum, and not a privately owned forum.

Especially with the economic disaster that the last bunch of presidents has left us with, independent film production is shutting down. The film and television industry is finding itself in the position the music industry found itself in [a few years ago]. The difference is they have a chance not to do what the music industry did, which was to ossify and to basically lock themselves in their fortress until they ran out of food.

They have an opportunity to try to stop the revolution by making evolutionary deals. They're not inclined to do that right now. So the trick is to create a venue that becomes attractive to them and [where] there is still an independent voice that can partner with them.

Ultimately, they have the power. They have the advertising dollars, they have the distribution systems and they're a force to be reckoned with. I would like to [sit] at the table as an equal, and not as one of the goddamn serfs who is giving them all my goddamn grain.

Knowledge@Wharton: You've made *Dr. Horrible* available through a number of different distribution channels. It was free for a short period. Then it was available for purchase as a video download through iTunes. The soundtrack can also be purchased online. It's now available once again for free, streamed over the web with advertising. And now there's a DVD. Can you give us an idea of how successful each of those has been?

Whedon: iTunes has been a great boon for us. And the DVD has done quite well—although I'd love to bump that up more. Streamed [online video] with advertising is probably the smallest revenue. Whether that's a viable monetization scheme . . . is the question. In some ways it acts as an advertisement and in some ways it might be pulling people away from bothering to download it or to buy the DVD.

In the case of the DVD, we went so ballistic with extra content that it took twice as long to make as the movie [laughs]. It wasn't just a question of: Here's another potential revenue stream. It was a question of: Here's something new, so that you don't feel like this is something you already have. We were trying to protect the monetization stream there and give people a new experience.

Knowledge@Wharton: You're a third generation television writer. Was it easy to land your first writing job in Hollywood?

Whedon: Well, it was definitely easier for me in the sense that someone would read my script. My father's agency said, "Look, we don't do any favors. We're not interested in this guy. But because he's your son, we will read the script." And that's a door that doesn't open for a lot of people.

Plus, I'd seen television scripts my whole life. I was raised by a tribe of funny people. Those things help. I understood the rhythms of the thing. Those advantages I never take for granted. But, ultimately, I still had to do the thing. And they read the script and I got an agent, and several spec scripts later—a job.

So, it always comes down to: Can you do it? Can you write it? I've made my way for a long time. But was I halfway down the track when the starting gun went off? I was.

Knowledge@Wharton: You've created content for television, for feature films, for the web. Do you view these as fundamentally different media or as merely different distribution channels for similar content?
Whedon: I see them as different media. They are connected and connecting in ways that I find both fascinating and appalling in the sense that everybody's trying to make every story work on every platform. Sometimes you're like, "Can you just make a frickin' movie! Can it not be a franchise and a comic book and a bobblehead? Can the characters just matter?"

Part of it is absolutely respecting that the media are different. That doesn't mean that you can only make things on the Internet that are two minutes long, like a lot of people believed. But it does mean that a movie and a television show and a limited Internet series are going be positioned differently, responded to differently and experienced differently. Ultimately, it's always going to boil down to: Did I [care]? Was I having a good time?

But the integration of the things can be exciting, if it's approached the way everything needs to be approached—which is artistically.

The problem now is the form that the integration takes. When I'm shooting my TV show I have to shoot it for four-by-three television ratio and widescreen—which means I can never compose a true frame. I'm always splitting the difference between frames. And that is destructive. So you do have to make a choice at some point.

Like when we did our commentary musical [on the *Dr. Horrible* DVD]. It's ridiculous. It's sophomoric, it's silly, it's off-topic. But, ultimately, we were striving to make a commentary musical, not just to pile on content for the sake of clocking more hours on the extras DVD. We wanted to use the idea of a commentary musical to at least have fun with the concept. Even if we didn't really break huge ground there, we were professionally silly.

Knowledge@Wharton: What do you think the media landscape will look like in another five or ten years?
Whedon: [Sarcastically:] I am exactly the kind of visionary who is so brilliant that he doesn't want to share that with other people. Meaning: I have no idea.

I still call my iPod "my Walkman." OK? I am old. I have gray in my beard—which, by the way, is terribly sexy. I've never been a maverick.

If you look at *Dr. Horrible*, it's a very old-fashioned story. And it's a very old-fashioned presentation. What I was going for was, basically, a television event. It's going to be on at this time, and this is going to be your opportunity to see it, because it's not going to be on after that. Tune in this night, this night, and this night when it premieres.

Obviously, it was slightly different than that. But that's the ethos I was going for. I'm a very old-fashioned storyteller. I am not, in any way, a visionary. I just try and make whatever I do good enough that people let me do it again. That's pretty much my scheme.

So, five years from now, we will all have antennae. I got nothing. The challenge for me now is to create some kind of formula for creation and monetization on a medium that may be completely different.

Right now, DVD is a great revenue source for an Internet-based venture. Most people are saying that in five years, DVD will be over. Sales are already way, way down from what they used to be. I don't understand how I'm going to ride that change. I'm just trying to make as much fun stuff as I can and stay, if not one step ahead of it, then not caught under the swell.

Knowledge@Wharton: Can you recall the first piece of popular entertainment—a TV show, a movie, a comic book—that really made an impression on you as a child?
Whedon: Umm . . . all of them?

Let's go with *Help, Help, The Globolinks*, a horror opera that I saw when I was five. It terrified me. They drove a van on stage—which was awesome. And then the van broke down, the Globolinks came, and the only thing that would keep them away was music. A young girl had a violin and she would play the violin at them and they would go away.

It just terrified me. But, at the same time, I adored it.

Knowledge@Wharton: Speaking of opera and musical theater, what are the chances that *Dr. Horrible* is going to make it to Broadway as a full-blown Broadway production?
Whedon: We talk all the time about all the possible venues for *Dr. Horrible*. And then we go back to our day jobs that we're supposed to be doing in the first place.

Broadway is something that we've talked about. I had a very funny experience talking with a Broadway veteran who basically said, "Oh, yeah, come to Broadway because there you'll have complete control and be treated with respect, and it will all go really easily."

[Sarcastically:] Right. And I was like, "Hmmm, I think I'll go back to the Internet, where you just put it on for free!"

I would love to do it. Broadway is a dream that we all have. But I'm not terribly interested in repurposing things I've already done. Obviously, I made a TV show out of one of my movies and a movie out of one of my TV shows, so it sounds like a crazy thing to say—except that I didn't tell the same story in either of them. I just took the story I had further.

And that's what I'm concentrating on with *Dr. Horrible*. It's not so much like: "How can I squeeze another media out of this story" but: "What happened to him after?"

Knowledge@Wharton: You felt that Fox didn't handle your TV series *Firefly* particularly well. I've heard that you swore to never go back to Fox, and yet you're working with them on *Dollhouse*.

Whedon: That is not, in fact, the case. I never swore not to go back to Fox. I left my deal at Fox because I couldn't think of any TV shows, and I didn't want to be paid to not do anything. Looking back—I can't imagine why I didn't want that [laughs]. It sounds so cool.

I was heartbroken, but I never swore not to work at Fox. The production people had not done anything bad. They let me make the show the way I wanted to. And the network—well, they're constantly changing, aren't they?

If it had been the same people running Fox now as it was then, I would not have come back. But you don't swear, because the ground is shifting under you constantly. It was doing that even before the new media made everyone cranky.

Knowledge@Wharton: What advice would you give to someone starting out that wants to make an independent film or web content? How can they get their work seen? How can they generate enough revenue to do another one?

Whedon: The fact of the matter is, if somebody has a story to tell there is no reason at all that they should not be telling it. The quality of the material that exists—I'm talking about the physical [equipment] like the cameras—[allows you to do] things that could not be done when I was a kid for almost nothing.

People aren't going to the Internet to look for IMAX [large-screen movies]. They're going to look for things that shock and delight and surprise and upset and all that good stuff. They're going for the most basic story.

A lot of people sit around and go, "How can I get this made?" The only answer is: By making it. By borrowing someone's camera. By buying a camera. They come cheap and they work well. And if you know where to point them—and the person that you point them at is saying something interesting—that's it! That's how it works.

I can't stress enough that I believe the best thing in the world is for everybody who feels like they have a story to tell, to tell it.

If they want to sell it, if they want to make a lot of money, they can do that—and they can kiss their story goodbye. Because, in general, that's the last they're ever going to see of it, because somebody else will own it and they will either not make it, or make it very differently than that person hoped.

So, if you really have a story you think you're ready to tell, what are you doing talking to me?

Joss Whedon Just Wants to Be Loved

JOY PRESS/2009

Joss Whedon looks rough and rumpled, as if he just tumbled out of bed and into his hotel lobby. Is this what a great television auteur looks like? The man who created *Buffy the Vampire Slayer*, *Angel*, and *Dr. Horrible's Sing-Along Blog* has earned a zealous cult following with his special blend of giddy fantasy, brainy humor, and beautifully constructed narratives.

Wearing an unbuttoned shirt covered in tiny retro TVs, Whedon doesn't resemble a Hollywood icon so much as a guy who spent part of the previous day at New York's fanboy festival Comic-Con. Where he was, by the way, the star attraction. Along with the various fantasy worlds that he has conjured on big and small screens, Whedon also writes comic books, contributing to hugely successful series like *X- Men* and *Runaways*, as well as penning comics based on his own TV shows.

Whedon's most surprising recent success was *Dr. Horrible's Sing-Along Blog*, a charming online musical about a lonely wannabe-supervillain (played by Neil Patrick Harris), which Whedon and his brothers (and sister-in-law) created on a shoestring budget during the writers strike. Originally intended to be streamed for free on the Internet last summer, the three episodes became a stone-cold smash via iTunes and later DVD. One might reasonably think that Whedon would now give up on network television for the creative freedom of the Internet—especially since his last TV show, the 2002 sci-fi western *Firefly*, was canceled by Fox after just eleven episodes. (Whedon later remade *Firefly* into the 2005 movie *Serenity*.)

And yet here he is, back on Fox with the new series *Dollhouse* (reviewed here). It stars former *Buffy* star Eliza Dushku as Echo, a young woman—known on the show as an "Active" or "Doll"—sapped of her memories and free will, who is sold to rich clients to fulfill their needs and fantasies. For each assignment she is imprinted with a fresh personality, complete with new skills, intelligence, and neurological information; sometimes she morphs into a sexbot, other times she takes on the life of a highly methodical negotiator. Echo and her fellow Actives live in a giant Zen loft called the Dollhouse, blissfully unaware that they are being remote controlled by a shadowy organization under investigation by a Fox Mulder–style FBI agent (played by *Battlestar Galactica* escapee Tahmoh Penikett).

The *Dollhouse* pilot may not immediately strike the Whedon lover as quite silly or talky or girl-powered enough. But this is a man who knows how to blow up genre expectations, and even in the debut episode we start to see cracks in Echo's vacant veneer that will undoubtedly force us to think about the nature of identity, memory, and sexuality, and even what it means to be a TV auteur who creates roles for sexy actresses to live out. Whedon swears that in *Dollhouse*, he has created a premise full of juicy possibilities for fun, fantasy, and intelligence, one that can also—he hopes—run the brutal gantlet of network TV execs.

Press: You went to New York Comic-Con this weekend. I assume that must be the epicenter of your fan base.
Whedon: Sometimes you go because you've got to promote something, and sometimes you go because you just want people to remember that you're still around, even though you have nothing to promote. I did that one year. I was terrified. I was like, uh, I just want to say, I'm still alive!

Press: What's that movie where the movie star goes to a mall when she's feeling insecure so that fans will recognize her and ask for an autograph?
Whedon: *Soapdish*! I was thinking about that yesterday. I understand that on a level I wish I didn't.

Press: You have a huge cult—it's not very often that TV show creators and writers get that kind of adulation.
Whedon: I was one of the first. The Internet community started forming right when *Buffy* started airing, and the notion of a show creator being anything other than a name people recognize on the screen was completely new. When you become a writer you assume it's this life of anonymity, and then all of a sudden it's this other thing. But at Comic-Con everybody's like that. There's a reason all the comic book artists trudge out there, because they do get, as they say, treated like rock stars.

Press: I don't know that there are a lot of other instances of people taking their own TV shows and continuing them on as comic books for years after the series ends. Do you have the same kind of emotional attachment to the characters in *Dollhouse*?

Whedon: It's different because this universe is so complicated. It's not a gut-punch like, "She's little and she beats up monsters." Echo is a much more complicated character by virtue of being hardly a character, and the premise itself is designed to be kind of distancing. I did pitch it with a six-year plan. But when we did the [first] thirteen episodes, we eventually said, instead of holding back, let's just go nuts. And by the second half of the season, we just started blowing shit up. And I don't mean literal explosions, because we couldn't actually afford those anymore.

Press: In the pilot, one of the men who works in the Dollhouse says, "There's nothing good or bad, but thinking makes it so." It seemed very much a trademark line of yours, because, aside from quoting Shakespeare, which you do—
Whedon: I do way too often.

Press: But you also like to play with the whole good-and-evil-are-relative thing in your shows. How is that gonna play out in *Dollhouse*?
Whedon: Constantly. The good and evil is kind of the point, the relativity of both and our assumptions about what's evil is something we want to explore all the time. The Dollhouse is by definition kinda sketchy. And very illegal. It's kind of a combination human trafficking/whorehouse/corporate fulfillment center.
   There's also some assassination. Actually, did we ever do that or did we just talk about it in the room? And of course the network is like, can we have more assassination and less sex?

Press: Fox asked for less sex?
Whedon: You'd be surprised. The networks are very prurient, especially after Janet [Jackson] decided to share with us. So the networks are like, we think this premise is hot. Just don't show anything or talk about it. Which can be so disingenuous that it becomes offensive.
   Obviously it's tough because—and this is the thing that kept me up nights—human trafficking in the real world is beyond heinous. What we were trying to do was create a situation in a science-fiction world where people gave themselves up for five years to the idea of, "I don't care what happens to me. I won't know about it. And as long as I'm not hurt, go with God. It's fine."

Press: So for whatever reason these "Actives" have voluntarily given up their bodies?
Whedon: Well, the question of whether they've actually volunteered or not is obviously somewhat dicey. And as we'll begin to learn, every Active has a

different backstory. What I wanted to do was talk about the idea of sex and what we expect from each other. Power, love, how these things are all connected. We're positing the idea of, if people were in a position to give up their lives, how many of them would?

Press: We saw a thing on *This American Life*, where guys had found a way to block a memory stream on mice and they got flooded with letters from people begging them to be test subjects, because they were like, I don't want to remember my life. Something bad happened or I want to cut out something. There is also this fantasy of not having control, of not having responsibility. These people are taken care of like children. They live in the best spa ever.

Whedon: I believe that prostitution is not, in concept, repulsive. I believe that people are gonna want to have sex for a long time. Eventually, I think that computers and TVs will become so awesome that they'll stop wanting to . . .

Press: Or they'll forget about it.

Whedon: Right. What interests me is that urge and what we do with it. People will always want to give up their power on some level. It's a nightmare and a fantasy. The nightmare is, I have no will. And the fantasy is, I have no responsibility or memory of what I've done.

Press: Along with *Buffy* expat Eliza Dushku, you have *Battlestar Galactica* star Tahmoh Penikett in *Dollhouse*. Are you a *Galactica* obsessive?

Whedon: Um, I think obsessive is too light a word. I absolutely adore it. It's my favorite show ever. Come on, it's *The West Wing* with space battles. It covers all of my needs. I watch their storytelling and go, "Oh, so that's how it's done. Fuck."

Press: Based on the pilot, *Dollhouse* seems much less playful than some of your previous shows.

Whedon: It is less playful, which doesn't mean we don't play. There's a lot of silliness and repartee and fun, but first we have to win over the world. I think the first episodes are trying to get people to understand and accept how this world works. But the show really finds itself in the second half. It's really where we start to go, "Ohhhhhh, we can do thiiiis. Right, this is why we showed up!" And so I'm hoping people will stick with it.

Press: So you're doing a bait and switch? You're tricking them with the more conventional stuff up front?

Whedon: Well, it's more that by episode six, people know the characters, they get it, now we can start to really mess with them.

Press: Viewers seem much more TV-literate these days. Certainly, your shows helped to create that literacy, but people seem able to cope with much more complicated ideas and structures.

Whedon: I think television is getting smarter and dumber at the same time. As it gets harder for the networks to figure out how to make their money and what's going to happen structurally with advertising, at the same time, on cable and even on some of the bigs, people are taking chances. It's a time of crisis, which means a lot of entrenching, a lot of let's just go for exactly what we know how to do, and a certain amount of let's shake it up. And those will be the shows people remember.

Press: I was startled to see that you were back on Fox, since you've had problems with networks supporting your previous series. There's so much good stuff on cable channels like Sci-Fi and AMC—and obviously you had a hugely successful experiment with *Dr. Horrible's Sing-Along Blog*.

Whedon: Yes, well, I made that after I made the deal for *Dollhouse*. [smiles] And um, [the Internet] is definitely a brave new world, in which I would like to live. But you know, TV is like a home for me, and Eliza obviously is a buddy [who had a production deal with Fox]. It just made sense. And since then, it's made less sense—and then it made more again, and then it made less again.

It was so clear to me what was interesting about this show—the idea of identity, and the idea that everybody is compromised. But knowing going in that the premise was going to be offensive to some people scared the shit out of me. Because I'm usually like, please love me. I actually had a lyric that was cut out of the commentary musical for *Dr. Horrible* where I just go, "Love me," very pathetically.

Press: So that's what motivates you—a desperate need for love?

Whedon: Yeah, hello! But this was one where I was just going to let that fall by the wayside because I wanted to deal with the issues. I wanted to actually deconstruct this love that I seemed to need so badly. But again, if the parallels to the horrors of the real world overwhelm the fantastical aspect of it, it won't work.

Press: Early in your career you worked as a writer on *Roseanne*, which was kind of a social realist comedy, and very much of its era. How much do you feel like your shows reflect their moment? Thinking about *Dollhouse*, where the clients are these zillionaires—are you going to have some of them being bankrupted by Madoff?

Whedon: Well, we wrote all of it before all this economic hilarity, so we were like, "Yeah, people are really going to want to see this show—a lot of billionaires, this is awesome!" Ultimately everything I do is pretty baldly classist—like, the powerful people are taking advantage of the poor people, and they don't get it.

Press: Looking at the set I was reminded of Wolfram and Hart, the creepy law offices in *Angel* that looked very normal and slick but were run by the devil.
Whedon: Yes, it is the same designer. And we wanted the same feeling of, "Isn't this attractive? You can't leave."

Press: And it's a similar idea of these mysterious people who seem very normal and slick, but are they . . . evil?
Whedon: Yeah. And we get to confront them with the consequences of what they do, and learn more about why they do what they do. Because very few people are entirely evil. I know it's hard to believe that after the last eight years of government in this country, but everybody has two sides, and I believe that not only are people often less or more righteous than they understand, but they often don't know what part of them is actually the good part. And a lot of the things that we prize in America might not actually be useful traits, and a lot of the things we vilify, to me, are not necessarily harmful, and that's something that's been in my work from the start.

Press: I'm always stunned by how much you appear to be doing. You seem to have a zillion comic books and ten movies in production.
Whedon: I create that illusion. I would like to become what I appear to be. I would like to have as much going on as other people do, but my problem is I get so attached to things, and there's my kids, and I need my sleep, and then there's being married, gotta check in on that, too. But living my life now is as important to me as telling stories, which it never used to be. Stupid kids.

Press: You grew up with a TV writer for a dad. Was it a different kind of a job for him?
Whedon: It was different, I think. He worked on other people's shows. He enjoyed what he did enormously, and I think his father enjoyed it too. But their love was really writing lyrics for musicals, off-Broadway musicals, and TV was something they did because they were good at it. But I got to incorporate all the things that I loved into my TV.

Press: Did you absorb stuff from your father?
Whedon: Oh, yeah, all of the most important lessons about writing I learned from my father. He never set out to teach me anything, it would just be something he said casually in conversation. In fact, he warned me, don't be a television writer. You'll have to work too hard.

Index